STUDIES ON VOLTAIRE
AND THE EIGHTEENTH CENTURY

224

GENERAL EDITOR   HAYDN MASON
DEPARTMENT OF FRENCH
UNIVERSITY OF BRISTOL
BRISTOL BS8 1TE

BARBARA WIDENOR MAGGS

Russia and 'le rêve chinois': China in eighteenth-century Russian literature

THE VOLTAIRE FOUNDATION
AT THE TAYLOR INSTITUTION, OXFORD

1984

ISSN 0435-2866

ISBN 0 7294 0311 4

Typeset by Cheney & Sons Ltd, Banbury, Oxon OX16 8EY

Printed in England at The Alden Press, Oxford OX2 0EF

To the memory of Margaret Ida Spencer
  Sinologist, Slavist, Friend

Contents

Acknowledgements

I WOULD like to take this opportunity to express my appreciation to many colleagues, friends, and members of my family, without whose help and support this book would not have taken shape. To my thesis adviser in the Program in Comparative Literature at the University of Illinois, Professor A. Owen Aldridge, who supervised the study in its original form when it was submitted in partial fulfilment of the requirements for the degree of Doctor of Philosophy, I owe the greatest debt of gratitude. Professor Aldridge's role in illuminating for me the ideas and ideals of the eighteenth century, his patient guidance and direction of this particular research project, as well as his continued support of my work, cannot be fully acknowledged. To Professor Evelyn Bristol of the Department of Slavic literatures at the University of Illinois, who offered numerous valuable suggestions on the original manuscript and much encouragement in all the later stages, I am also greatly indebted. To Professor Michael A. Curran, formerly of the Department of Slavic Languages and Literatures, who read the original thesis and made many helpful comments, I also wish to express my gratitude. For his informed advice, particularly on Chinese matters, I thank my fellow comparatist Professor David Wei-Yang Dai, and for consultation on an esoteric Chinese problem, I also thank my friend Professor Yen Lo. For any errors of fact or interpretation, I alone take complete responsibility.

A large debt of gratitude is owed to the many librarians who obtained for me materials often difficult to locate. The assistance of the staffs of the Slavic and East European Library at the University of Illinois, the rare book division of the Lenin Library in Moscow, and Hamilton Library at the University of Hawaii was very much appreciated.

For her expert typing of a very difficult manuscript I am very grateful to Ms Janet Sanderson, and for Cyrillic typing I want to thank Dr Ilene Levine.

Finally, for their patience with this project my thanks go to my family, especially to my husband Peter; his assistance with footnote typing, proofreading, Russian terminology, and countless other matters, as well as his encouragement over the years, made the book possible

B. W. M.

A note to the reader

THE transliteration system for Russian is the modified Library of Congress system used in the *Slavic review*. Names of persons have been given in their most commonly accepted English form, except in citations and quotations, where numerous variations in spelling will be noticed. Chinese words and names have been given according to the modified Wade-Giles transliteration system, except in a few cases where I have been unable to identify a Chinese name on the basis of the eighteenth-century French or Russian transliteration. In these cases I have used the French form or have simply transliterated the Russian form into English.

The spelling for nineteenth- and early twentieth-century Russian titles has been silently modernised. Eighteenth-century Russian booktitles have usually been given in the modified eighteenth-century form in which they appear in the *Сводный каталог русской книги XVIII века 1725-1800* (Union catalogue of the Russian book of the eighteenth century 1725-1800) (Moscow 1963-1967). Titles of articles in eighteenth-century publications have generally been given in modernised form, following the other bibliographies that were consulted.

Introduction

COMMENTING on the educational value of travel literature, Daniel Defoe observed that the armchair traveller 'may go round the globe with Dampier and Rogers, and kno' a thousand times more in doing it than all those illiterate sailors'.[1] The creator of *Robinson Crusoe* certainly had valid reasons for propagandising the literature of travel, and may well have overstated his case. Perhaps readers of travel narratives did not succeed in learning more than did the sailors who actually made the voyages. Still, at a time when travel was difficult, dangerous, and time-consuming, the reading of travel accounts became, if not the best way, at least the most feasible way of acquiring knowledge of foreign lands. In the eighteenth century it was generally with the reports of authentic travellers that the image which one nation held about another part of the world began to take shape. The picture that emerged from the travel narratives, augmented gradually by other genres of literature, was often in fact a mirage, a representation more illusory than real, but nevertheless accepted as fact by the non-travelling reading public.

The need for systematic studies of the formation and effect of literary images was first stressed in the early part of the twentieth century by the French school of comparative literature, the group of comparatists who emphasised the importance of influences and direct literary relations between authors and between different national literatures. Theoretical studies of image and mirage were a particular concern of the well-known pioneer in comparative literature studies, Jean-Marie Carré. Investigating the 'reciprocal interpretations of peoples', Carré showed the relevance of such images to literary and cultural history studied from an international rather than a national point of view.[2]

The image studies which comparatists have undertaken since the early part of the twentieth century have varied greatly in scope and purpose. Some have been conceived on a broad scale, such as Gilbert Chinard's monumental *L'Amérique et le rêve exotique* (1913),[3] which deals with the French view of America in the seventeenth and eighteenth centuries. Chinard correlates the literary depictions of America with the trends developing in French literature during this period. Other image studies have been concerned with more limited periods of time or with selected genres of literature. This type of analysis is useful not only for specialists in literature, but also for other scholars, for instance social scientists who have a particular interest in the period being studied.

A great amount of attention has been given in the past, and is still being given today, by comparatists – as well as by specialists in the history of ideas, art history and other disciplines – to the development of a literary image which had a broad influence upon many aspects of Western culture, the European image

[1] Daniel Defoe, *The Compleat English gentleman* (London 1890), p. 225.
[2] Jean-Marie Carré, 'Avant-propos' to M. F. Guyard, *La Littérature comparée* (Paris 1951), quoted in *Connaissance de l'étranger* (Paris 1964), p. 29.
[3] Gilbert Chinard, *L'Amérique et le rêve exotique dans la littérature française au dix-septième et au dix-huitième siècle* (Paris 1913).

of China in the seventeenth and eighteenth centuries. Among the numerous studies that have been made of this image in Europe as a whole are Adolf Reichwein's *China und Europa: geistige und künstlerische Beziehungen im 18. Jahrhundert* (1923), Wolfgang Franke's *China and the West* (English translation, 1967), and Raymond Dawson's *The Chinese chameleon: an analysis of European conceptions of Chinese civilisation* (1967). Donald F. Lach's monumental *Asia in the making of Europe* (1965-1977) considers Europe's views of China as well as other Far Eastern Asian nations. Specifically French impressions of the Middle Kingdom (as well as the Near East) were set forth in 1906 in the pioneering work by Pierre Martino, *L'Orient dans la littérature française au dix-septième et au dix-huitième siècle*. Particularly useful on French points of view are Basil Guy's *The French image of China before and after Voltaire* (1963), A. Owen Aldridge's 'Voltaire and the cult of China' (1971-72), and Arnold H. Rowbotham's 'Voltaire sinophile' (1932). *A cycle of Cathay* (1951) by William Appleton concerns the eighteenth-century English image of China, while the German view is presented by Ursula Aurich in *China im Spiegel der deutschen Literatur des 18. Jahrhunderts* (1935) and by Eduard Horst von Tscharner in *China in der deutschen Dichtung bis zur Klassik* (1939) and in a series of articles. *La Cina e l'età dell'illuminismo in Italia* (1974) by Sergio Zoli is a study of Italian *chinoiserie*. Chinese influence on European art and architecture is discussed by Hugh Honour in *Chinoiserie: the vision of Cathay* (1961), and by Henriette Belevitch-Stankevitch in *Le Goût chinois en France au temps de Louis XIV* (1910). Arnold Rowbotham's *Missionary and Mandarin: the Jesuits at the Court of China* (1942) deals with the Jesuits' role in creating the European image of China.[4]

The analysis of this image offers some striking insights into Carré's 'reciprocal interpretations of peoples'. The West, in sending to China in the mid-sixteenth century its cultural emissaries, the Roman Catholic missionaries, had hoped to

[4] Adolf Reichwein, *China und Europa: geistige und künstlerische Beziehungen im 18. Jahrhundert* (Berlin 1923); English translation, *China and Europe: intellectual and artistic contacts in the eighteenth century*, trans. J. C. Powell (New York 1925); Wolfgang Franke, *China and the West*, trans. R. A. Wilson (Columbia 1967); Raymond Dawson, *The Chinese chameleon: an analysis of European conceptions of Chinese civilisation* (London 1967); Donald F. Lach, *Asia in the making of Europe* (Chicago 1965-1977); Pierre Martino, *L'Orient dans la littérature française au dix-septième et au dix-huitième siècle* (Paris 1906); Basil Guy, *The French image of China before and after Voltaire*, Studies on Voltaire 21 (Geneva 1963); A. O. Aldridge, 'Voltaire and the cult of China', *Tamkang review* 2, no. 2 and 3, no. 1 (Oct. 1971-April 1972); Arnold H. Rowbotham, 'Voltaire sinophile', *PMLA* 47 (1932), pp.1050-65; William W. Appleton, *A cycle of Cathay* (New York 1951); Ursula Aurich, *China im Spiegel der deutschen Literatur des 18. Jahrhunderts*, Germanische Studien, Heft 169 (Berlin 1935); Eduard Horst von Tscharner, 'China in der deutschen Dichtung des Mittelalters und der Renaissance', *Sinica* 9 (1934), pp.8-31; 'Die Erschließung Chinas im 16. und 17. Jahrhundert', *Sinica* 9 (1934), pp.50-77; 'China in der deutschen Literatur des klassischen Zeitalters', *Sinica* 9 (1934), pp.185-98 and 269-80; 'China in der deutschen Dichtung, i: Barock', *Sinica* 12 (1937) pp.91-129; 'China in der deutschen Dichtung, ii: Aufklärung und Rokoko', *Sinica* 12 (1937), pp.181-207; *China in der deutschen Dichtung bis zur Klassik* (München 1939); Sergio Zoli, *La Cina e l'età dell'illuminismo in Italia* (Bologna 1974); Hugh Honour, *Chinoiserie: the vision of Cathay* (London 1961); Henriette Belevitch-Stankevitch, *Le Goût chinois en France au temps de Louis XIV* (Paris 1910); Arnold H. Rowbotham, *Missionary and Mandarin: the Jesuits at the Court of China* (Berkeley 1942).

change radically the nature of the Eastern world. But the result was far from what had been anticipated. While Christian converts were indeed made in China, the greater cultural impact was not that of Europe on China, but that of China on the Western world.

Through the narratives written by the early missionaries, the West began to acquire a broad spectrum of information about the Middle Kingdom. The missionaries' accounts were not, of course, the first descriptions of China to catch the imagination of the Western World. The famed Cathay of the medieval travellers Marco Polo, Friars Odoric, Giovanni de Plano Carpini, and William of Rubruck had long been a subject of great interest. But with the appearance in 1585 of the *Historia de las cosas mas notables, ritos y costumbres del gran reyno de la China*, written by the Augustinian Juan Gonzáles de Mendoça[5] (and translated into English three years later), a great succession of contemporary accounts of China written by keen and generally sympathetic observers began. The works of fathers Trigault, Semedo, Navarrete, Lecomte, and Magalhaens of the seventeenth century, Amiot, Gaubil and Parennin of the eighteenth century, along with the narratives of many other missionaries, some presented in carefully edited compendiums, enjoyed tremendous success. The early missionary reports were to be augmented by accounts written by the members of occasional trade missions, such as that of John Nieuhof. By the eighteenth century fascination with China had developed into full-fledged sinophilia. Although certain critics attempted to dampen the public's enthusiasm, admiration for almost all aspects of Chinese culture was intense and sustained. Inspired by the accounts of authentic travellers, writers of fiction incorporated Chinese themes into stories, poems and plays. Objects of Chinese art were imported and copied, and Chinese styles of architecture appeared throughout most of Europe. Moreover, in the realm of ideas European philosophers expanded on Chinese or supposed Confucian theories, reworked and incorporated these ideas into their own philosophic systems and in so doing added new dimensions to the picture of the kingdom in the east. Particularly in France, was the utopian 'rêve chinois' cultivated and nurtured. This Chinese mirage remained distinct and bright in France until mid-century.

Western Europe was not alone in its fascination with China during the eighteenth century. Russia, much closer geographically to the Middle Kingdom than were the countries of Western Europe, was also highly concerned with China, and by roughly the middle of the eighteenth century began to develop in her published (as well as manuscript) literature her own image of her neighbour to the east. The analyses which have been made of Russian китайщина or *chinoiserie* are, however, few. Studies of general European views of China, such as Reichwein's early work and Dawson's more recent one, do not survey Russian attitudes. In the introduction to his *China and the West*, a work which deals primarily with Chinese views of the West, but which also concerns itself with Western Europe's images of China, Wolfgang Franke states that Russia's relationship to China is unique and has therefore has not been given a place in

---

[5] Juan Gonzáles de Mendoça, *Historia de los cosas mas notables, ritos y costumbres del gran reyno de la China* (Rome 1585).

his study.[6] Donald Lach's *Asia in the making of Europe*, which analyses in its first two volumes (in five parts) sixteenth-century Europe's knowledge and views of China and which will eventually also cover the seventeenth and eighteenth centuries, will deal with Russia, Lach states, as 'one of several intermediaries in the transmission of knowledge about Asia to Europe',[7] and not, evidently, as a constituent part of Europe with its own images of the East.

But while no comprehensive studies have emerged, so far as I know, of Russia's eighteenth-century literary image of China and how it derived from, but in its totality was quite different from that developed in France and Western Europe, a number of useful studies and reference works have dealt with separate aspects of the subject. A short but valuable and stimulating discussion is found in M. P. Alekseev's 'Pushkin and China'.[8] A brief Marxist interpretation of Western European and Russian *chinoiserie* appears in A. Ikonnikov's *The Chinese theatre and chinoiserie at Detskoe Selo*.[9] O. L. Fishman touches on the comparison of Western European and Russian images of China in *The Chinese satirical novel*,[10] and Eric Widmer in his engaging study *The Russian ecclesiastical mission in Peking during the eighteenth century*[11] deals extensively with impressions held by Russian religious and political emissaries to China. A very informative work on all aspects of Russian cultural ties with China in the seventeenth and eighteenth centuries is P. E. Skachkov's *Outline of the history of Russian sinology*.[12] Skachkov is also the compiler of the *Bibliography of China*,[13] the invaluable bibliography of all works about China published in Russian up to 1957. The latter work along with A. N. Neustroev's *Index to Russian periodicals*,[14] and the *Union catalogue of the Russian book of the eighteenth century 1725-1800*,[15] served as the bibliographic basis

[6] Franke, p. vii.

[7] Lach, vol. i, Book i, xv.

[8] M. P. Alekseev, 'Пушкин и Китай' (Pushkin and China), in *А. С. Пушкин и Сибирь* (A. S. Pushkin and Siberia) (Moscow, Irkutsk 1937), pp.108-45.

[9] A. Ikonnikov, *Китайский театр и ‹китайщина› в Детском селе* (Moscow, Leningrad 1931).

[10] O. L. Fishman, *Китайский сатирический роман: эпоха Просвещения* (The Chinese satirical novel: the Enlightenment era) (Moscow 1966), p.168.

[11] Eric Widmer, *The Russian ecclesiastical mission in Peking during the eighteenth century* (Cambridge, Mass. 1976).

[12] P. E. Skachkov, *Очерки истории русского китаеведения* (Outline of the history of Russian sinology) (Moscow 1977). See also Skachkov's earlier 'История изучения Китая в России в XVII и XVIII вв. (краткий очерк)' (History of the study of China in Russia in the 17th and 18th centuries – a brief outline), in Академия наук СССР, Институт истории (Academy of Sciences of the USSR, Institute of History), *Международные связи России в XVII-XVIII вв. (Экономика, политика и культура)* (International ties of Russia in the 17th and 18th centuries – economics, politics and culture) (Moscow 1966), pp.152-80.

[13] P. E. Skachkov, *Библиография Китая* (Moscow, Leningrad 1932; 2nd ed., rev. & enl., Moscow 1960).

[14] Aleksandr Nikolaevich Neustroev, *Указатель к русским повременным изданиям и сборникам за 1703-1802 гг.* (Index to Russian periodicals and Collections of 1703 to 1802) (St Petersburg 1898; Cleveland, Ohio 1963).

[15] *Сводный каталог русской книги XVIII века 1725-1800* (Moscow 1963-1975); see also the definitive bibliography of Russian works published in the period 1689-1725, *Описание изданий, напечатанных при Петре I* (Description of publications printed during the reign of Peter i), compiled by T. A. Bykova & M. M. Gurevich (Moscow 1955-1972).

for the present study, which attempts to fill in the gap in scholarship on eighteenth-century European views of China, exploring the reception and development of the 'rêve chinois' in Russia.

Russia, like the countries of Western Europe, began to establish ties with the Middle Kingdom in the sixteenth century. While the first important Western European contacts with China in the modern period concerned trade, but more significantly religion, the first Russian-Chinese relations were of a commercial and political nature. These Sino-Russian affairs led in time to exchanges of official representatives between the Russian and Chinese capitals on a scale unmatched in the history of Western European-Chinese relations. In addition, by the beginning of the eighteenth century, Russian Orthodoxy became firmly established in Peking. Although the aims and accomplishments of the Orthodox mission differed greatly from those of its Roman Catholic counterparts, this early cultural contact between Russia and China was eventually to be of considerable importance to the formation of Russia's view of the Middle Kingdom.

By the end of the eighteenth century the authentic accounts of persons involved in these Russian religious, political and economic missions to China constituted a sizeable body of literary material. Fictional representations of the Middle Kingdom, philosophic works dealing with Chinese themes, as well as scholarly works by Russian sinologists who translated and edited many works of Chinese literature, complemented the travel narratives, producing a picture of the Middle Kingdom not lacking in colour or detail, in facts and in opinions.

Curiously, this picture contained many unflattering depictions of the Empire to the East. The old narratives we are about to peruse will reveal the specific reasons why various groups of Russian visitors to China returned with negative impressions. One key to understanding why the Russian views so often differed from those of Western Europeans can, however, be found in the perceptive observation of that genuine admirer of China, Voltaire. Commenting on the literature of travel, which played such an important part in the formation of one nation's vision of another, and pointing out the existence of some inaccurate and unreliable travel accounts, the French writer remarked, 'Our European Travellers for the most Part are satyrical upon their neighbouring Countries, and bestow large Praises upon the Persians and Chinese.'[16] This can be explained, Voltaire continued, by the fact that nations tend to be critical of those nearby with whom they are in competition, and to admire more distant lands which are not perceived as rivals. Voltaire's 'geographic' theory of images, as we will see, does much to explain Russia's dissatisfaction, which stemmed so often from disagreements over matters of politics and trade and evolved from day to day dealings over these practical matters; and it elucidates as well the reason for France's glorification of a distant Shangrila.

In reading the old accounts one should also keep in mind the point developed by Nicholas Riasanovsky in his article 'Asia through Russian eyes', that Russia, especially in the early part of the eighteenth century, viewed Asia as a backward

---

[16] F. M. A. Voltaire, 'Advertisement to the reader', *An essay upon the civil wars of France*, 2nd ed. (London 1728), second page.

region, associating it with the Mongol hordes which had invaded Russian
territory centuries earlier. By the eighteenth century, as Riasanovsky notes,
Russian hostility to Asia had ceased, but the feeling of apartness remained, and
even those aspects of Asian culture, such as Buddhism or Japanese aesthetics,
which Russians might admire, were generally found interesting precisely because
they were different.[17]

The richly diverse, if heavily tarnished, image of China which the Russian
writings produced formed, however, only a part of Russia's view of her eastern
neighbour. The mirage was made even more complex by the addition of a large
representative selection of Western European, particularly French works on
China which came into Russian literature in translation; typically, though not
always, these glorified their subject. That so many Western European works on
China appeared in Russia at this time is not surprising. Although modern
Russian literature was still in the early stages of its development, Western
European literature, and indeed Western culture in general, was becoming
known, and was highly esteemed and generally emulated by Russian society.
French literature and the French language (which was often used socially by
the educated elite) were held in especially high regard.

The simultaneous appearance then of translated French and Western
European works on China, along with the original Russian discussions of first-
hand contacts with the Chinese, as well as writings translated by Russians
directly from Chinese and Manchu is not remarkable. When Leibniz wrote to
Peter the Great in 1716 about Russia's unique opportunity, because of her
geographical position, to absorb wisdom from both Western Europe and China,
he was referring to the acquisition of many types of knowledge, not, of course,
merely to insights about Russia's eastern neighbour herself; and he was suggesting that Russia should facilitate an East-West exchange of ideas. But his starting
point that Russia's location permitted her to observe widely differing cultural
patterns and institutions, and 'to draw from Europe on one side and from China
on the other' was well taken.[18]

The merging of these varied sources of information on China brought a
number of conflicting elements into contact with each other, creating in Russia's
picture of the Middle Kingdom an ambiguity that became one of its most
intriguing characteristics. This feature, strangely enough, was seldom commented upon in eighteenth-century Russian publications. Russian travellers to
China occasionally compared their own observations with the literary impressions of Western Europeans, but apart from this there were few contemporary articles, editorial comments or reviews which pointed out national differences
in the attitudes of various writers toward the Middle Kingdom.

While even modern observers have so far not studied in detail this peculiarity

---

[17] Nicholas V. Riasanovsky, 'Asia through Russian eyes', in *Russia and Asia: essays on
the influence of Russia on the Asian peoples*, ed. Wayne S. Vucinich (Stanford, California
1972), pp.3-29 at p.8.

[18] David E. Mungello, *Leibniz and Confucianism: the search for accord* (Honolulu 1977),
p.7; Gottfried Wilhelm von Leibniz, *Selections*, ed. Philip P. Wiener (New York 1951),
pp.596-97; Donald F. Lach, 'Leibniz and China', *Journal of the history of ideas* 6 (1945),
pp.436-55 at pp.439-43.

of Russia's image of China, several scholars have commented upon it. In his brief illuminating remarks on the differences between the 'French Orient' and that which was developed by eighteenth-century Russian writers, M. P. Alekseev, for example, cites several instances in which the Russian writers either imply disagreement with their Western European colleagues our indicate a sense of competition with them in regard to China. Such an attitude constitutes in Alekseev's words a 'unique and mute struggle with Western tradition'.[19] While Alekseev does not elaborate upon it, the reason for the mute nature of such conflicts with Western views seems clear: because of Russia's almost fanatical attraction to Western culture and her desire to emulate Western European taste, disagreements with that culture were seldom voiced. Most Russian Europophiles were probably too blinded by the dazzle of Western cultural attractions to notice any discrepancies between native Russian views and those of Western Europeans. Cultural fashions such as French *chinoiserie* were therefore assimilated without question, and Russian writings and opinions about China were permitted to coexist peacefully beside the French import.

Because of her Europocentrism, as Eric Widmer notes in his study of the Russian religious mission in Peking, Russia tended to ignore the opinions of her own experts on China. Discussing how little attention eighteenth-century Russian sinologists, for instance, received from the government and the public, Widmer points out that Russian salons were more interested in what was being said about China by the French philosophers than in what their own leading China-trained scholar was writing.[20]

This respect for the supposed superiority of Western Europe's tradition, it seems to me, must also have been the reason that those Russian readers, critics, and editors who did in fact notice contradictions between Russian and Western European appraisals of China, said little. The comment of Catherine the Great in a letter to Voltaire perhaps reflects this reticence. Complaining about her own difficult dealings with the rulers of China and referring to the glowing reports of French and other European missionaries there, she wrote, 'Ainsi je me tais, et j'admire les relations des délégués de la Propaganda sans les contredire.'[21] While she goes on to note quite realistically that the missionaries were after all describing Ming China before the days of the Manchu conquerors with whom she now had to deal, one still feels that it is partly her respect for French writings themselves that prevents her from making more of the discrepancy to which she alludes.

It is impossible to establish whether the typical Russian reader attempted to differentiate between the Russian and non-Russian points of view about China which he encountered in print. But whether or not he attempted to sort out varying national points of view, the Russian sinophile of the period would

[19] M. P. Alekseev, 'Pushkin and China', pp.117-18.

[20] Widmer, pp.166-67.

[21] Catherine II, in F. M. A. Voltaire, *Correspondence and related documents*, in *The Complete works of Voltaire*, ed. Theodore Besterman (Genève, Banbury, Oxford 1968-1977) [hereafter Best.D], Best.D16861. The *Congregatio de propaganda fide* was the official missionary organisation in Rome.

have read simultaneously both the original Russian and the French and other European works about China that appeared in Russian translation. For this reason I have considered the Russian and the translated literature together, grouping the material according to the activity with which the writers were primarily concerned or to the genre of the works discussed. Within this framework I have then generally attempted to separate the 'rêve chinois' of the Europeans from the China of the Russian writers.

An alternative to this topical method of organisation might have been a chronological approach in which works were considered in the order in which they appeared. In analysing the image of China in a Western European nation, for example in France where the image, developing over the course of two centuries, passed through certain noticeable phases, a chronological approach, such as that used by Basil Guy, is most appropriate. But in the case of Russia the period we are dealing with is a much shorter one, namely the last half of the eighteenth and the early part of the nineteenth century, particularly the years from 1770 to about 1815. It would be very difficult to show a discernible pattern in the nature of the image during this short period. This difficulty results not only from the limited duration of the period considered, but also from several other factors. First, there was a considerable time lag between the writing and the publishing of many of the Russian works. Certain seventeenth-century travellers' journals, for instance, did not appear in print until the end of the eighteenth and the beginning of the nineteenth centuries. In addition, translations of Western European works reflecting one attitude toward the Middle Kingdom appeared in Russian simultaneously with translations of more recent material that expressed an entirely different point of view. Analysing these works in the order in which they were published would, I feel, lead to confusion. It seems to me that the clearest view of the image and especially of the peculiar dual nature of its sources can be achieved by reconstructing its various topical components, placing more emphasis on the form which the image attained toward the end of the eighteenth century and the beginning of the nineteenth century, than on strict literary chronology.

Following this principle, I have not, even when discussing one genre or segment which made up the image, attempted to deal with the individual works in the order in which they appeared. In some sections, for instance, in the discussion of the Russian religious missions, I have organised the material in such a way as to show the events in the order in which they actually occurred. This methodology might be questioned, since an image study is, of course, concerned not with actual history, but rather with literature and literary reflections of history. Still, it seems to me that in regard to this particular source of information about China, historical chronology is important for an understanding of the events which gave rise to the image. In creating a historical framework for the ecclesiastical mission I have, however, tried to use only material that was written during the eighteenth century, remaining generally within the limits of what was known during the period.

A few unpublished documents have been included in the analysis of writings from which Russian readers derived their impressions of China. These are mainly unpublished manuscripts of substantial works which are known to have circulated widely. In considering published literature I have limited the analysis, with a few exceptions, to Russian language material published during the period under consideration since it would be virtually impossible to identify the books in Western European languages that were imported into Russia, or to analyse their influence. Several works about China written in German were, however, published in Russia, and these have been included in the study.

The literature of travel constituted a large proportion of all of the works pertaining to China to which Russian readers had access. These travel narratives, as eyewitness commentaries on the Chinese, must, I feel, have made a special impression on readers, and for this reason I have given considerable emphasis to them. As many of these works, which are located in obscure Russian books and periodicals, are not easily accessible today, I have discussed their contents rather extensively, relating a great many details, and attempting to recreate the spirit and flavour of the narratives. I have stressed in particular the personal opinions and emotional reactions of the writers of these narratives since the general attitude of each visitor to the Middle Kingdom had a significant influence on the final picture which the travel literature projected. I have not, except in a very few instances, tried to comment on the reliability of any of these eyewitness reporters, the purpose of the study being, of course, to review all of the material – the prejudiced accounts as well as the most objective records of historical truth – which came into the readers' hands.

Russia's eighteenth-century image of China was, in the final analysis, made up of many historical truths, as well as many half-truths and artistic fictions. The Russian image of the Celestial Empire, composed as it was both of the visions of French and other European writers on the one hand, and the views of Russian writers on the other, consisted to a great extent of conflicting and irreconcilable elements. It perhaps presented a confusing picture to a reader who demanded an accurate and concise picture of the neighbour to the east. But from the contradictory facts and opinions which were to be found in Russia's literature about the Middle Kingdom there emerged an image that perhaps more closely approximated historical truth than did Western Europe's ethereal dreams of Cathay. Journeying through this diverse literature, the armchair traveller of eighteenth-century Russia could indeed 'go round the globe', and know a great deal in doing it.

1. The missionaries and the Middle Kingdom

'China is the largest and best of known governments.'
Diu Gal'd (Du Halde)[1]

'The praises attributed by Europeans to the present Manchu-Chinese government do not deserve the slightest credence.'
Archimandrite Sofronii Gribovskii[2]

AMONG the earliest and most permanent contacts between Russia and China were those established at the end of the seventeenth century by the Russian Orthodox Church. Labouring under difficult conditions, and often, as it must have seemed, without support from their countrymen and government, Russian priests set up and maintained a centre of Russian Orthodoxy in Peking which was to endure until 1949.

About a century before the arrival of the Russians, the Roman Catholic Church, particularly the Society of Jesus, had begun its own mission work in China. By the time of the establishment of the Russian Mission, the Jesuit effort was reaching its highest point of success. It was to a large extent the descriptive and scholarly works written by these Jesuit missionaries in the seventeenth and eighteenth centuries that stimulated the intense interest in China and the great admiration for her institutions that developed throughout Western Europe at this time. As the main interpreters of Chinese culture to Europe, the Jesuits produced travel accounts, geographic and historical studies, treatises on Chinese philosophy, translations of the Chinese classics and numerous other types of works dealing with various facets of Chinese life.

From the middle of the eighteenth century on, the writings of many of these Western European missionaries, especially works by French Jesuits, began to be published in Russian translation.[3] How did these publications and the views expressed in them compare with those of the Russian priests in Peking?

Among the French missionary works translated into Russian were portions of two of the most influential contributions to early Western sinology, the

[1] Diu Gal'd (Jean Baptiste Du Halde) *Географическое, историческое, хронологическое, политическое и физическое описание Китайския империи и Татарии Китайския* (trans. of vol. i of Du Halde, *Description géographique, historique, chronologique, politique, et physique, de l'empire de la Chine* (Paris 1735)) (St Petersburg 1774-1777), i (1774), p.2. (The Russian translation gives 'the best' for 'plus beau'.)

[2] Sofronii [Gribovskii], 'Известие о Китайском, ныне Манджуро-Китайском государстве' (News about the Chinese, now the Manchu-Chinese government), *Чтения в Императорском Обществе истории и древностей российских при Московском университете* (Papers of the Imperial Society of History and Antiquities of Russia at Moscow University), no. 1 (1861), pp.23-119, at p.30.

[3] A manuscript translation of a short excerpt from at least one Western European missionary work, that of Athanasius Kircher, is known to have circulated as early as the seventeenth century: Athanasius Kircher, *China monumentis* (Amsterdam 1667). See Dmitrij Čiževskij, *History of Russian literature from the eleventh century to the end of the Baroque* (The Hague 1960), p.327.

Description géographique, historique, chronologique, politique et physique de l'Empire de la Chine of J. B. Du Halde (1735), translated in part in 1774 and 1777,[4] and the *Mémoires concernant l'histoire, les sciences, les arts, les mœurs, les usages, etc. des Chinois. Par les missionaires de Pékin* by Amiot, Bourgeois, Cibot and others (1776-1814), parts of which began to appear in Russian translation between 1786 and 1790, relatively soon after the publication of the original.[5] Beginning in 1744 and continuing through 1747 one of the earliest Russian literary periodicals, the *Календарь или месяцослов* (Calendar) carried in instalments parts of father Gerbillon's description of the 'Grande Tartarie', taken from the last volume of Du Halde's monumental four-volume work, published only nine years earlier in Paris. The excerpts from Gerbillon were also reprinted later in a collection of materials from the *Calendar* in 1785.[6] In 1780 a short translation from the French appeared in the Russian journal *Академическия известия* (1780) (Academic news), entitled 'Filial piety in China, taken from the latest news of the Christian missionaries in Peking and published last year, 1779, in Paris.'[7] In the same year there appeared portions of the work by Philippe Couplet and others, *Confucius Sinarum philosophus*.[8] An excerpt from the abbé Grosier's *Description générale de la Chine* was translated in 1788,[9] and portions, at least, of

---

[4] Du Halde, *Description géographique, historique, chronologique, politique, et physique, de l'empire de la Chine* (Paris 1735). (See note 1 for Russian citation.) Subsequent citations, included in text, are to this original French edition.

[5] *Mémoires concernant l'histoire, les sciences, les arts, les mœurs, les usages, etc. des Chinois. Par les Missionaires de Pékin* (Paris 1776-1814), xii: *Vie de Koung-tsée, appellé vulgairement Confucius* (Paris 1786). *Записки, надлежащия до истории, наук, художеств, нравов, обычаев, и проч. китайцев, сочиненныя проповедниками веры христианской в Пекине* (Moscow 1786-1788), i-vi (translation of vols i-iii of original). The translation of volume twelve of the *Mémoires, Vie de Koung-tsée*, appeared several years later: Amio (Amiot, Joseph Marie) *Житие Кунг-Тсеэа или Конфуциуса, как именуют его европейцы, наиславнейшаго философа китайскаго, возстановлятеля древния учености* (The Life of Kung-tsee or Confucius as he is called by Europeans, the most famous Chinese philosopher, the renewer of ancient learning), trans. M. I. Verevkin (St Petersburg 1790).) (Subsequent citations, included in the text, are from the Russian translation of Amiot.)

[6] Gerbillon (Jean François Gerbillon), 'Описание и известие о Великой Татарии' (Description and information about the Great Tartary), *Календарь* (1744-1747); *Собрание сочинений выбранных из месяцословов* (Collection of compositions selected from calendars), i (1785), pp.227-50. Commentary by G. F. Müller.

[7] M. S. 'О благоговении сыновнем у китайцев, почерпнуто из последних известий христианских проповедников, находящихся в Пекине и издано в Париже прошлого 1779 года' (Filial piety in China, taken from the latest news of the Christian missionaries in Peking, and published last year, 1779, in Paris), *Академическия известия* (Academic news), pt. 4 (April 1780), pp.516-28. This article was probably taken from the fourth volume of Amiot's *Mémoires concernant les Chinois*, entitled *Doctrine ancienne et nouvelle des Chinois, sur la piété filiale* (Paris 1779).

[8] *Confucius Sinarum philosophus, sive scientia sinensis latine exposita, studio et opera Prosperi Intorcetta*, ed. Philippe Couplet (Paris 1683); Russian translation: *Описание жизни Конфуция, китайских философов начальника* (Description of the life of Confucius, the leading Chinese philosopher), Shcheglov, corrector (Moscow 1780).

[9] Groz'er (Jean Baptiste Grosier), 'Описание китайских войск и военного их порядка' (Description of the armed forces of the Chinese and their military organisation), *Новыя ежемесячныя сочинения* (New monthly compositions) 28 (Oct. 1788), pp.47-55. It is

J. Bouvet's life of K'ang-hsi, *Histoire de l'empereur de la Chine*, appeared as part of another publication in 1787.[10] All of these works reflect the great esteem which the Jesuit missionaries had for life and thought in China, particularly for Confucian philosophy and for China's system of political and social organisation.

Among the varied Jesuit works translated from the French, many of which are of a purely scholarly nature, the volumes which one suspects made the greatest contribution to Russian readers' impressions of China are the Amiot materials, and the abridged version of Du Halde, especially the narratives of the missionaries' travels within the Middle Kingdom, and their eyewitness accounts of the country. Several of the Amiot articles in particular projected vividly the missionaries' image of China as a land ruled by wisdom and philosophy. The 'Portraits des chinois célèbres', for example, a collection of fifty-two short biographies of famous Chinese rulers, governmental figures and philosophers, illustrated how traditional virtues and ideals were exemplified in the lives of public servants. The 'Requête à l'empereur pour la cérémonie du labourage', another selection, which described the ceremony in which the emperor himself took part in the spring planting, demonstrated the closeness of the emperor to his people, and the traditional respect for the cultivation of the land.

Also contributing to this theme were the two translations in Amiot from the Chinese classics, the *Ta Hsüeh* (The Great learning) and the *Chung Yung* (The Doctrine of the mean), both of which illustrated the emphasis which the Chinese placed on a meditative approach to life and to government. The *Chung Yung*, which described the state of calm achieved when the passions are controlled by reason, was concerned not only with the goal of perfecting oneself, but also with the mutual responsibilities of rulers and subjects.

Finally, the twelfth volume of the *Mémoires*, Amiot's long biography of Confucius, provided Russian readers with a wealth of material about the great thinker who, as the subtitle of the work indicates, was 'the most famous Chinese philosopher, the renewer of ancient learning' (Vie de Koung-tsée, Russian translation, title page).

The missionaries' personal impressions and evaluations of China and the Chinese are also brought out clearly in Du Halde's *Description de la Chine*.[11] Du

noteworthy that this translation from Grosier and one of the translations from Amiot concern Chinese military organisation. The choice of this material for translation reveals Russia's practical political interest in her neighbour, a concern which will be constantly evident in eighteenth-century Russian literature about China.

[10] Joachim Bouvet, *Histoire de l'empereur de la Chine*, translation as contained in *The Present condition of the Muscovite empire, till the Year 1699*, J. Crull, trans. (London 1699), translated into Russian in F. O. Tumanskii, *Собрание разных записок и сочинений [...] о жизни [...] Петра Великого* (Collection of various notes and works on the life of Peter the Great) (St Petersburg 1787-88), i (1787).

[11] It should be noted here at the start that certain aspects of life in seventeenth- and eighteenth-century China were not in fact Chinese in origin, but rather derived from the Manchus who had conquered China in 1644. This point is not always clear to a present-day reader of these excerpts, nor one supposes, would it always have been evident to a Russian reader of the eighteenth century. The attribute 'Chinese' will consequently sometimes be used rather imprecisely here and throughout this study to describe what

Halde, a Jesuit though not a missionary himself, utilised for the work much of the missionary material to which he had access as editor of the well-known *Lettres édifiantes et curieuses* which were published periodically during the eighteenth century. Du Halde's introduction to the *Description* sets the tone well for the first volume, stating at the outset that China is the largest and most beautiful of known kingdoms, a land where live 'un Peuple puissant, policé, habile dans les Arts, et appliqué aux Sciences' (Du Halde, i.1-2). A description of some of the areas and peoples of China is followed by the colourful first person accounts by the Jesuit fathers of several trips made by them within China. The first is a narration of the journey of the French priests, fathers Bouvet, de Fontaney, Gerbillon, Lecomte and de Visdelou from the port of Ning Po to Peking in 1687. Their impressions of the countryside, and their discussions of the receptions they received along the way by Christian converts and by local officials are almost entirely favourable. Uncomfortable inns, dust on the road, and a few unpleasant villages receive bare mention. Even the awareness that their hosts, in theory at least, consider all people outside of China as barbarians does not dampen their enthusiasm (Du Halde, i.79). Commenting on this basic attitude of the Chinese, the missionaries, incidentally, offer the advice and warning that any gifts sent by European governments to the emperor will cause the giver to be registered among the tribute states of the Empire, and add that the 'Moscovites' had objected greatly to this custom (Du Halde, i.80). The Chinese requirements for humility on the part of foreign visitors were not, however, of great concern to the Jesuits personally; they were willing to adapt themselves to the Chinese procedures in order to further their cause.[12]

The accounts of father de Fontaney's trip from Peking to Kiang Tcheou in 1688 and father Bouvet's long journey from Peking to Canton in 1693 are similarly full of praise for the Chinese. Both priests laud the industriousness of the people, as evidenced by their careful cultivation of the soil (Du Halde, i.91 and 99). Unpleasant situations, such as father Bouvet's encounter with a dishonest local official, are glossed over quickly (Du Halde, i.102).

The description by father Bouvet of a night spent in a Chinese temple illustrates the typical realistic attitude taken by the Jesuits toward problems of conversion. Although the bonze of the temple, to whom Bouvet spoke for several hours that night, showed an interest in Christianity, the missionary notes that the prospects of a miserable life of poverty that would await someone like this priest should he leave his position constitute a powerful factor in preventing conversion. Bouvet, who states that he has learned this from experience, seems to accept the fact and is not bitter (Du Halde, i.100-101), an attitude which will be seen to differ considerably from that of the Russian priest Gribovskii, who would arrive in China about a century later.

The travel accounts of the missionaries are followed by Du Halde's detailed 'Description géographique des provinces de la Chine'. This section provides a

should often technically be designated as 'Manchu'. For our purposes, though, the distinction does not seem of great importance. What is significant is that the Russians, like other Europeans, were now becoming familiar with the Middle Kingdom and were beginning to evaluate its ways.

[12] Arnold H. Rowbotham, *Missionary and mandarin: Jesuits at the Court of China*, p.216.

wealth of information on local scenery, climate, industries, customs, and traits of the inhabitants of each of the main cities of each province. Although Du Halde describes some regional groups in an uncomplimentary way (certain mountain peoples, for example, are said to be of a hard and savage character without the usual Chinese politeness), a favourable characterisation is made of almost every area. The descriptions of Nanking, the cultural centre, with its libraries and well stocked book stores, and of Peking are quite colourful. Du Halde praises the beauty of the capital, as well as the orderliness and lack of crime, achieved through a curfew and well organised guard. The system of justice is also commented upon briefly. While there is little formal protection against the abuse of authority by local officials, Du Halde states, the system of public 'censors' who report grievances to the emperor on behalf of the people, is very effective (Du Halde, i.121).

Russian readers of the *Description* could not have failed to perceive the enthusiasm that Du Halde and the missionary contributors to the work felt for their subject. The picture that emerges from the missionary narratives and Du Halde's own commentary is that of an almost utopian society. But while the narratives of the missionaries' travels and their scholarly works on China tended to present a very favourable view of the country, other materials concerning the Western European missionaries became available to Russian readers in the eighteenth century which indicated that the position of the Jesuits themselves in China was far from being a comfortable one.

A translation by the Russian sinologist Leontiev of a Jesuit petition presented to the emperor K'ang-hsi, and published in a Peking newspaper in 1692 appeared in a Russian journal in 1764.[13] A note included with the translation indicates that although Du Halde had mentioned this document, as far as the writer of the note knew, the *Petition* itself had not previously been published outside of China. In the *Petition*, which was occasioned by the compulsory closing of Jesuit churches in one of the provinces, the missionaries reviewed their activities in China and the favours that they had enjoyed, and asked that they be allowed to continue their work. Among the services alluded to by the missionaries, interestingly enough, was their assistance to the Chinese in an attack against the Russians, a reference, no doubt, to one of the Sino-Russian clashes over the fort at Albazin in the second half of the seventeenth century. In his answer to the petition, which is also given in the Russian translation, the emperor K'ang-hsi commended the work of the Jesuits (including their manufacturing of weapons used against the Russians). Pointing out that there was no law against idolatry, the emperor granted the petition. While the Chinese principle of religious toleration (a subject often discussed in the Jesuits' works) was brought

---

[13] 'Переводы с китайского языка. II Перевод с китайской газеты публикованной в 5 день 2 луны 31 года царствования Хана Кансия (1692) коя содержит в себе Езуитскую челобитную, и по челобитной решительную резолюцию' (Translations from the Chinese. II Translation from a Chinese newspaper published on the fifth day of the second month of the thirty-first year of the reign of the emperor K'ang-hsi (1692) which contains a Jesuit petition and an affirmative reply to the petition), *Ежемесячныя сочинения и известия о ученых делах* (Monthly compositions and news of scholarly matters) (Dec. 1764), pp.516-36 at 528-36.

out by the emperor's statement, the fact that the churches had been summarily closed must have indicated to Russian readers that there were also forces in China operating in opposition to this principle.

That the Jesuits are seen in the *Petition* to have cooperated with the Chinese against the Russians at the end of the seventeenth century may well have caused Russian readers to view them and their works about China with some suspicion. Later writers would speak of Jesuit intrigues against the Russian missionaries themselves. That there was, however, no personal hostility between the Jesuit missionaries and their Orthodox counterparts in Peking at the middle of the eighteenth century is brought out in another work, a manuscript which remained unpublished in the eighteenth century, but which may have been known at least to those closely associated with the mission. This is a Russian document entitled *Об иезуитах в Китае* (The Jesuits in China), written by the priest Feodosii Smorzhevskii, who served at the Russian mission in Peking between 1745 and 1755.[14] While excerpts that have been found from other writings by Smorzhevskii will be seen to shed some light on the history of the Russian religious venture in Peking, this work deals almost exclusively with the Jesuits and their successes and failures in China. The narrative, which to the best of my knowledge has not been reprinted since its appearance in *Сибирский вестник* (Siberian Herald) in 1822, has been generally neglected by historians of the Jesuit mission. But because most of the contemporary reports of the Jesuits' activities in China came either from the hands of the missionaries themselves, as in their *Lettres édifiantes*, or from their adversaries in other orders, such as father Ripa, Smorzhevskii's attempt to present an impartial and detached account of his Roman Catholic colleagues merits careful consideration. Perhaps most important is Smorzhevskii's discussion of the persecutions that members of the Society of Jesus suffered, since the Jesuit writers did not dwell on this aspect of their experiences. The Orthodox missionary's respect for the Jesuits and his close ties with them are evident from his description of their difficulties.[15]

Altogether then there appeared in Russia between 1744 and the end of the century a good selection of scholarly Jesuit works about China, as well as an impressive amount of material by other writers about the activities of the Jesuit missionaries in China. Paradoxically, the Russian public had very little published material during this period about its own religious mission in Peking. Histories and accounts of the mission, as well as the Russian missionaries' descriptions and views of China did not appear in published form or even circulate in manuscript copies until the period 1810-1814. Before this time, however, the Russian reader had several sources of information about the mission. One consisted of incidental comments in the translated narratives of Western European travellers. A second and probably more significant source

[14] Feodosii Smorzhevskii, 'Об иезуитах в Китае. (Отрывок из китайских записок иеромонаха Феодосия Сморжевскаго)' (The Jesuits in China. [Excerpt from the Chinese notes of the priest Feodosii Smorzhevskii]), contributed by E. F. Timkovskii, *Сибирский вестник* (Siberian herald), pt. 19 (1822), pp.107-32, 181-210; pt. 20 (1822), pp.227-54, 295-310, 329-56.
[15] See Barbara W. Maggs, '"The Jesuits in China": views of an eighteenth-century Russian observer', *Eighteenth-century studies* 8 (Winter 1974/75), pp.137-52.

was the unpublished correspondence and reports of the missionaries, students, diplomats, couriers, traders and others who came in contact with the mission, and the directives of the government and church to them. Although these documents remained classified during the eighteenth century,[17] it can be assumed that at least some of the impressions they contained were disseminated by word of mouth by the many persons who wrote them, and by the members of the inner circles of church and government who had the opportunity to read them. This material, concerned as it is with the activities of the mission itself, rather than with formal descriptions of China, throws considerable light on the attitudes and position of the Russian religious workers, and helps to explain why the Russian missionaries were not producing the quantity of commentaries that their Jesuit counterparts were. And indirectly it also reveals the attitudes of the members of the mission toward China and its culture. In their own way then these classified documents and oral reports no doubt enriched the Russian image of China.

During this period the mission also contributed to the Russian view of China through its various official and unofficial functions. Of considerable importance was the institution's undeclared but very significant role in Russo-Chinese political relations. While its main purpose was simply to serve the religious needs of the Orthodox who happened to be in Peking, the mission in fact acted as a kind of Russian embassy in China performing for the Russian merchants, couriers and diplomats who passed through Peking, many of the services which an embassy normally provides. In this capacity the religious institution facilitated communications between the Russian and Chinese governments.

Equally important was the mission's achievement in producing the first generation of genuine Russian sinologists. In England at mid-century an anonymous writer could suggest satirically that since war on the Continent interfered with the grand tour by young noblemen, they should instead complete their education by going to Peking; in Russia the extended tour of scholarly duty in China became in fact for certain promising youth an often trying reality. Almost from its very beginning the mission included, in addition to the priests, a fixed number of Russian students, stipulated by treaty, who were sent to Peking to study Chinese and Manchu. Some of these students died in Peking. Others did not succeed in their studies; but a number eventually returned to Russia where they performed several important tasks. Their literary work, mainly translations from the Chinese classics, rather than travel accounts or personal impressions of China, gave the Russian reader direct access to works previously unknown in Russia, and an introduction to the ancient culture of China, known earlier only through translations from Western European sources.[18] In addition, these

[17] Even the invaluable compilation of archival material made at the end of the eighteenth century by the historian N. Bantysh-Kamenskii, *Дипломатическое собрание дел между российским и китайским государствами с 1619 по 1792-й год* (Diplomatic collection of affairs between the Russian and Chinese states from 1619 to 1792) (Kazan 1882), could not be published until the late nineteenth century.

[18] Hugh Honour, *Chinoiserie: the vision of Cathay*, p.130; eight of the twenty-one Russian students sent between 1727 and 1794 died in Peking: P. E. Skachkov, 'History of the study of China in Russia in the 17th and 18th centuries – a brief outline', p.174.

specialists in Chinese and Manchu served, upon their return to Russia, as government translators, making possible direct communication between the tsar and the emperor. The preparation of Russian sinologists at the Peking mission therefore gave both the Russian people and the Russian government, for the first time, direct contact with their eastern neighbour, without intermediaries.[19]

The Peking mission's contribution to the Russian image of China in the form of manuscripts and published accounts delineating the missionaries' views of the nation in which they worked were not to appear until the early years of the nineteenth century. The first history of the mission, by the priest Feodosii Smorzhevskii, was written as early as the period 1745-1755 when the author served in Peking; this work was, however, suppressed by the Church because, according to a later 'official' historian of the mission, Amvrosii Ornatskii, it was full of 'gall and malignant gossip' about the priest's colleagues.[20] The early document by Smorzhevskii was apparently utilised to some extent by a second chronicler of the mission, archimandrite Sofronii Gribovskii, for his manuscript, also unpublished, entitled *Information about the beginning of the presence of the Russians in Peking and the existence there of the Greco-Russian faith*, a work which contains a considerable amount of material unfavourable to the priests.[21]

While this history by Gribovskii did not appear in published form, it can be assumed that it circulated in manuscript in the early years of the nineteenth century. The work contains a great many colourful details of human interest about life at the mission. Standing in sharp contrast to it is the first 'official' history of the mission published in Moscow in 1810 by Amvrosii Ornatskii. Ornatskii was not a missionary himself, but a professor of theology. His *Short description of the Peking monastery* (*Краткое описание пекинского монастыря*) presents only the bare facts of the mission's history, and, undoubtedly to preserve the reputation of the clergy and their position in China, omits anything which might create an unfavourable impression of either the missionaries or of relations between Russia and China.[22]

[19] G. Cahen, *Histoire des relations de la Russie avec la Chine sous Pierre le Grand (1689-1730)*, (Paris 1912), p.273.

[20] Amvrosii [Ornatskii], 'Краткое описание Китайского Пекинского монастыря' (A short description of the Chinese Peking monastery), ii (Moscow 1810), pp.439-500 at p.480 in *История российской иерархии* (History of the Russian Church hierarchy) (Moscow 1807-1815).

[21] Sofronii [Gribovskii] 'Уведомление о начале бытия россиян в Пэйдзине и о существовании в оном грекороссийской веры' in *Материалы для истории Российской духовной миссии в Пекине* (Materials for the history of the Russian religious mission in Peking), ed. N. I. Veselovskii (St Petersburg 1905), pp.1-45. How much Gribovskii relied on the Smorzhevskii history is not known, however, as the earlier manuscript, which remained in Peking until the mid-nineteenth century, has never been wholly recovered (Veselovskii, pp.vi-vii). An extract from Smorzhevskii's writings about the mission is entitled 'Выписка из замечаниев о Пекинских духовных миссиях' (Extract from remarks on the Peking ecclesiastical missions), in Veselovskii, pp.65-71.

[22] See note 20 above. A German version of the work appeared in Russia soon afterward in G. F. Müller, *Eröffnung eines Vorschlages zu Verbesserung der russischen Historie* (St Petersburg 1732-1764), vol. x, Supplement: *Sammlung russischer Geschichte* (Dorpat 1816), at pp.277-96, 'Schicksale der russischen Kirche in China'. See Cahen, p.clxv.

Although various modern histories give more complete and detailed accounts of the Peking Mission,[23] the details revealed by these early sources of information – the classified documents, Gribovskii's and Smorzhevskii's manuscript histories, and Ornatskii's 'official' history, all of which were written before 1814, give some idea of the mission and the life of the missionaries in China which Russian sinophiles at the end of the eighteenth and in the early years of the nineteenth century would have had.

Ornatskii's very favourable account of the mission begins with a brief description of the early seventeenth-century Russian trading caravans, bringing back friendly messages and gifts from the Mongolian and Chinese 'Khans' to the Tsars. The failure of one of the earliest Russian diplomatic missions to China, that of Nikolai Spafarii in 1675, to negotiate trade agreements is mentioned but passed over quickly. Ornatskii tells of the Russian settlements, especially the forts at Nerchinsk and Albazin on the Amur River, used by traders in Mongol territory as they expanded their commercial dealings in this area.[24] The siege of Albazin in 1685 by the Chinese (who had become apprehensive over Russian encroachment in the area) is, however, glossed over, with the emphasis being put instead on a description of the community established in Peking for the small group of Albazinians, who, according to Ornatskii, had been captured during the fighting (or who according to a modern view, had voluntarily emigrated over the years to China).[25] Among the Russians in Peking was an Orthodox priest who was permitted to conduct religious services for the members of the group. (The fact, incidentally, that the Albazinians were allowed to organise their own church provided Russian readers with another illustration of the Chinese attitude of religious toleration.)

Not many years after the arrival of the Albazinians, Ornatskii relates, the emissary of the Russian government, Ysbrants Ides, who had set out for China in 1692, requested but did not receive permission from the Chinese government for the establishment of a permanent Orthodox Church in Peking. In 1713 this permission was granted, and in 1715, the first Russian religious mission, headed by the archimandrite Ilarion Lezhaiskii, with nine other persons, arrived in Peking (Ornatskii, ii.449).

Both Ornatskii and Gribovskii relate that the first mission was favourably received. Gribovskii does, however, admit that archimandrite Lezhaiskii encountered serious difficulties in Peking. Although he received an adequate salary from the Chinese government, and a modest one from Russia, his funds were not sufficient for entertaining official guests. The generous archimandrite, giving away furs in exchange for gifts brought by the people, finally exhausted his resources. He applied at times to the Jesuits for help. Eventually he began to

---

[23] The best history of the mission is the account by Eric Widmer, *The Russian ecclesiastical mission in Peking during the eighteenth century* (Cambridge Mass., London 1976). The most recent 'official' history of the mission is that of Nikolai [Adoratskii], *Православная миссия в Китае за 200 лет ее существования* (The Orthodox mission in China during the 200 years of its existence) (Kazan' 1887); *Православный собеседник* (The Orthodox companion) (Feb.-Oct. 1887).

[24] Ornatskii, ii.446.

[25] Widmer, pp.13-16.

drink, evidently ruined his health in this way, and died a few years later (Gribovskii, *Information*, pp.14-16).

The friendly reception given the First Mission was not forthcoming for Peter the Great's appointee to replace Lezhaiskii, the bishop Innokentii Kul'chitskii, who arrived in Siberia in 1722 but was refused admittance to China. Ornatskii explains that political disagreements at this time concerning refugees and border disputes had caused the change of attitude on the part of the Chinese. More specifically, Ornatskii notes, the position of Christians in the Empire had deteriorated. The emperor Yung-cheng, in contrast to his father K'ang-hsi, who had permitted Christians to worship rather freely, had given orders to make things more difficult for the Christians and to confiscate their churches, and had forbidden his subjects to convert to Christianity. Ornatskii also lays part of the blame for the new Chinese position on the intrigues at the Court by the Jesuits, who, he claims, feared competition from the Russian priests.[26]

Eventually in 1729 a second mission, headed by a new appointee, Antonii Platkovskii, and a party of nine, was accepted in Peking. Included in this group were three students, one of whom, Ilarion Rossokhin, was to become an outstanding Russian sinologist. But Platkovskii's administration was ill fated; according to official reports, letters of complaint, and the extant portion of Smorzhevskii's manuscript history of the mission, it was marred by dissension between the archimandrite and his subordinates, mutual accusations of drunkenness, and even scandals such as an attack on the archimandrite by a Russian priest. The emperor himself sent the following report to Petersburg: 'The priest Ivan is unable to live quietly with the students who are in our country, and as a result disagreement and great arguments occur. He severely wounded the priest Antonii [Platkovskii] in the hand, and because of this we are sending the priest Ivan to the official in charge at your border.'[27] The students were said to be playing chess, cards and dice, and two of them were accused of being frequently intoxicated.[28] Platkovskii, who, according to Smorzhevskii, was such a 'strange person' that no one among the Russians, the residents of Peking, the Chinese officials, or the Jesuits had a good word to say about him and his work (Smorzhevskii, *Extract* in Veselovskii, p.69), was in 1734 ordered back to Petersburg, where he was brought to trial and reduced in rank to a simple monk.

While the affairs of the Third Ecclesiastical Mission under the new archimandrite, Ilarion Trusov, began well, the situation eventually began to resemble that which had developed under the previous administration. A report in 1741 from a student, Alexei Vladykin (also to become a Russian sinologist), accused archimandrite Trusov of insulting his subordinates, of not performing church services even on high holy days, and of succumbing to drunkenness and blasphemy, wearing a Chinese woman's dress, at times even in church.[29] Gribovskii's outspoken history of the mission states also that Vladykin accused archimandrite

---

[26] Ornatskii, pp.460-65. Authorities disagree on the question of Jesuit intrigues against the Russian Mission. See J. Glazik, *Die Russisch-Orthodoxe Heidenmission seit Peter dem Großen* (Münster 1954), p.56 and Rowbotham, p.234.

[27] Materials cited in Bantysh-Kamenskii, p.189.

[28] Materials cited in Cahen, pp.260-61.

[29] Materials cited in Bantysh-Kamenskii, pp.242-43.

Trusov of stealing church silver (*Information*, pp.22-23). The Synod responded by depriving the archimandrite of his jurisdiction over the clergy and students. Trusov died, however, in 1741, before the order reached him.

A report by the caravan director Erofei Firsov, presented to the Ministry of Foreign Affairs in 1742, noted that the Russian clergy, according to reports of the Chinese, were for the most part spending their time drinking and quarrelling among themselves. Firsov contrasted their conduct with the temperate ways of the Roman Catholic clergy, some of whom, he noted, even held local public offices.[30]

Ornatskii's official history, stressing continuously the friendly relations between Russia and China, states that the two succeeding missions under archimandrites Lintsevskii and Iumatov were praised by the Chinese; Ornatskii alludes only briefly to the fact that in 1760 the emperor, because of a dispute with Russia involving Chinese fugitives, had the Orthodox mission sealed off. A guard prevented the archimandrite Iumatov, the rest of the clergy and the students from leaving the compound, and a notice on the gates threatened death to any Chinese who tried to enter. Ornatskii tries to minimise the seriousness of the situation, stating that upon the insistence of the Russian Senate the mission was soon reopened.[31]

The incident involving the temporary sealing off of the mission by the Chinese raises the question, to what extent was the mission involved in diplomatic activity? Specialists do not agree on an answer. Soviet historians accuse the missionaries outright of espionage. The late nineteenth-century official historian of the mission, Adoratskii, states that occasionally the priests carried out diplomatic missions. Source materials seem to indicate that from the time of Iumatov's administration of the mission, 1755-1771, until the mid-nineteenth century missionaries did in fact participate in the diplomatic relations between the two countries, and that they were expected to engage in clandestine political activities. Iumatov, for instance, took part in negotiations in the 1750s regarding the navigational rights of the Russians on the Amur River. (His attempts at bribing the Chinese with gifts and feasts, however, were not successful.)[32] Later, archimandrite Tsvet, Iumatov's successor, was accused by the Russian students in Peking both of 'stupid administration' and of not gathering any information for the Russian government.[33] In 1780, according to another document, a directive was sent to archimandrite Shishkovskii cautioning against sending any secret information in private letters.[34]

---

[30] Bantysh-Kamenskii, p.244.

[31] Ornatskii, ii.480-81 and 486, and materials cited on p.299 in Bantysh-Kamenskii, who gives the date for the sealing off of the mission as 1759.

[32] Albert Parry, 'Russian (Greek Orthodox) missionaries in China, 1689-1917: their cultural, political and economic role', *Pacific historical review* 9 (1940), pp.401-24 at pp.401-403.

[33] I. Korostovets, 'Русская духовная миссия в Пекине' (The Russian ecclesiastical mission in Peking), *Русский архив* (Russian archives) 3, Issue 9 (1893), pp.57-86 at p.64.

[34] *Святейший Правительствующий Всероссийский Синод* (Most Holy Governing All-Russian Synod), 'Инструкция от Святейшаго Правительствующаго Всероссийскаго Синода' (Instructions from the most holy governing all-Russian synod) in Veselovskii, pp.53-58 at p.58.

The twentieth-century Roman Catholic historian of theology, Josef Glazik, who claims vigorously that the religious purpose of the mission was always secondary to its diplomatic one, furthers his argument by citing statistics showing the small number of converts to Russian Orthodoxy made by the mission. In 1778, for instance, the Russian Orthodox Baptismal Register indicated only twenty-four new registrants.[35]

Although there appears to be no definitive answer to the question of the extent of the mission's involvement in diplomacy, it seems probable that its political activity consisted mainly in serving as a medium for communication between the Russian and Chinese governments. The absence of aggressive missionary work on the part of the priests would seem to be the natural result of their situation: first, the purpose of the Orthodox Church in Peking had been originally to serve the Orthodox who happened to be there, rather than to make new converts; and second, although later missions were urged to make greater efforts at proselytising, they never really had the facilities or staff for it. That the Chinese government, which may have been cautious at first, evidently had little fear in the long run of the missionaries' espionage potentialities can be inferred from the fact that during the course of the eighteenth century, while the official diplomats sent by the Russian government were often given a less than friendly reception in Peking, the missionaries' relations with the government with a few exceptions were good.[36] Both sides evidently realised that it was the presence of the mission in Peking that made it possible for Sino-Russian relations to continue throughout the century.[37]

Thus the scope of the missionaries' political as well as religious activities appears to have been somewhat circumscribed. Similarly, their scholarly interests and endeavours were limited, for as the old documents and histories show, most of the Orthodox priests who were sent to Peking, unlike the Jesuits, were not scholarly men. One reason for this is that the general level of education and culture in Russia at this time was not high. The lack of academic interests on the part of the personnel of the mission is a reflection of this and of the general state of the Russian clergy. Furthermore, the best of the Russian clergy were not appointed to this post.[38] Peter the Great himself had stated in 1689, 'What is needed there are priests who are not so much learned, as reasonable and obliging [подкладный] men.'[39] Some of those who were sent to Peking went unwillingly;[40] others considered the position a quiet retreat or alternatively, and, unrealistically in most cases, a step in hierarchical advancement.[41] Confronted with numerous difficulties within the mission itself, few of the priests had the ambition or energy to learn Chinese, mingle with the people, or record their impressions of the community in which they found themselves. While they were

[35] Glazik, p.59.
[36] Korostovets, p.67.
[37] Widmer, pp.168-80.
[38] Korostovets, p.62.
[39] V. P. Petrov, *Российская Духовная миссия в Китае* (The Russian ecclesiastical mission in China) (Washington, D.C. 1968), p.17. Petrov quotes materials in Adoratskii.
[40] Archimandrites Kul'chitskii and Lintsevskii. Widmer, pp.60 and 136.
[41] Korostovets, p.66.

not harrassed by the Chinese government, as were the Jesuits at times, their situation was indeed difficult for several reasons. Besides lacking the experience which the Jesuits had been acquiring in China for more than a hundred years before the Russians arrived, the Orthodox mission was also hampered by the smallness of its staff, the lack of discipline among its members, and especially by insufficient financial support. Lacking impressive scholarly backgrounds, the Russians were not sought out at the Chinese court as were a number of the Jesuit scholars, even during the periods when the Jesuits' activities in the provinces were being restricted. The isolation from both the government and the Chinese people, and the lack of success in proselytising, as well as more personal factors such as ill health and aversion to the climate led to loneliness and boredom, and as has been seen, in numerous cases to hard drinking and dissolute living. Returning to the documentary chronicle of the mission's past, one finds in Gribovskii's pathetic description of the archimandrite Iumatov an illustration of the state of mind that many of the Russian missionaries apparently reached. After his ten years of service were over, Iumatov began to look with inceasing desperation for approaching Russian caravans and couriers, both of which seemingly had stopped coming. When three more years had gone by, the archimandrite gave up hope of ever returning home, began drinking excessively and died (*Information*, p.28).

It was Gribovskii himself who, arriving in Peking in 1794 as the eighth archimandrite of the mission, was the first to overcome the many difficulties facing the mission and provide for the Russian people descriptions both of the mission and of China, its history and its people. In addition to his manuscript history of the mission, discussed above, Gribovskii produced a manuscript account of his return trip from Peking to Kiakhta in 1808.[42] He is also the reputed author of a *Note, unsigned, concerning the difficulties facing an archimandrite in Peking in converting the Chinese to Christianity*.[43] Most important, though, is his account (running to almost 100 pages in print) entitled *News about the Chinese, now Manchu-Chinese Government*.[44] Although this work could only have been read in manuscript form in the eighteenth century, it is significant, both because it corroborates much of the information about the mission that must have been filtering back to Russia, and also because it is the first exposition by a Russian missionary about China, and as such invites comparison with the Jesuits' descriptions of the country.

Although he was criticised by his successor, Bichurin, for being an obstinate person and for accomplishing nothing at the mission (Veselovskii, p.iv), Gribovskii seems to have been considerably better prepared for his work, and of a more inquisitive and practical nature than his predecessors. In his history

---

[42] Sofronii [Gribovskii], 'Путешествие архимандрита Софрония Грибовскаго от Пекина до Кяхты в 1808 г.' (The Journey of archimandrite Sofronii Gribovskii from Peking to Kiakhta in 1808), *Siberian herald* 1 (1823), pp.1-14, 15-30, 31-44, 45-62.

[43] Sofronii [Gribovskii], 'Записка, без подписи, о трудностях, с которыми приходится считаться архимандриту в Пекине при обращении китайцев в христианство', in Veselovskii, pp.59-64. This title was used in an earlier collection, cited by Veselovskii (p.iv). Veselovskii calls the work 'Note without title'.

[44] Sofronii [Gribovskii], *News* (note 2 above).

he describes the state of complete disorganisation that existed at the mission when he arrived there. Insubordination, drunkenness, and even fights with the Chinese were among the disorders he encountered. Among the practical ideas he had for eventually improving the situation was that of recording his experiences for the benefit of his successors (*Information*, p.26).

While Gribovskii did not learn Chinese or Manchu during his thirteen-and-a-half-year stay in Peking, the archimandrite devised various methods of learning about his surroundings. He stated in his history, for instance, that it was essential for a Russian archimandrite to get to know the Jesuits in Peking – not only because they were the only source of companionship (the Chinese being ruled out because within a month after making one's acquaintance they would ask to borrow money which they would not be quick to repay), but also because evidently the Western Europeans were a good source of foreign news; for a Russian, Gribovskii stated, got no news from Russia. In addition, through Jesuit contacts one could become informed about local affairs (p.28).

Gribovskii, was not, of course, the first of the Russian missionaries to become friendly with the Jesuits. Smorzhevskii's contacts with them have been discussed. Lezhaiskii had turned to the Jesuits for money, and both Lintsevskii and Iumatov had been, according to Gribovskii, on good terms with their Jesuit counterparts. Gribovskii mentions that many Jesuits spoke well of archimandrite Iumatov, although it appears that they may have taken advantage of the superiority of their position in relation to the Chinese Court, for Gribovskii adds that Iumatov had to 'conduct himself with them as if with an older Russian' (pp.26-27).

The Synod of the Orthodox Church, it might be noted, took a dim view of fraternisation between members of the two rival missions. Among the numerous instructions received by archimandrite Trusov in 1734 was the admonition to refrain from discussions with the Jesuits.[45] Peter the Great had warned as early as 1698 that representatives of the Orthodox Church in Peking must 'for the sake of God, proceed carefully and slowly so as not to anger the Chinese officials, as well as the Jesuits, who have had their nest there for a long time'.[46] Shishkovskii, in the early 1780s was given the following directive: 'If, for some reason, you as Archimandrite have occasion to see or be in the company of any Jesuits or other Roman Catholic clergy who are in Peking, deal with them cordially but carefully, then and in further conversations, but most important, do not under any circumstances enter into debates with them about faith and the law.'[47] Gribovskii evidently ignored this general policy against collegial association, for he often mentions his contacts with 'Western European missionaries.'

The archimandrite was familiar with several published descriptions of China by Western Europeans, probably in Russian translation, and in his *News about the Chinese government* he frequently compares his own impressions with those found in these works. It is at once apparent that the archimandrite disagrees with much of what he has read. Unfortunately, he seldom gives direct citations,

---

[45] Materials cited in Cahen, p.263.
[46] Petrov, p.17. Petrov quotes materials in Adoratskii.
[47] 'Instructions' (note 34 above) in Veselovskii, pp.57-58.

and it is not possible to determine to which Western European works he is referring. It is strange in this connection that Gribovskii does not refer to the published reports of the Russian diplomatic missions which he could have cited to support many of his own arguments. But perhaps because of his long residence in Peking and association there with the Jesuits, Gribovskii was simply more familiar with Western European than with Russian accounts of China.

After a brief historical introduction concerning the Manchu conquest of China in 1644 (for more background on which he refers the reader to Aleksei Leontiev, the sinologist trained at the mission), Gribovskii describes the weak condition of the government of China at the end of the eighteenth and beginning of the nineteenth century. He discusses not only the ineffectiveness of the army in dealing with recalcitrant peoples in one of the western provinces, but also the corruption within the capital. As proof of the situation he claims that the emperor Ch'ien-lung (1736-1796), in return for bribes, pardoned on two occasions a provincial governor who had been convicted and sentenced to death. The emperor, he states, in addition violated the imperial laws through his cruelty to his wife, and finally, made plans to rob the graves of his ancestors. Opening his account in this way, the Russian priest presents a point of view strikingly different from the panegyrical approach of fathers de Fontaney, Gerbillon and Bouvet, whose accounts had appeared in the Russian translation of Du Halde about forty years earlier.

It is in fact true that the internal political situation at the end of the reign of Ch'ien-lung and during that of Chia-ch'ing (1796-1820) had deteriorated badly. Gribovskii, however, while giving the latter emperor credit for trying to end the corruption, generally gives the impression that conditions in China had not altered between the time the earlier Western European accounts to which he refers were written, and his own day. He implies rather, that the former descriptions are simply in error. For instance, at the beginning of his fourth section entitled 'The kind of justice that exists in China' Gribovskii states: 'The praises attributed by Europeans to the present Manchu-Chinese government do not deserve the slightest credence, the praises, that is, in the books they publish, in which plain facts, which have no relation to the essence of a thing are somewhat fair, but are mixed half and half with lies. I, having had the opportunity to know about the justice of the Manchu government and their actual observance of their laws, write here only the truth' (*News*, p.30).

The archimandrite lays much of the blame for the corruption in government on the dishonest ministers surrounding the emperor. He cautions the Russian government to be careful in its dealings with imperial counsellors, particularly in connection with gifts sent to the emperor. (It would seem, incidentally, that the presentation of gifts proved a greater source of annoyance to the Russians, as evidenced as early as the seventeenth century in the journals of the Russian envoys, and mentioned specifically in connection with the Russians in the accounts by fathers Bouvet, Fontaney and others, discussed earlier, than it did to the Western European ambassadors: *News*, p.58.)

Stressing that the main principle of government in China is respect for superiors and obedience to ancient tradition, whether or not it is 'incompatible with reason' (p.29), Gribovskii labels the Chinese government a monarchy, and states that the Western European history and geography books which refer to the system as a despotism are in error. Because he is so bound to tradition, especially in regard to religion, the emperor, according to Gribovskii, cannot be described as a despot, who would in contrast be a free agent (p.34). While he does not refer here to any specific sources, Gribovskii probably has in mind Montesquieu's *L'Esprit des lois* (1748) (translated into Russian in 1775), or to later works reflecting Montesquieu's classification of the government of China as a despotism.

In addition to presenting the view that justice is difficult to obtain, Gribovskii appears to be quite critical of the system of punishments when he discusses 'the severity of Chinese law' (pp.85-91). Like Du Halde, Gribovskii notes the extensive use of corporal punishment, and states that in no other country is it used to such an extent. (Du Halde, however, as we have seen, even while admitting that a privileged segment of the population, the mandarins, were exempt from the bastonade, had concluded that this did not obstruct the workings of justice (Du Halde, i.5)).

The laws regarding parental treatment of children are singled out for particular criticism by the archimandrite. In conformity with the principle of absolute respect for those higher in authority, children must obey their parents. But, Gribovskii asks, what if the parents are unjust? According to law parents can even sell their children as slaves, or if the children fail to respect them, the parents can have them executed. The only right a child possesses is to report his parents for treason (pp.50-51, 89-90). Elsewhere Gribovskii states that because of the improper conduct of parents toward their children, and the disobedience of the latter toward their parents, many children in fact run away from home and become indigents. His discussion of this point forms an interesting contrast with the ideal of filial piety referred to many times in Amiot's *Mémoires*.

The poverty he encountered made a great impression on the Russian priest. Europeans, he states, who read about the great wealth of China, would find it difficult to believe how much poverty exists there, or how many people, to take a specific example, are without clothing even in winter. Gribovskii attributes the existence of so many poor persons to various causes. In addition to the unhappy family relations which produce runaway, indigent children, he cites the national tendency toward extravagance, and the laziness of the people. While the government provides some assistance for these people, as well as hospitals for the elderly, the personnel who operate the programmes, Gribovskii claims, have no interest in the recipients and often embezzle the government's funds (pp.51-52).

In his chapter 'Cleanliness and order in Peking and how zealously they are maintained by the police', the archimandrite makes some caustic remarks comparing what he has read with what he has personally observed. While the 'perfection' of the system of sanitation is much trumpeted in Europe, Gribovskii states, there are times in March, when the canals are opened throughout Peking, that the smell is so overwhelming one can hardly go out on the street. Most of the canals are kept open until residents and local merchants pay the officer of the street and the soldiers to close them up again. The local use of night soil contributes to the unpleasant atmosphere of the city. Gribovskii, like other foreign commentators, notes the enormous quantities of dust on the roads, but in addition he describes the custom of sprinkling the roads with water from the offensive smelling canals, which adds considerably, he says, to the general stench (p.49).

Much of Gribovskii's report consists of information about climate, crops, and livestock which is, for the most part, presented objectively and without comment.[48] He does make an occasional disparaging remark in connection with this material, however, such as the statement that the lack of land for cultivation results from the 'stupid rites of the Chinese, dictated by their empty theory' regarding the preservation of the graves of their ancestors (p.68).

In his discussion of the various religions of China, the archimandrite, while making clear his view that the Chinese are idolatrous, tries to remain unemotional. Without mentioning any specific works, Gribovskii states that in certain European accounts it is said that the emperor, nobles, and learned people, 'having minds rather enlightened by natural religion', believe in and worship the one true God (pp.101-102). This opinion, the archimandrite says, is erroneous. While the Chinese use a term, 'Shang-ti', meaning Heavenly Ruler, this refers, Gribovskii states, to one god who is merely higher than other gods.[49]

The term mentioned by Gribovskii, 'Shang-ti', was interpreted by the Jesuits during the seventeenth and first half of the eighteenth century as having a meaning similar to 'Jehovah', or the one true God. Disagreement over the meaning of the term eventually became one of the main points of dispute in the long and involved 'Rites controversy' which racked the Roman Catholic missionary effort during this period. The exact meaning of the term 'Shang-ti' was in fact ambiguous even in Chinese. The Jesuits, who claimed that Confucian philosophy, since it recognised one Supreme Deity in the concept of 'Shang-ti', did not basically conflict with Christianity, were opposed by the Dominicans and other orders within the Church, who claimed that Confucians did not in fact worship a Supreme Ruler; the term 'Shang-ti', they said, referred to the head of the four hierarchical classes of spirits. 'Shang-ti' was therefore not in

---

[48] Gribovskii's disagreement with a European source in regard to the climate of China includes one of his few direct citations; it is to an *Историческое и географическое описание Китая*, translated into Russian from German (*News*, p.75). This is possibly the *Историческое и географическое описание Китайской империи, с изъяснением различных названии Китая* (Historical and geographical description of the Chinese empire with explanations of the various names of China), translated from German in 1789, five years before Gribovskii arrived in Peking.

[49] Gribovskii was not, incidentally, the first to express this point of view to Russian readers. One of the few commentaries on Chinese religion to be published in a Russian periodical in the eighteenth century was an anonymous article, probably a translation, appearing in 1763, which had presented a quite prejudicial survey of the indigenous Chinese religions, concluding that the worship of the one true God had in general died out: I. F. Bogdanovich, 'Диссертация о древнем Китайском законе' (Dissertation on ancient Chinese canon law), *Невинное упражнение* (Innocent pastime) (1763), pp.90-96, 114-32. *Union catalogue*, vol. iv, entry 188, p.153 indicates that this is a translation from Voltaire; I have, however, been unable to verify this fact.

any way comparable to the Christian concept of a deity who is a personal entity and the creator and ruler of the universe.[50]

The Catholic controversy had already come to a close, with the Jesuit point of view being rejected by the Roman Catholic Church, when Gribovskii made his comments. It would seem that the archimandrite made his interpretation independently of the Russian Orthodox Church, which was apparently not concerned with controversial points of Chinese religious doctrine.[51] In view of his rather close association with the Jesuits and his ignorance of the Chinese language, it is noteworthy that Gribovskii reached conclusions which were similar to those of the Jesuits' opponents.

In spite of his many negative criticisms of the Chinese, Gribovskii does praise certain aspects of their culture. Commenting on the matter of religious freedom, he joins the Jesuits in crediting the Chinese with allowing foreigners complete freedom in this 'and in their national customs' (p.81). The archimandrite also registers approval of the Chinese when he states that they carry out their business agreements with foreigners quite faithfully; but, Gribovskii seems to hasten to add, this is mainly because they fear a foreigner might register an official complaint against them if they do not (p.83).

The Western European accounts which describe the Chinese as moderate in matters of eating and drinking, except on certain ceremonial occasions, are in general accurate, the archimandrite notes. Heavy drinkers may possibly be found inside the taverns, where, the priest has to admit, he has never been. But during his thirteen years in Peking, Gribovskii writes, he saw drunkards on the streets on only two or three occasions (pp.95 and 101).

Gribovskii concurs with the Western European travellers upon another point – their admiration for Chinese landscape gardening. The Chinese concept of seemingly free, natural gardens differed radically from the principle of formally organised landscaping which had previously dominated in England and on the Continent. Russian readers were already familiar with some of the views of William Chambers, the British architect who wrote enthusiastically about Chinese gardens. A translation of Chambers's *Designs of Chinese buildings, furniture, dresses, machines and utensils … to which is annexed a description of their temples, houses, gardens, etc.* (London 1757), was published in Russian in 1771 and a commentary on this work appeared in 1786.[52] (The Russian royalty showed its own approval of Chinese architecture and landscaping by constructing a replica of a Chinese village on the grounds of the palace at Tsarskoe Selo.) Much of what Chambers

---

[50] Rowbotham, pp. 128-31.

[51] That the Synod of the Russian Orthodox Church assumed, however, that the Chinese did not worship the same divinity honoured by Christians can be inferred from a document of 1742 which noted that China as a nation 'lives in almost complete idolatry' (cited in Widmer, p.136).

[52] Cheimbers (William Chambers), *О китайских садах. Перевод из книги сочиненной г. Чамберсом содержащей в себе описание китайских строений, домашних их уборов, одеяний, махин и инструментов*, trans. of Chambers, *Designs of Chinese buildings, furniture, dresses, machines and utensils [...] to which is annexed a description of their temples, houses, gardens, etc.* (London 1757; St Petersburg 1771); Anon., 'О садах в Китае' (On gardens in China), *Экономический магазин* (Economic magazine), pt. 25 (1786), pp.321, 337, 353.

had attributed to the Chinese, however, was really his own proposal for a new style of landscaping. The true facts about the Chinese system of gardening, including its propensity for forcing trees into various shapes, such as forms of animals, did not come out until the nineteenth century.[53] But Gribovskii's discussion of Chinese gardening, which he calls 'the imitation of nature through delusion' (*News*, p.96) combines both the early European admiration for the so-called Chinese system, and a realisation that it is achieved through considerable artifice. They 'purposely distort living trees', Gribovskii writes, 'and do the same with the new branches when they appear', creating a very attractive sight (p.96).

In these favourable comments on certain aspects of Chinese life the archimandrite can be seen to agree with and to share some of the enthusiasm of the Western European authors that he has read. His overall impressions, however, particularly as seen in the section 'Morals and characteristics of the Chinese', in which he compares his own observations with those of certain European writers, are definitely uncomplimentary. The Europeans are correct, writes Gribovskii, in saying that the Chinese are very proud, and that they do not consider persons of other nationalities to be people, or that at best they view them as very stupid people. Gribovskii, for his part, finds the Chinese intelligent, of a rather melancholy disposition, with a wrathful nature. They are not dependable, he says, do not keep promises, and engage in thievery. Stressing that Chinese standards are different from those of Christians, Gribovskii dwells particularly on the concept of deception, which, he claims, is not considered a sin by the Chinese. They are experts at keeping secrets and specialise in tricky dealings; if you should need an undercover agent (фискал), you will not find a better one than a Chinese, writes the priest bitterly (p.94). Not only are they dishonest among themselves in public, but even within families brother deceives brother.

Gribovskii provides an illustration of the concept of deception in his other work, that dealing with the history of the mission, in his comments on Chinese converts to Christianity. When a caravan would arrive from Russia, he states, the Chinese, who knew that the director of the caravan was authorised to trade only with the baptised, would appear in great numbers to receive this sacrament. While the Russian merchants remained in Peking, the newly baptised would attend church. Afterwards they would not be seen inside the church again – until the next caravan arrived. The archimandrite also accuses some of accepting baptism as an easy way of access to the Russian compound, where opportunities for theft abounded (*Information*, pp.41, 43).

While the French Jesuits also took a realistic view toward conversion, as was seen in the example of father Bouvet and the Buddhist bonze, they did not, at least in their writings available to the Russians, exhibit the bitterness of tone that can be felt in the Russian priest's remarks. The Jesuits in fact were very optimistic about their success in making conversions, amassing statistics which, if perhaps questionable, were certainly impressive. In 1705, for example, during the high point of their success in China, it is claimed that there may have been

[53] Honour, pp.117, 148-49, 158.

as many as 300,000 converts to Christianity.[54] But Gribovskii's pessimistic comments about deception and the motivation of at least some Chinese converts cannot be written off entirely to the fact that the Russian mission had relatively little success in this venture. The official journal of the Russian ambassador Vladislavich-Raguzinskii contains a declaration made by certain Chinese ministers at a meeting with him in December 1726 which tends to corroborate the view later expressed by Gribovskii. The Chinese ministers, according to Vladislavich, stated that the Chinese people

do not adopt the Orthodox faith, and only deceive the Russian priests; some have pretended to adopt the Orthodox faith: it was to receive a certain present and a cross [of silver], but all the time, and afterward, they remain Chinese. [...] For more than one hundred and fifty years the Jesuits have endeavored to introduce the Roman Catholic faith throughout China, and it is true that a number of Chinese deceivers have accepted the Roman Catholic faith for an hour, in order to receive some presents; but afterwards they actually live in the [Chinese Buddhist] faith and deceive the Jesuits. [...] The Jesuits write that they have already led more than 200,000 Chinese to the Roman Catholic faith; it is possible that they have really baptised this number, but there are actually not more than 2000 in the whole Empire who now believe in the Roman Catholic faith. The Jesuits think they are deceiving our people: they are openly deceiving themselves and their kings, for [the kings'] money, sent to them, the Jesuits, remains with [the ministers of China], in China. And the Chinese maintain their faith as before.[55]

Gribovskii expresses his conclusions about the Chinese in this way: 'Thus, if this nation is examined very thoroughly, in all fairness it can be said to be in great need and distress' (*News*, p.92). One feels in reading the archimandrite's account, that he has indeed attempted to be fair. While disagreeing in the main with the Western European writers he has read, Gribovskii's aim is not simply to refute their opinions, but rather to give a description of China as seen from the Russian Orthodox Mission. While his assessment of Chinese life is generally uncomplimentary, the archimandrite does not hesitate to praise certain aspects of it. Although he often uses information supplied to him by contemporary missionary sources in Peking, Gribovskii seems to draw his own conclusions, and tries to give examples from his own experience for the judgments he makes. A good example of his attempt at objectivity is found incidentally in his work entitled *Note*, when, reversing the position of the observed and the observer, the missionary describes the Russian priests as seen through the eyes of their hosts. The Chinese, he writes, 'are ashamed to have as teachers uncouth and uneducated people who do not know the customs or language of the Chinese, and who go about with long beards and wear strange repulsive clothes' (p.59).

Gribovskii's generally unfavourable views about China are also reflected in his 'Journey', which recounts the return journey from Peking to Russia in 1808. Tired, and in failing health, the archimandrite found the trip extremely arduous. Only when he once again saw vegetation similar to that of Russia, did Gribovskii begin to seem happy. The missionary's pleasure at the sight of mushrooms provides the reader with a poignant glimpse into the life of loneliness and

[54] Rowbotham, p.210.
[55] Document in Cahen, pp.xcvii-xcviii.

isolation which Gribovskii, like his predecessors, must have endured during his long sojourn in Peking.

Gribovskii did not make as great a contribution to Russian scholarship on China as did his immediate successor, archimandrite Bichurin, whose *Описание Пекина* (Description of Peking) (1829), based on an eighteenth-century Chinese work, was recognised by nineteenth-century sinologists as an authoritative study and was often drawn upon by them.[56] Gribovskii does, however, deserve considerable credit as the first of the Russian missionaries to make a systematic exposition of his views.[57]

At the time Gribovskii wrote his *News about the Chinese government* the sinomania in Western Europe, which had reached its height in the 1760s, had abated greatly. Certain European works, such as Grimm's *Correspondance littéraire* as early as 1773, and Condorcet's *Esquisse d'un tableau historique des progrès de l'esprit humain* in 1793, had expressed the same sceptical conclusions about the superiority of Chinese culture as those drawn by Gribovskii. Two of the most important travel accounts which had been to a great extent responsible for the reversal of Western European opinion about the attributes of Chinese culture were admiral Anson's *A voyage round the World* (1748) and the Staunton account of lord Macartney's embassy (1797). Although these two travel accounts had been translated into Russian in 1751 and 1804 respectively, Gribovskii was evidently not familiar with them or with the changing tide of taste in Western Europe. He makes no mention of these accounts or of other descriptions by Russian travellers, such as the journals of the seventeenth-century and eighteenth-century diplomats, which contained unfavourable appraisals of Chinese civilisation. His work is therefore the more remarkable in that he appears to have reached his conclusions about the fallacies of the Chinese superiority theory quite independently of other writers.

The question that arises as a result of the comparison of Jesuit and Russian Orthodox evaluations of Chinese society is why did the views of the two missionary groups differ so much from each other? We have seen that the position of the Russian missionaries in Peking was quite difficult, even though the Orthodox Church was not persecuted by the Chinese government. In view of the problems with which the Russian missionaries were beset, it is understandable that even a scholarly archimandrite such as Gribovskii, in spite of his attempt to be objective in his appraisals, could have come to view Chinese life with a jaundiced eye. But the practical position of the Jesuits, who were actually persecuted by the Chinese, was in fact even more formidable, and still these missionaries were full of praise for Chinese culture.

Since the differences in the missionaries' outlooks cannot be explained by the physical conditions of their lives, other aspects of their situation might be

---

[56] N. Ia. Bichurin, *Описание Пекина* (Description of Peking) (St Petersburg 1829). Bichurin also wrote numerous other books about Chinese life and culture; see Juliet Bredon, *Peking* (Shanghai 1931), Preface.

[57] By the middle of the nineteenth century a sufficient number of scholarly articles had been produced by members of the mission to form a four-volume work, *Труды членов Российской духовной миссии в Пекине* (Works by the members of the Russian ecclesiastical mission in Peking) (St Petersburg 1852-1866).

considered. One of these is the ideological basis on which the missionaries operated. The motivation for much of the praise of Chinese culture on the part of the Jesuits can be understood by examining the questions of Chinese converts to Christianity and the Rites Controversy within the Roman Catholic Church. The Jesuit missionaries, who sincerely felt that the Chinese could convert to Christianity and at the same time retain some of their ancient customs, wanted to convince the rest of the world that these customs were of a social rather than a religious nature and that they were not in fact pagan. They hoped that by showing the moral superiority of the Chinese people they could demonstrate that China was not a pagan nation.[58] It may well be that the Jesuits were thus predisposed to see the best in Chinese life, and becoming attracted to the ideals of the society, particularly to the concepts of justice and morality, were inclined to overlook any all too human discrepancies between theory and practice. Gribovskii, in contrast, while he may have been somewhat prejudiced against the Chinese for circumstantial reasons, was not bound by any ideological necessity to look for either the bad or the good aspects of the society. For this reason he was able, at times at least, to present the analysis of an objective observer.

Psychological factors connected with this issue must also ultimately have influenced the missionaries' appraisal of their hosts. Perhaps the differing points of view between the Western and the Russian missionaries are mainly attributable to the human tendency to react to a new environment in accordance with the way one's own affairs prosper there. The Western Europeans felt that they were in fact accomplishing their goals of making Christian converts among the Chinese and of convincing the rest of the world that China was a morally superior and not a pagan nation. This feeling of success may account for their optimistic outlook both on their work and on the milieu in which they found themselves. The Russian missionaries, however, who had the quite limited objective of maintaining Orthodoxy among Russian residents in Peking, found themselves without even the proper support to perform this task, and as a result could not have felt that their efforts were totally effectual. Their less than sanguine view of the environment in which they found themselves may have developed in part from this situation.

From the works of the French Jesuit missionaries that were translated into Russian in the eighteenth and early nineteenth centuries, and the material provided during the same period by those connected with the Russian mission in Peking, Russian readers received a considerable amount of valuable factual information, as well as widely differing impressions of the Middle Kingdom. The majority of the published material consisted of the highly laudatory works of the Jesuits. In contrast to them the few travel accounts and unpublished literary impressions that the Russian missionaries produced, along with the documents revealing the history of the mission – especially the personal histories of the Orthodox priests in Peking, reflected the fact that there was little enthusiasm on the part of the Orthodox missionaries for Chinese life and culture. At the same time, the first history of the Russian mission that was actually

[58] Basil Guy, *The French image of China before and after Voltaire*, pp.44-50.

published, that by Ornatskii, attempted to present a favourable picture of China, at least of the life lived by the Russian missionaries in Peking. More important, the Russian students attached to the mission, who returned to Moscow and St Petersburg to produce the first direct translations of the Chinese classics from Chinese into Russian, demonstrated an appreciation of Chinese culture similar in some ways to that of the Jesuit sinologists.

If Russian readers had tried to form an impression of China solely on the basis of the works of those connected with the Western European and Russian missionary ventures there, their task would have been a very difficult one. The image that emerges from these works contains perplexing contradictions. The missionary reports were, however, only one part of the broad range of literature about China that was available to Russian sinophiles of this period.

2. Chinese visitors in Russia

'We replied [...] that [...] we had previously only heard
about their Russian state, but had never been there, but
since we now had had the occasion to travel through their
Russian land [...] and see so much of their goodwill, we
too were extremely pleased.'

The Chinese Consul, Tulishen[1]

WHILE missionaries, merchants, explorers and other travellers from Russia and
Western Europe were making their way eastward to Peking and back, and
providing their compatriots with their first-hand impressions of the Middle
Kingdom, a smaller but very significant number of travellers journeyed westward, from China to various countries in Europe, where they were generally
received with great interest, and where their personal appearances, conversation,
and writings made a unique contribution to the European view of the Celestial
Empire.

It was the Christian missionaries to China who were responsible for bringing
many of these Chinese visitors to Western Europe. Among the first were Michael
Chin Fo-Ts'ung and his compatriot Huang, who returned with father Philippe
Couplet to France in 1684. Chin Fo-Ts'ung was entertained by the king himself,
an event described in some detail by the *Mercure galant*. He later visited both
England and Italy. Huang stayed in France in order to work on a Chinese
dictionary. Other protégés of the missionaries were Arcade Wang, who was
taken back to Rome and later Paris by the vicar apostolic to Szechwan in 1703,
and who is said to have provided Montesquieu with the inspiration for the *Lettres
persanes*, and John Hoo, who accompanied father Foucquet on his return to
Europe in 1721, but became insane after reaching France.[2] Five Chinese converts
accompanied father Ripa of the Sacred Congregation of the Propaganda on his
return to Italy in 1724.[3]

Later in the century, in 1756, a Chinese named Loum Kiqua was received
by members of the royal family in England.[4] A Chinese page of the duke of
Dorset, Whang-At-Ting, was immortalised by becoming the subject of two

---

[1] Tulishen, 'Описание путешествия, коим ездили китайские посланники в Россию,
бывшие в 1714 г. у калмытского хана Аюки на Волге' (Description of a journey to Russia
by the Chinese consuls who visited the Kalmuk Khan Aiuki on the Volga in 1714),
trans. A. Rossokhin, *Ежемесячныя сочинения и известия о ученых делах* (Monthly
compositions and news of scholarly matters) 2 (1764), pp.3-48, 99-150, 195-234, 291-
353, 387-413, 414-28, at 403-404.

[2] Basil Guy, *The French image of China before and after Voltaire*, pp.158-59. The names of
the Chinese visitors in Europe appear in various transcriptions; William W. Appleton,
A cycle of Cathay, p.131. Appleton gives the date of Couplet's return as 1685.

[3] George Macartney, *An embassy to China*, ed. J. L. Cranmer-Byng (Hamden, Conn.
1963), pp.384-85, note 91.

[4] Beverly Sprague Allen, *Tides in English taste (1619-1800): a background for the study of
literature* (Cambridge, Mass. 1937), ii.18.

portraits by sir Joshua Reynolds,[5] and a Chinese portrait sculptor named Chit-qua (or Tan Chetua), who was working in England, gained renown by having attributed to him the 'explanatory discourse' that appeared in the second edition of William Chambers's *Dissertation on oriental gardening*. Chambers, who had actually written the discourse himself, felt it would lend authority to his work to put it in the name of a genuine Chinese artist.[6]

These and other Chinese travellers, through their mere presence as well as through the influence they exerted upon writers such as Chambers and especially Oliver Goldsmith, who was to create in his *Citizen of the World* the prototype of numerous fictional Chinese visitors in Europe, made a considerable contribution to the Western view of the Orient. In addition, at least one of the real-life visitors was to help formulate the European image of the Middle Kingdom through his own interpretations of Chinese culture. This was the Chinese convert Kao Lei-Ssu, who, with his compatriot Yang Te-Wang, was sent to Paris by the Jesuit missionaries in the early 1750s to receive a European education. After many years of studies supervised by the French Academy and by the Jesuits, the Chinese were ordained as priests and returned to China in 1766 to help in the work of the mission. A series of questions regarding political economy, which had been submitted to them by the French Minister of Finance, Turgot, formed the basis of Turgot's influential treatise, *Réflexions sur la formation et la distribution des richesses* (1766).[7]

Kao and possibly Yang also contributed to the monumental *Mémoires concernant [...] les Chinois* (1776-1814) discussed earlier; the preface explains that in addition to the material supplied by the European missionaries in Peking, the work includes writings by two Chinese who had studied in Paris and then returned to China. The first volume of the *Mémoires* contains a lengthy article signed by Ko, Jéf. entitled 'Essai sur l'antiquité des Chinois', in which in addition to discussing the beginnings of the Chinese empire and the origins of the Chinese language, and describing the Chinese literary classics, the writer draws upon his experience as a Chinese visitor in Europe to make some comparisons between the lives of scholars in China and France. He speaks favourably of the attitude of the French toward him as a foreigner, and of the scholarly atmosphere in Paris. Another article by a Chinese, found in the second volume of the *Mémoires*, constitutes a lively, indignant, and sarcastic commentary on a work by Cornelius de Pauw (whose name is not actually given in the text), a Dutch geographer whose description of China, published in 1770, was far from favourable.[8]

---

[5] Appleton, p.103.

[6] William Chambers, *A dissertation on oriental gardening, to which is annexed an explanatory discourse by Tan Chetua, of Quang-chew-fu, gent.*, 2nd ed. with additions (London 1773); Hugh Honour, *Chinoiserie: the vision of Cathay*, p.158.

[7] A. R. J. Turgot, 'Questions sur la Chine adressées à deux Chinois, suivies de Réflexions sur la formation et la distribution des richesses', in *Œuvres et documents*, ed. Schelle (Paris 1913), vol.ii, 1st ed., 1766; Guy, pp.354-56; Kao is alternatively spelled Ko; see A. H. Rowbotham, *Missionary and mandarin: the Jesuits at the Court of China*, p.286.

[8] *Mémoires concernant l'histoire, les sciences, les arts, les mœurs, les usages, etc. des Chinois – par les missionaries de Pékin*, i.i-iv, 9-11 and ii.365-574; see Cornelius de Pauw, *Recherches philosophiques sur les Egyptiens et les Chinois* (Berlin 1773); Lewis A. Maverick, *China a model for Europe* (San Antonio, Texas 1946), p.59.

The two articles in the *Mémoires* by Chinese authors are among the very small number of works by Chinese who had visited the West that eventually found their way in the eighteenth century into Russian literature about China. The first three volumes of the *Mémoires*, as discussed earlier, appeared in Russian translation in Moscow in 1786-1788. The Chinese commentary on de Pauw, containing several references to visits of Russian ambassadors to China, was probably of particular interest to Russian readers. De Pauw's unfavourable views on China, while given only in excerpts, form a striking contrast to most of the Western European impressions of the Middle Kingdom that appeared in Russian translation.

While these two articles undoubtedly had some effect on the formation of the Russian reader's image of China, more substantial contributions to the image were made by several considerably earlier accounts concerning Chinese who in the capacity of official diplomats had travelled in Russia itself. The most impressive of these is a narrative which was originally published in Chinese and Manchu in Peking in 1723 and was subsequently translated, in whole or in part, into French, German, English and Russian. The account, entitled in Russian translation, 'Описание путешествия, коим ездили китайские посланники в Россию, бывшие в 1714 г. у калмытского хана Аюки на Волге' (Description of a journey to Russia by the Chinese consuls who visited the Kalmuk Khan Aiuki on the Volga in 1714)[9] was written by the Mandarin Tulishen, the official historian of a group of six chief emissaries sent by the Manchu emperor K'ang-hsi in 1712 to the Torgut Mongols. These were a Kalmuk people who at the beginning of the seventeenth century had emigrated westward from the region called Dzungaria on the western borders of China to the area of the Ural Mountains along the Volga River. The Russian government had attempted through successive treaties from 1673 to 1710 to secure an alliance with the Torguts. At the same time the Chinese government showed great interest in these people, attempting to exert its own influence over them.

The sending of an embassy by the Chinese to a foreign government outside of Asia was an unprecedented step. The reasons behind the mission were not fully known to diplomats of the eighteenth century, nor are they entirely clear to historians in the present century. It seems probable though that one purpose of the embassy was to encourage the Torguts to return to China. This they were in fact to do in the 1770s.[10]

---

[9] There were two eighteenth-century Russian translations. The title quoted in the text is from the translation by I. Rossokhin, see above, note 1. The second Russian translation is by A. Leontiev: Tulishen, *Путешествие китайскаго посланника к калмытскому Аюке хану, с описанием земель и обычаев российских* (The Journey of the Chinese consul to the Kalmuk Khan Aiuki with a description of the Russian lands and customs) (St Petersburg 1782; 2nd ed. 1788). Both Russian translations were from Tulishen's original Manchu text, rather than his Chinese version.

[10] G. Cahen, *Histoire des relations de la Russie avec la Chine sous Pierre le Grand (1689-1730)* (Paris 1912), pp.116-19, 130-33; the first of Tulishen's epilogues to his narrative, which discusses inter alia Chinese difficulties with the Kalmuks of the border area, is one of the few contemporary explanations of the complicated political situation in this area that appeared in a Russian periodical.

The proximity of the Torgut people to Russian territory during the first three quarters of the eighteenth century had considerable effect on Sino-Russian relations. Because of the Torguts, official Chinese diplomatic missions were to cross through Russia several times in the early part of the century, the second group visiting the Russian ruler as well as the Torgut Khan. The personal contacts of these Chinese ambassadors with the Russian people, as well as the literary accounts of their visits, were to be an important factor in the formation of the Russian image of China. In addition, matters concerning the Torgut people caused the exchange of numerous communications between China and Russia during the eighteenth century, a correspondence which revealed much to the Russians about the Chinese national character and interests. Although they were known only to government personnel, and to researchers or historians of the period, these letters constitute a unique source for the formation of the Russian view of China, one which did not in any comparable degree exist in Western European countries.

The narrative by the consul Tulishen is an exceptional travel account for the period, not only in terms of its factual content relating to the people, the geography, and the flora and fauna of Siberia, southeastern Russian and the other areas visited, but also for its colourful vignettes, and for the creation, mainly through an unusual amount of dialogue, of a number of persuasively real Russian and Chinese figures. For these scholarly and artistic reasons, and simply because of the popularity in Europe at this time of travel accounts, especially ones relating to Russia and China, it is not surprising that the first translation of the narrative in a Western European language appeared in 1729, only six years after its publication in Chinese and Manchu. This was an abridged French translation by the Jesuit missionary Antoine Gaubil, one of the leading French sinologists.[11]

Soon afterward, a German translation was made from the French by the German sinologist G. F. Müller, who resided in St Petersburg and who contributed significantly to scholarship about China both in Russia and in Western Europe. His translation of Gaubil's version of Tulishen's work, which he included in his nine-volume Russian history, appeared in 1732.[12] Müller was dissatisfied, however, that a complete version of the narrative was not available, and when the Russian sinologist Ilarion Rossokhin, who had studied in Peking under the auspices of the Russian Orthodox Mission, returned to Russia with a copy of the full Tulishen text in the original, Müller persuaded him to make a complete Russian translation. Rossokhin's carefully annotated translation was made from Tulishen's Manchu text rather than from his Chinese version, which had been

[11] (Tulishen), 'Relation chinoise', abridged trans. by A. Gaubil in E. Souciet, *Observations mathématiques, astronomiques, géographiques, chronologiques et physiques, tirées des anciens livres Chinois ou faites nouvellement aux Indes et à la Chine; par les pères de la Compagnie de Jésus,* i (Paris 1729), pp.148-75.

[12] (Tulishen), 'Auszug einer Chinesischen Reise-Beschreibung von Peking durch Sibirien nach der Astrachanischen Calmuckey'. German trans. based on French trans. by A. Gaubil in G. F. Müller, *Eröffnung eines Vorschlages zu Verbesserung der Russischen Historie durch den Druck einer Stückweise herauszugebenden Sammlung von allerley zu den Umständen und Begebenheiten dieses Reichs gehörigen Nachrichten,* i (St Petersburg 1732), at pp.327-48.

used for the French abridgement and which contained numerous distortions in place names. Because of its fulness and faithfulness to the original, Rossokhin's translation is generally agreed to be superior to the previous translations. Müller added his own notes and comments to those of Rossokhin and published the work in 1764 in one of the most important Russian journals of the day, *Monthly compositions*, which he edited.[13] Later in the century another Russian sinologist, Aleksei Leontiev, also a former student of the Orthodox Mission in Peking, produced a second Russian translation, and in 1821 George Staunton, a member of the British Macartney expedition to Peking in 1793-1794, translated Tulishen's narrative into English.[14]

During the course of a century then, Tulishen's account became known from Peking to London. Probably the most significant parts of the narrative for Russian readers were the exchanges of views presented in the work between the hosts and the consuls who had been in Tulishen's words 'sent to the farthest ends of the earth'.[15] By this time, the second half of the eighteenth century, the sinophilia then at its height in Western Europe had extended into Russia. This general cultural interest, combined with a growing awareness of China as a neighbour through increasingly frequent contacts between the two governments, must have aroused the curiosity of Russian readers about Chinese attitudes and viewpoints. A narrative by a Chinese commenting on Russian life of the not too distant past was therefore a source from which the Russian could learn much about his Eastern neighbour.

In his narrative Tulishen indeed reveals much about himself and Chinese national character. But the Chinese diplomat was not destined to speak entirely for himself to his Russian readers. Instead, the editor Müller, through his outspokenly negative criticisms contained in the notes to the text, conducted a running verbal battle with Tulishen throughout the narrative, a battle which the reader could hardly ignore. The reasons behind Müller's antagonistic attitude are probably to be found, in part at least, in the fact that as a historian and sinologist he was aware (as the public may not have been) of the increasingly uneasy state of relations existing between Russia and China in the 1760s owing to disagreements over such matters as trade, fugitives on both sides of the border, and various problems of protocol. The German sinologist set the tone for his notations at the outset, stating in his introduction that the emperor's instructions to the emissaries before their departure for Russia provide a good example of 'the arrogant, boastful Chinese people, who scorn everyone else, who are famous for their moral admonitions but worthy of contempt because of their actions, and who are in deep ignorance about foreign states' (Müller in Rossokhin, pp.5-6).

These instructions from the emperor, a vital part of the text missing from the French version of the narrative, do seem to give important insights into Chinese

[13] Cahen, p.125; Müller, at pp.4-5 of the Rossokhin translation. See above, note 1.

[14] Leontiev, above, note 9. (Tulishen), *Narrative of the Chinese embassy to the Khan of the Tourgouth Tartars*, trans., George Thomas Staunton (London 1821); Cahen, p.125.

[15] Rossokhin translation, p.22. The title of the narrative as given within the Russian edition of the work is 'The Notes of the journey of the consuls sent to the farthest ends of the Earth'. Rossokhin translation, p.6.

conceptions of themselves and of other nations. Forewarned by Müller of Chinese 'scorn' for foreigners, the Russian reader was probably not surprised to encounter the emperor's admonition to the consuls that if en route to Aiuki Khan they are invited for an audience with the Russian tsar, they are to conduct themselves as Russian custom dictates, and to tell the Russian authorities that they 'are not such stubborn people as was [the emissary of the Russians] Nikolai, who, when he was with us some years past, acted in an absolutely stubborn manner' (Rossokhin, p.28). (This reference to Nikolai Spafarii, the seventeenth-century ambassador who refused to kowtow to the Chinese emperor, is explained in a note by Müller). The emperor continues his instructions by stating that if the Russian tsar should ask what is most highly esteemed in China, they are to answer 'loyalty to the Emperor, obedience to parents, a clear conscience, knowledge of the truth, and keeping one's word' (Rossokhin, p.29).

The emissaries are carefully coached on presenting a positive image of their country. They are instructed, for instance, to inform the Russians, if they should be asked to provide their hosts with any Chinese artillery weapons, that it has been impossible for them to bring any (showing, says Müller, how little the Chinese know of Europe, to think that their Jesuit-made artillery should be superior to that of the Russians). Explaining that the Russians enjoy showing off unusual items to foreigners, the emperor tells his representatives to show no surprise or disdain at seeing new things, but merely to state that in China some of these things exist and others do not, but that of course, no one person has seen everything in the empire. Müller points out that this attitude on the part of the Chinese only shows their 'weakness of intellect', for all intelligent people like to see rare things (Rossokhin, p.33, note). Later when the journey itself has begun, the consuls, using the formula they are to repeat again and again, tell local officials from the Russian town of Selenginsk that they are the 'ambassadors sent out from the kingdom lying in the centre of the world from the highest, most Holy and great Emperor'. A note points out that 'these expressions are in complete accord with the pride of the Chinese court' (Rossokhin, p.102 and note).

The first of the revealing dialogues between the Chinese and their Russian hosts occurs in the account of the consuls' reception in Irkutsk when Tulishen tells the Russian colonel, their escort, about the peaceful and just ways of his country. 'We have no wars or battles with anyone,' he claims (an example of the 'shameless boasting of the Chinese Consul', notes Müller, explaining that the Chinese at that very moment were at war with the Kalmuk leader and that the embassy itself was on a mission to get Aiuki Khan to join them in their war). The Russian colonel replies that his country is different. It is burdened by continual wars, and, he states, 'we strive to achieve only empty glory'. The sceptical Müller asks if a Russian officer would in fact be likely to make these remarks, and suggests that Tulishen might have heard praiseworthy reports of Peter the Great's achievements in his current war with the Swedes, and being envious, simply invented this speech for the colonel (Rossokhin, pp.122-24).

The account of the emissaries' eight-day stay in the Siberian town of Tobolsk, and their discussions there with Matvei Petrovich Gagarin, the Governor of Siberia, are central to the narrative's revelation of Chinese and Russian attitudes.

The conversations are also stylistically noteworthy because the reader seems to sense here the sincerity of the author, and Tulishen is felt to begin to triumph subtly over the attacks of his commentator. The present-day reader is persuaded that Gagarin and the consuls actually like each other.

The Chinese ambassadors speak proudly to Gagarin of their nation and their ruler. They stress the great 'generosity', 'kindness', and 'magnanimity' of the emperor, as exemplified, for instance, in his pardoning of several Russian trespassers found in a Chinese forest. They extol the way of life in China, the prosperous passing of the days, the longevity of the people, the abundance of the harvests, and the 'quiet of sweet peacefulness' enjoyed by everything under the sun. Gagarin does not seem to feel that his guests are boastful, for he generously replies that he has known for a long time that their emperor was 'most gracious' and 'very wise', that their government was 'rich and peaceful', and that they were able to pass their time in 'entertainments and amusements only' (Rossokhin, pp.206-208). The Russian nobility formerly led this type of life too, the Russian explains, but years of warfare have changed this. The consuls then discuss their philosopher-emperor's well-rounded activities, which include studying the Chinese classics, the sciences and the history of various nations, as well as spending time in archery and fishing.

Several details in the account of the emissaries' stay in Tobolsk would have indicated to Russian readers that their guests were well disposed toward Gagarin himself and that they were kind and personable individuals. In reply to Gagarin's questions about their journey, the consuls assure him, for instance, that they have been well received everywhere, that the tsar's supplies have been overabundant, and that they have no needs or worries. Their genuine desire to show their appreciation to Gagarin is felt in Tulishen's long discussion of the plan to present a gift to the Governor (Rossokhin, pp.213-19). Some criticism of the Russian people as a whole, however, emerges later in a section entitled 'Condition of the Russian State, the manners and religion of the Russian people'. A note of warning at the beginning by Müller states, 'When the kind reader sees something written here in censure of the Russians, he must remember that this was written by a hostile Chinese who tried in every way to abase the Russians so that his nation would seem superior to theirs' (Rossokhin, p.309 note). Tulishen comments that the Russians are habitual braggarts and inclined toward being mercenary and envious, and that they dress and live poorly (скупо) in rather unclean houses. He does, however, give them credit for getting along honestly and agreeably with each other, preferring to settle their differences through law suits rather than fights (Rossokhin, pp.312-14).

Tulishen's narrative continues with an account of the journey from Saratov across the Volga to the consuls' ultimate destination, the headquarters of Aiuki Khan. In June of 1714, about two years after their departure from Peking, the emissaries finally reached the Torgut's nomadic encampment. As the visit lasted only two weeks, Tulishen treats it rather briefly; but the controversy between the author of the account and Müller continues energetically here. The picturesque description of Aiuki Khan kneeling to receive the official document that had been brought from the emperor provides Müller with another opportunity to cast aspersions on the Chinese visitor's integrity. Müller claims that it is unlikely that the Khan knelt. As he ordinarily sat crosslegged, Müller explains, Aiuki on this occasion probably only raised himself up slightly to receive the paper. But, he continues, 'the arrogant Chinese, flattering their Emperor', claim that he knelt (Rossokhin, p.324, note).

Having completed their diplomatic mission, the consuls leave the Torgut territory, and after a tedious journey lasting several months, return to Tobolsk. Again, a series of frank and cordial conversations is held with Governor Gagarin. These talks, which continue to project the image of the Chinese as knowledgeable diplomats and as honest and idealistic people who are sincere in their desire to foster Russian-Chinese good will, reflect, in addition, Russia's continual concern with Chinese military and political affairs. The conversation, touches, for instance, on the tsar's use of Torgut troops in his war against Sweden and how unsatisfactory they have proved to be; on the question of weapons and discipline in the Chinese army (Gagarin telling the consuls that the Russians, unlike them, have not used bows and arrows for twenty years); and on the problem of Russian fugitives in China. The Chinese, reminding Gagarin of the longstanding peaceful accord between Russia and China, assure him that if the tsar should need any of the Russian troops stationed along the Chinese border for his wars in Europe, he can remove them with no fear of attacks on the border from the Chinese (Rossokhin, pp.393-98).

Eventually Gagarin begins to question one of the consuls, named In'dzhan, about religion in China. The consul replies with a fine statement of the Chinese attitude toward religion and virtue. In'dzhan in a general way equates 'faith' with the virtues and ideals most highly esteemed in China: loyalty to the ruler, respect for parents, a clear conscience, knowledge of the truth, and keeping one's word. He explains:

Even if fortunate or disastrous consequences are presented before one's very eyes, still from beginning to end we maintain these virtues inviolably, with such force, that we would rather accept death than forsake them. Today every nation on earth prays to the gods and brings sacrifices according to its own faith, but if they do good deeds, and do not maintain these virtues as the head of all of their undertakings, then their prayers cannot help them at all. Heaven, earth, ruler, father and mother – there is our God. Happiness will increase by itself, if we can serve these entities diligently and with due respect; but nothing is dependent on God, whether anyone prays to him or not.[16]

'This is indeed the truth,' Gagarin replies approvingly. 'I spoke to you this way,' he says to the group, 'because from him, as an old man, I wanted to hear good words.' Tulishen's narrative, like the journey itself, has at this point come nearly full cycle. The statement of Chinese principles given by the emperor at the opening of the work and the old man's concluding words on the same subject form an ideological frame within which the events of the journey have been presented.

One is reminded, in considering this last exchange of views, of the often quoted remarks by Leibniz concerning Chinese ideas on natural theology;

[16] Rossokhin, p.401; the Manchu word 'futsikhi', translated as 'God' in Russian, is given in Russian transliteration and explained by Rossokhin in a note at page 400 of his translation.

Leibniz commented that the Chinese should send missionaries to Europe to teach their approach to this subject. Leibniz and other Western Europeans concerned with Chinese religion, such as the missionary Navarette and the deist Matthew Tindal, speculated on such a prospect and upon what visitors from the Far East might in turn think of Europe's religious attitudes. But while these Western Europeans merely contemplated the concept of direct East-West discussions of natural religion, the Russian governor Gagarin and the elderly Chinese visitor In'dzhan in the Siberian town of Tobolsk in 1714 actually engaged in just such a theological dialogue.[17]

Müller included in the *Monthly compositions* publication of Tulishen's narrative two excerpts from another travel account describing the same journey, which were written originally in Swedish. The work was entitled 'Note by the Swedish captain J. Ch. Schnitscher who escorted the Chinese consuls who visited Aiuki Khan in 1714, with a copy of a map printed in Peking'.[18] Schnitscher, or Snidskii (the name he used in Russia), a captain in the Russian army, accompanied the Chinese consuls from Tobolsk to the headquarters of the Torgut Khan. One of the excerpts from Schnitscher's work concerns the audience of the consuls with Aiuki Khan and is significant because it corroborates Müller's contention that Tulishen, because of his inordinate pride, was not always truthful in his account. Schnitscher tells how the emissaries entered the Khan's tent, where, after presenting the imperial letter, the chief consul embraced Aiuki's knees. A footnote by Müller points out the discrepancy between Tulishen's version of the meeting in which it was the Khan who knelt, and this account by Schnitscher.[19]

Aleksei Leontiev's new translation of the Tulishen narrative appeared in St Petersburg in 1782, eighteen years after the publication of the Rossokhin-Müller version. This translation is said to be inferior to that of Rossokhin for several reasons, including errors in figures, the absence of the prefaces and epilogues, the unsatisfactory form in which dialogue is presented, and the arrangement of the geographic information in a systematic order, all of which tend to detract from its usefulness.[20] In spite of these defects, the translation went into two editions, which attests to the public's continued interest in the work.[21]

[17] Gottfried Wilhelm von Leibniz, 'Preface' to *Novissima sinica*, in *Opera omnia*, ed. L. Dutens, iv (Geneva 1768), pp.78-86 at 82; Matthew Tindal, *Christianity as old as the Creation* (London 1730), pp.404-405; Appleton, pp.50-51.

[18] 'Записка Шведского Капитана И. Х. Шничера, который был у Китайских посланников бывших в 1714 году у Аюки-Хана в провожатых', *Monthly compositions* (Nov. 1764), pp.428-40. Müller had also published a German translation of the work in his *Eröffnung eines Vorschlages*, iv (St Petersburg 1760), pp.275-364. Cited in Cahen, p.clxiv.

[19] J. C. Schnitscher, *Berättelse om Ajuckiniska Calmuckiet, eller om detta Folkets Ursprung, huru de kommit under Ryssamas Lydno, deras Gndar, Gndsdyrkan och Prester [...] deras Politique och Philosophie, etc.* (Stockholm 1744). 'Zapiska', above, note 18, p.431 note.

[20] Cahen, p.125.

[21] Still another account, which gives the impression of being a caricature of Tulishen's original, appeared in a Russian periodical in 1810 with the title, 'The conversation of the Chinese consul with a Russian official'. This curious, unsigned work, which gives no sources, presents in dialogue form a conversation between an unnamed Russian official and Tulishen: 'Разговор китайского посла с русским чиновником', *Русский вестник* (Russian herald) 12 (Dec. 1810), pp.1-14.

The accounts of Tulishen's journey, appearing in two Russian translations (the first in one of the leading journals of the day, the second in book form), made valuable contributions to the eighteenth-century Russian view of China. Whether the reader accepted Tulishen's image of himself and his colleagues, or whether Müller's commentaries, continually casting aspersions on the Chinese visitors, resulted in prejudicing him against the narrator, cannot, of course, be known. The tension created by the contradictions between the text and Müller's notes heightens considerably the appeal of the work today. For the eighteenth-century reader, however, these contradictions must have added to the ambiguity that was already apparent in the Russian view of China. The impression of the reasonable, idealistic, humane Chinese fostered by Tulishen is comparable in many ways to that presented to Russian readers in the translations of French missionary works. Müller's unfavourable views, however, are similar to those of the Russian religious emissaries, who viewed their neighbours to the East more circumspectly.

Some fifteen years after the visit of Tulishen, another group of Manchu-Chinese diplomats arrived in Russia. Part of the delegation went to Moscow, bearing congratulations to tsar Peter II on his accession to the throne. Another section of the party visited the Torgut Khan. This new embassy, the first ever sent by the emperor of China to a European head of state, received a fair amount of attention in Russian publications at the time of the visit. An article entitled 'The Chinese embassy to Russia' in the periodical *Примечание на ‹Ведомости›* (Commentary on The News) in 1730 heralded the visit of the diplomats,[22] and the *Санктпетербургские ведомости* (The St Petersburg news) mentioned the ambassadorial visit in nine separate numbers, two of which contained considerable detail. The description of the official reception of the embassy and the ceremonial audience with the empress, Anna Ioannovna, who had just succeeded Peter II, was contained in one of these articles, and was also reprinted as a small brochure.[23] The visit of the consuls occasioned too the publication of an article entitled 'Chinese history', intended, no doubt, as a demonstration of politeness to the visiting ambassadors.[24] But the details concerning this mission were most likely forgotten by the time Russian sinophilia began to flourish during the last quarter of the century, and there was no substantial human interest account of the visit comparable to Tulishen's narrative that could be reprinted for a curious public.

The Manchu government's second official embassy to a European monarch, again directed to Russia, followed close upon the heels of the earlier delegation. Arriving in Petersburg in April of 1732, the ambassadorial party brought formal

[22] 'О Китайском посольстве в Россию', *Commentary on The News* (1730), p.195.

[23] *St Petersburg news* (1731), nos. 6, 8, 20, 22, 25, 56, 72, 82, 99 (Cited in P. E. Skachkov, *Outline of the history of Russian sinology*, p.301, note 35. The brochure, 'Обстоятельная реляция церемонеи ...' (Detailed account of the ceremonies) is cited in *Union catalogue*, ii.329, entry 4786.

[24] 'История Хины или китайская' (Chinese history), *История, генеалогия и география – примечание к ‹Ведомостям›* (History, genealogy and geography – commentary on the News), no. 13-18 (1731); cited in P. E. Skachkov, 'History of the study of China in Russia in the 17th and 18th centuries – a brief outline', p.176.

congratulations and gifts for the Russian empress, Anna Ioannovna. While this ambassadorial party also met with a cordial reception, news coverage was rather brief. The *Saint Petersburg news* again devoted an article to the ambassadorial party, commenting in some detail on its visit to the Academy of Sciences. Here the Chinese were presented with issues of the Academy's publication *Комментарии* (Commentaries), and with copies of the work written in Latin by the academician T. Z. Baier, entitled *The Chinese museum, where the characteristics of the Chinese language and literature are taught*. One can infer from the newspaper article that the Chinese were pleased to learn of the Russian Academy's interest in their literature and language, and that a congenial atmosphere prevailed during the consuls' visit.[25] But among later sinophiles, knowledge of the mutual impressions produced during the visit of the Chinese was probably slight.

While both these official Chinese embassies received hospitable receptions in Russia, considerable friction was now beginning to develop between Russia and her neighbour. Official representatives of the tsar did in fact continue to visit Peking, but no further embassies were sent by the emperor to Russia during the century. Russia's Chinese visitors from this point on were persons who came as private individuals, sometimes remaining to live and work in their adopted country. It was, for instance, with a Christian convert, Chou Ko, the first teacher of the Chinese and Manchu languages in Russia, that the future Russian sinologist Aleksei Leontiev began his study of these languages at the end of the 1730s. Later, in the early 1760s another Chinese, a Christian convert named 'Vasil'ev', assisted Leontiev in the sinologist's language school in Moscow.[26] The presence of these individuals in Russia must have contributed to Russian views of China, but it was probably the Chinese ambassadors and, particularly, the literary accounts of their visits that influenced the Russian public most.

What was the overall image that the Chinese ambassadors projected in Russia? On the basis of the accounts written early in the century and contemporaneous to the events described, it would appear that the visitors created a quite favourable impression. The envoys are seen to have been received on the official level with honour, and personally with considerable warmth. Reports of the visits indicate that many Russians – in Moscow, St Petersburg and the provinces – had the opportunity to form first-hand impressions of the ambassadors. It seems likely, however, that the narrative by Tulishen, appearing for the first time in Russian some thirty years after the last of the three embassies had visited Moscow, and being published again in a new translation eighteen years after this, reached a far greater number of people, and had an even greater impact on the Russians'

[25] *St Peterburg news* (1732), no. 46, pp.206-207. Cited in P. E. Skachkov, *Outline of the history of Russian sinology*, p.301, note 36; see also M. I. Radovskii, 'Первая веха в истории русско-китайских научных связей' (The First milestone in the history of Russian-Chinese scholarly relations), *Вестник Академии наук СССР* (Herald of the Academy of Sciences of the USSR), no. 9 (1959), pp.95-97; T. Z. Baier, *Museum sinicum, in quo sinicae linguae et litteraturae ratio explicatur* (St Petersburg 1730).

[26] Eric Widmer, *The Russian ecclesiastical mission in Peking during the eighteenth century*, pp.159 and 164. See also P. E. Skachkov, 'Первый преподаватель китайского и маньчжурского языков в России' (The first teacher of the Chinese and Manchu languages in Russia), *Проблемы востоковедения* (Problems of oriental studies), no. 3 (1960), pp.198-201.

views of their Chinese visitors, than did the personal appearances of the diplomats themselves. By the time Müller's edition of Tulishen's work appeared in
1764, Russian interest in China, in travel accounts by Russians and Western
Europeans, in works by missionaries, and in other forms of literature relating
to the Middle Kingdom, was running high.

By this time, however, relations between Russia and China were considerably
less friendly than they had been at the time of the visits of the ambassadors,
and this change in the political climate appears to be reflected in the accounts
which readers of the latter half of the century were to receive of the early
eighteenth-century Chinese visitors. In particular, Müller's commentaries on
the Tulishen narrative and on the selections from Schnitscher, presenting the
Chinese as hostile, lying braggarts, contributed features to the image which
were not a part of the original writings.

How the public interpreted the conflicting viewpoints in Müller's edition of
Tulishen's work is impossible to tell. Perhaps the very careful reader saw the
work – with its favourable portrait of the wise and good Chinese and its conflicting
picture of the hypocritical Chinese boaster – as a virtual microcosm of the image
of China then taking shape throughout the various genres of Russian literature.

3. Other roads to Cathay

THROUGHOUT the second half of the eighteenth century and at the turn of the 1800s, while both the glowing accounts of China by Western European Jesuits and the less than complimentary reports from the Russian Orthodox mission were becoming known in Russia, a considerable number of narratives by other travellers were making their own contributions to the Russian image of Cathay. These accounts seem to fall naturally into two main groups: the first is a heterogeneous collection of reports by several navigators, two popularised compendiums of Western European travellers' narratives, and two accounts by Western European diplomats. The other is a larger group of works by writers all associated with the same activity – Russian governmental embassies to the Middle Kingdom. Would the Russian reader have seen any patterns in these disparate travel accounts? In particular, would he have seen in these works, as he may have seen in the narratives of the Western European and Russian missionaries, a 'French' China that differed from that of the other travellers?

i. Diverse travellers

'It is a veritable paradise on earth.'

Marco Polo[1]

'The happiness and tranquillity of China are only imaginary, and we are entirely deceived by appearances.'

I. F. Krusenstern[2]

One of the most engaging in the first of these two groups of narratives is the highly influential report by the British admiral George Anson of his voyage around the world in 1740-1744.[3] Anson's account, appearing in Russian translation in 1751, was among the earliest works about China to be published in Russia, a fact which is significant for a comparison of the eighteenth-century Western European and the Russian image of China.[4] For while in Russian literature Anson's work, presenting a scathing criticism of China, came at the very beginning of the Russian sinophile movement, in the West the narrative served as the beginning of the end of European sinomania. Preceded by a century and a half of eulogistic reports about the Celestial Empire by Jesuit missionaries, Anson's biting commentary came as a surprise and shock to

[1] Quoted in Jean François de La Harpe, *Abrégé de l'histoire générale des voyages* (Paris 1780), vii.10.

[2] Adam Johann von Krusenstern, *Voyage round the World in the years 1803, 1804, 1805, and 1806*, trans. Richard Hoppner (London 1813), ii.305.

[3] George Anson, *A voyage round the World in the years 1740, 1741, 1742, 1743, 1744*, compiled by Richard Walter, 2nd ed. (London 1748). Subsequent references to this work will be to this original English edition and will be included in the text.

[4] Uolter (Richard Walter), *Путешествие около света, которое в 1740, 41, 42, 43, 44, годах совершил адмирал лорд Ансон* (A voyage around the World made by admiral Anson in the years 1740-1744) (St Petersburg 1751).

Western European readers. Certain *philosophes* and scholars had, it is true, presented negative opinions about the Middle Kingdom prior to this time.[5] Western Europeans also had available the accounts of several seventeenth- and early eighteenth-century travellers who had been attached to Russian diplomatic missions to China, narratives, which, as will soon be seen, presented views contrasting sharply with those of the Jesuit missionaries. These works, however, had very little effect on the almost entirely favourable reputation that was enjoyed by the Middle Kingdom in Western Europe until about the middle of the eighteenth century. Only with the much publicised report of lord Anson did this popular image begin to be seriously questioned. From this time on ever greater doubts began to arise concerning the theory of Chinese superiority until, by the end of the century, the once glorious image had faded altogether.

In Russia the situation was quite different. The translation from Gerbillon entitled 'Description and information about the Grand Tartary', taken from Du Halde, which had begun to appear in a Russian periodical in 1744, only seven years before the Anson translation made its appearance in Russia, was the only published Jesuit work on China available in Russia at this time. In Russia, therefore, Anson's relation did not challenge a strongly established image of China based on Jesuit writings.

In his *Voyage around the World* admiral Anson presents a forceful account of his experiences in China and the conclusions he drew from them. The report of his visit to Canton in 1742-43 is an exasperated tale of continuous difficulties and frustrations. Anson was in command of a naval squadron sent out to attack Spanish possessions in South America. Eventually the ships became engaged in a search for a richly laden Spanish galleon in the area of the Philippines. Hoping to resupply his one remaining ship in the port of Canton, Anson finally succeeded by means of threats and great perseverance to enter the harbour. But the Chinese, according to Anson, at first demanded payment of customs duty (which, as the commander of a warship and not a merchant vessel, Anson declared he would not pay), denied him access to the viceroy of Canton for a considerable length of time, promised but failed to deliver the provisions he had ordered for the ship, and in fact carried out too many 'artifices' for him to relate all of them (Anson, p.524).

Infuriated by this treatment, Anson was also irate at what he observed of Chinese society. An educated man of his day, he was, of course, familiar with the Jesuit literature about China, and he was indignant at the disparity between what he encountered and what he had been led to expect. His account contains numerous references to the missionaries' descriptions of the empire. Relating several examples of theft and fraud which he had observed, Anson states, for instance, that these may 'serve as a specimen of the manners of this celebrated

---

[5] These included among others the voyager captain William Dampier (who was more indifferent than hostile to China), the scholar Cornelius de Pauw, William Wotton, George Berkeley, and lord Bolingbroke (the latter of whom along with Samuel Johnson at first favoured and then questioned the Chinese superiority theory), Daniel Defoe, Fénelon, and in the period closer to that of Anson's report, Montesquieu, Rousseau and Grimm. See Appleton, *A cycle of Cathay*, pp.53-64, and Adolf Reichwein, *China and Europe: intellectual and artistic contacts in the eighteenth century*, pp.92-98.

Nation, which is often recommended to the rest of the world as a pattern of all kinds of laudable qualities' (Anson, p.525). He relates other incidents so that, in his words: 'I may not be thought too severe in ascribing to this Nation a fraudulent and selfish turn of temper, so contradictory to the character given of them in the legendary accounts of the Roman missionaries' (Anson, p.519). 'Jesuitical fictions', 'boundless panegyric', 'fustian elogiums', Anson terms the missionaries' descriptions, insisting that they do not represent the truth (pp.543, 544, 482). Admitting that he himself has observed only a 'corner of the Empire', the admiral, nevertheless, warns that those who have commented on the interior of the country 'have been evidently influenced by very ridiculous prepossessions' (pp.541-42).

In regard to national character Anson is particularly incensed by the dishonesty and inordinate cupidity of the Chinese with whom he comes in contact. He states (pp.518-19):

after all, it may perhaps be impossible for an European, ignorant of the customs and manners of that nation, to be fully apprized of the real incitements to this behavior. Indeed, thus much may undoubtedly be asserted, that in artifice, falsehood, and an attachment to all kinds of lucre, many of the Chinese are difficult to be paralleled by any other people; but then the combination of these talents and the manner in which they are applied in particular emergencies, are often beyond the reach of a Foreigner's penetration.

On a different level Anson's analysis of the Chinese national character clearly reflects the eighteenth-century preoccupation with the study of the nature of man. Anson observes: 'Indeed, the only pretension of the Chinese to a more refined morality than their neighbours is founded, not on their integrity or beneficence, but solely on the affected evenness of their demeanour, and their constant attention to suppress all symptoms of passion and violence' (pp.543-44). It may be, he continues, that the 'calm and patient turn' on which the Chinese pride themselves so much 'is in reality the source of the most exceptional part of their character'. Perhaps with Pope's explication of the 'ruling passion' in mind Anson concludes that as those who make a study of the nature of man tell us, 'it is difficult to curb the more robust and violent passions, without augmenting, at the same time, the force of the selfish ones: So that the timidity, dissimulation, and dishonesty of the Chinese, may, in some sort, be owing to the composure, and external decency, so universally prevailing in that Empire' (p.544).

The Admiral does grant, however, that the Chinese are a 'very ingenious and industrious people' (p.541). He also acknowledges that they were quick to come and express their appreciation to him and his men for their aid in extinguishing an almost disastrous fire in the warehouse region of Canton (p.535).

Judged on the basis of his own account, Anson's behaviour in Canton seems to indicate a highhanded manner, which might well have precipitated the unpleasant treatment he claims to have received. This in turn may have coloured his entire outlook.[6] But whether or not it was justified, Anson's negative

[6] Some of Anson's commentators of both the eighteenth and twentieth centuries have asserted that the admiral's complaints consist of fabrications and exaggerations. Voltaire,

commentary on the Chinese was for Western Europeans indeed iconoclastic; to Russian readers it became a valuable, but in all likelihood, hardly shocking contribution to the fund of information and opinion on a little known subject.

While more than half a century separates the visit to Canton by Anson from those of two Russian voyagers, it is worthwhile to compare the experiences and the conclusions of three visitors who were all professional navigators.

The Russian voyagers Iurii Lisianskii and Ivan Fedorovich Krusenstern, commanding the ships *Neva* and *Nadezhda*, set out in 1803 by order of tsar Alexander 1 on the first Russian voyage around the world. Their primary objectives were the opening of sea trade with Japan and China and the discovery of a practical sea route by which to provide supplies to Russian fur trading settlements on the northwest coast of North America. Upon returning to Russia, Lisianskii prepared an account of his experiences which was published in St Petersburg in 1812. An English translation appeared in London two years later.[7] Krusenstern's account was published in both Russian and German in St Petersburg between 1809 and 1813 and was translated into English in 1813.[8] The accounts of Krusenstern and Lisianskii do not overlap entirely; the ships the two men commanded were sometimes separated from each other for considerable lengths of time. But in regard to their impressions of China, Krusenstern and Lisianskii are very much in agreement with each other.

The Russian navigators relate in their accounts that they had succeeded in exchanging a cargo of North American furs for Chinese goods in Canton (a trade pattern which the Russians had hoped to establish by this first expedition to the Chinese port) and were prepared to set sail for home, when they were unexpectedly detained by local officials. Krusenstern succeeded in remedying this 'hostile measure' only with considerable difficulty. Upon reaching St Petersburg the navigators learned that immediately after their departure an order had

as the defender of the image of the 'ideal' China, tried to minimise the effect of Anson's remarks. Suggesting that Canton, a provincial outpost, was hardly representative of China as a whole, he noted: 'Anson méprise les Chinois, mais si des Chinois avaient debarqué au nord d'Angleterre!' (*Notebooks, The Complete works of Voltaire* 81-82, ed. Theodore Besterman (Genève 1968), i.136). Voltaire discusses the Anson voyage further in his *Précis du siècle de Louis XV*, chap. 27, *Œuvres complètes*, ed. Moland [hereafter M.], xv (Paris 1878), pp.312-20. A Chinese view of the affair is found in Arthur Waley, *Yuan Mei: eighteenth-century Chinese poet* (London 1956), pp.205-209. Basil Guy accuses Anson of 'wilful blindness and partiality' and 'lack of good faith' in his appraisal of the Chinese, and also questions the fact that an incident described by Anson resembles very closely an event related by Le Gentil twenty years earlier (*The French image of China before and after Voltaire*, p.210).

[7] Iurii Lisianskii, *Путешествие вокруг света в 1803, 4, 5 и 1806 гг.* (A voyage around the World in 1803-1806) (St Petersburg 1812); Urey Lisiansky, *A voyage round the World in the years 1803, 1804, 1805, and 1806* (London 1814). Subsequent references are to the English translation and will be included in the text.

[8] Kruzenshtern (Adam Johann von Krusenstern), *Путешествие вокруг света в 1803, 4, 5 и 1806 годах* (St Petersburg 1809-1813). Adam Johann von Krusenstern, *Reise um die Welt in den Jahren 1803, 1804, 1805, und 1806* (St Petersburg 1810-1812; 2nd ed. Berlin, 1811-12). Adam Johann von Krusenstern, *Voyage round the World in the years 1803, 1804, 1805, and 1806*, trans. Richard Hoppner (London 1813). Subsequent references are to the English translation and will be included in the text.

arrived from Peking to detain the Russian ships. If they had remained a day longer, Krusenstern speculates, they would 'have fallen into the absolute power of these savages' (Krusenstern, ii.290-91, 299).

Both Lisianskii and Krusenstern, like Anson, make comparisons between their own impressions and the established literary image of China, specifically that presented by the Jesuit missionaries. Like Anson, the Russian navigators cannot contain their irritation at the glaring discrepancies they feel exist between the picture given by the Jesuits and the facts as they see them.

By now, at the turn of the first decade of the nineteenth century, many important Jesuit works had made their way in translation into Russian literature. The attack, therefore, by Krusenstern and Lisianskii would probably have had far more significance for Russian readers than did the criticisms of admiral Anson in 1751. Referring to the 'vast approbation' of the Jesuits, Krusenstern states: 'There may be many things in China deserving of admiration; but the wisdom of the government, and the morals of the people, however favourably the world may be disposed to judge of them, are far from praiseworthy' (Krusenstern, ii.303). Lisianskii writes, in the same spirit: 'The European missionaries, in their account of China, speak highly of its laws. I know not what policy there may be in this; but sure I am, that there is no country in the world where the people are so much oppressed as in this great empire (Lisianskii, p.292).

Awareness of the fact that their refutation of the Jesuit image is not entirely new is seen in Lisianskii's reference to China as a country 'formerly so highly extolled for its just laws' (p.280) and in a comment by Krusenstern about the 'well-known barbarous laws' of China (ii.317). But the vigour of the attack indicates that both writers felt that it was still necessary to speak out against the praises of earlier reporters.

It is surprising, however, that in their denial of the Jesuits' idealised portrayal Krusenstern and Lisianskii (like the Russian missionary Gribovskii) do not cite any of the accounts written by persons associated with Russian diplomatic missions to China, despite the fact that these accounts had been appearing in Russian journals for several decades prior to this first Russian voyage around the world. The Russian navigators in order to emphasise their own points do in fact cite harsh criticisms of the Chinese contained in two recent accounts of the British diplomatic mission to China under lord Macartney. Perhaps the explanation for the fact that they fail to draw also upon Russian sources for corroboration of their views is simply that the navigators, both of whom had at one time served in the British fleet, and who were of course cosmopolitan because of their profession, were mainly concerned with Western European literature about China, and were not in fact aware of the accounts of Russian diplomatic missions.

Lisianskii and Krusenstern single out the Chinese system of justice and law for particular criticism. Lisianskii observed that 'the abject state in which the people are held by their rulers is such, that every species of injustice, however great, must be submitted to' (p.280). The widespread poverty, which, Lisianskii feels, is 'ascribable to the oppressive nature of the laws, and the corresponding oppression of those who execute them' (p.283), made a great impression on the

Russian. His remarks on the Chinese practice of quartering as a method of capital punishment sum up his opinion of Chinese culture: 'From this it would appear, as if the Chinese, who boast of having been enlightened when Europe was plunged in barbarism, have made but slow advances since in improvement' (p.293).

Krusenstern, whose views are stated somewhat more moderately than are those of Lisianskii, draws similar conclusions in regard to the 'purely tyrannical' government of the Chinese (ii.303-305). Discussing Chinese institutions, which, Krusenstern asserts, decidedly do not merit the fine reputation they have acquired, he states: 'It is evident that the government, although some brilliant points in their laws and maxims of state may give an advantageous appearance to the whole, has not attained to that degree of perfection which they would willingly persuade us.' He continues, 'The happiness and tranquillity of China are only imaginary, and we are entirely deceived by appearances.' Krusenstern, it would seem, has touched here on one of the basic problems inherent in many eighteenth-century accounts of China, that of differentiating between the ideal and reality in Chinese life. While the Jesuits, as we have seen, concentrated on the ideals and aspirations of the Chinese, later unfriendly commentators, shocked by obvious evils, could neglect to acknowledge the merits to be found in the theories and goals of the society. The Russian navigator is apparently aware of this problem.

Krusenstern, as can be seen in the observation quoted above, attempts to write objectively, generally supporting his comments with factual material, and he often qualifies his remarks. For instance, like Anson, he admits that one cannot make generalisations about the entire country on the basis of life in Canton. (He then, however, elaborates on this qualification by asserting that the character of the Cantonese has in fact been somewhat refined by constant contact with Europeans! (ii.303)).

As to Chinese character in general, the Russian commanders are just as uncomplimentary, if somewhat less bitter, than admiral Anson. Krusenstern is appalled at the 'hateful traits' of parents murdering their children, and of incest (ii.304). While commenting generally on the 'knavery of the Chinese merchants', Krusenstern does find praise, however, for the members of the hong, the company in charge of European trade in Canton, who, he states, are completely reliable and quite efficient (ii.340-41). Lisianskii finds commendation for the intelligence, politeness and obedience that he observed. His uncomplimentary remarks, however, overshadow this praise (Lisianskii, pp.280-87). He claims that the Chinese are 'greatly addicted to sensual pleasure', cites the 'thirst for wealth' of the rulers, and states that the Chinese have no equals 'in the arts of cunning and deceit'. As if in summary, he states: 'In a word, fraud and deceit are the prevailing practice here; and the misfortune is, that, to whatever extent it may be carried, no justice can be obtained.'

Lisianskii's commentary on the religious practices of the Chinese people constitutes one of the few favourable observations that he makes on the Chinese way of life. He relates that in the corner of each Chinese house and shop a candle is kept burning in honour of the idol venerated by the owner. He states that he finds this 'an attention which seems to prove that its inhabitants are sincerely attached to their religion' (p.288).

Considerable attention is devoted by both Russian navigators to the state of discontent and disorder among the Chinese populace at the time of their visit to Canton. Krusenstern describes various insurrections and attempts on the life of the emperor himself to bolster his point that tranquillity exists in appearance only (Krusenstern, ii.306). Both navigators, like Anson sixty-three years earlier, comment on the insignificance of the Chinese military force. But unlike Anson, who merely evaluated Chinese strength, Krusenstern (ii.341-42) pushes his observation through to the conclusion that if the Chinese should refuse to grant Russia trading privileges in Canton, the realisation that 'force will be met with force', would compel China 'to act with more justice'. 'The political importance and vicinity of Russia are arguments too powerful in the eyes of the cowardly Chinese', he states, for China to try to prevent this trade from being established. The harsh realities of politics reflected in the Russian's statements constitute an element in the Russian picture of China, not typically found in its Western European counterpart.

The persecution of the Catholic missionaries by the Chinese government constitutes another negative element in Krusenstern's picture of the Empire. The fact that the Russian Orthodox priests were not treated with the same suspicion during this period as were the Catholics is indicated in Krusenstern's relation of the following incident. Several letters written by European missionaries in Peking to their colleagues in Macao were intercepted by the Chinese government which turned them over to the Russian bishop, evidently with the expectation that he would inform them of the contents. The Russian cleric, however, claimed that he was unable to read the languages in which the letters were written. 'This declaration of the Russian bishop', Krusenstern states, 'was the means of saving many, and they have gratefully acknowledged it.'[9] This is one of the few glimpses one encounters in Russian accounts of China, by any except the Russian missionaries themselves, of the activities of the Orthodox mission in Peking.

The episode with which Lisianskii concludes his account of the visit to Canton can be seen as a microcosm of his and Krusenstern's China experience (pp.294-95). The commander is invited to visit the country home of a wealthy Cantonese, where he is taken on a tour of the garden. Noting the 'taste displayed in the arrangement, so different from ours', Lisiansky comments favourably on the elaborate stonework representing, 'on a small scale, precipices, and different excavations of mountains, with astonishing accuracy'. The Russian, however, seems ultimately to question the traditional European admiration for Chinese landscape gardening, pointing out discrepancies between reality and the highly praised image of the Chinese garden in the same way that he and Krusenstern have spoken out throughout their accounts about the defects in the image of China as an ideal state. In describing the garden he notes: 'In vain did my eyes search every where for a lawn: nothing of the kind was to be seen in this extensive

---

[9] The English translator uses the title 'Bishop', referring no doubt to the archimandrite of the Russian mission; Krusenstern ii.320.

place; the best parts of which, instead of containing, as in Europe, grass-plots variegated with beds of flowers, were taken up by ponds of stagnated water, which occasioned no very agreeable smell.'

As the narratives by Krusenstern, Lisianskii and Anson show, the three navigators had more in common than just their profession. Krusenstern's English translator provided the following epigram for the *Voyage round the World*: 'Les Marins ecrivent mal, mais avec assez de candeur. – De Brosses' (ii, title page). Testing this generalisation against all three navigators' accounts considered here, most readers would probably not agree that mariners write badly. As for candour, however, it is indeed a quality that characterises and makes memorable all three narratives. The most significant common denominator seen here in the navigators' accounts is, of course, their scepticism in regard to China as a utopian kingdom.

A similar attitude characterises another of the most influential of the eighteenth-century travel documents about China, one which made its way into Russian translation in the early years of the nineteenth-century. This was the official account by sir George Staunton of the British embassy to Peking led by George Macartney in 1793-1794. While admiral Anson's narrative in the middle of the eighteenth century had signalled in Western Europe the beginning of the breakdown of the glowing image of the Middle Kingdom, at the end of the century reports of the Macartney mission marked for Western Europeans the final stage of the disintegration process.

George Macartney, an able and experienced diplomat, who incidentally had served as ambassador to Russia from 1764 to 1767, went to Peking with the aim of establishing official diplomatic contacts with the Chinese government and formalising and improving the commercial dealings which British merchants had been carrying on at Canton for almost a hundred years. The ambassador and his suite were treated respectfully by their Chinese hosts, but in the long run the mission failed to achieve its objectives.

The embassy returned to London in 1794, and accounts of the journey by members of the diplomatic party began to appear almost at once. At least five narratives had been published by 1804. The best and most important account, however, the personal journal kept by Macartney himself, remained in manuscript form, and a full and accurate edition was not available until rather recently.[10] The official account of the mission, composed by sir George Staunton, the secretary of the embassy, who utilised the papers and journal of lord Macartney and other officials of the suite, appeared in 1797. A Russian translation of this work was to become available in 1804-1805. Excerpts from the first published account of the mission, that by lord Macartney's personal servant, Aeneas Anderson, which had appeared in London in 1795, were, however, printed by a Russian periodical, *Политический журнал* (Political magazine), as early as 1796.[11] Anderson's account proved to be superficial and of little

[10] George Macartney, *An embassy to China*, ed. J. L. Cranmer-Byng.
[11] 'Китай. Многолюдство. Армия. Полиция. Земледелие. Из путешествия Аглинскаго Посла Лорда Макартнея' (China. Populousness. Army. Police. Agriculture. From the journey of the English ambassador lord Macartney), *Политический журнал* (Political journal), pt. 2 (1796), pp.21-33.

worth,[12] but the fact that the excerpts were translated almost immediately after the work was published in England is a sign of Russia's curiosity about the embassy's experiences.

Nine years after the Anderson material was published in Russia another short excerpt 'from the Journey of the English Ambassador Lord Macartney', came out in the periodical *Вестник Европы* (Herald of Europe).[13] At about the same time there began to appear a four-volume edition, running to almost 1200 pages, of George Staunton's official account of the mission.[14]

The objectiveness of approach, the moderate tone, and the tendency toward understatement which characterise the Staunton report comprise the major differences between this account and the controversial narrative by Staunton's British predecessor, admiral Anson. The surprise and indignation registered by Anson at his discoveries in China do not emerge from the Staunton narrative. In terms of content, however, the Staunton report corroborates the basic conclusions of Anson, through its presentation of the inflexibility of the Chinese government in its dealings with foreign governments, as well as through its revelation of noteworthy defects in Chinese society.

The difference in the tone of the two works is quite possibly due less to the personalities of the writers, than to the changes that had taken place in the climate of opinion in Western Europe regarding China between the middle of the eighteenth century and its final decade. While Anson refers repeatedly to the deceptive nature of the missionary reports on China, for example, the Staunton narrative does not elaborate on such discrepancies. What was needed in Western Europe at this point were not refutations of previous writers but explanations of the true nature of the ambiguous Eastern nation. This is what Staunton, within the specific framework of English thought and culture, attempts to present.

In recounting the experiences of the embassy, Staunton creates few dramatic moments. There are no gross provocations, insults, or confrontations to be related. Still there are several memorable scenes reflecting the inevitable conflict concerning homage and honour. One of these is the description of the ambassadorial party moving regally along the river route toward Peking on yachts and in land carriages provided by the emperor and adorned with flags which proclaimed in large Chinese characters 'Ambassador bearing tribute from the country of England'. Russian readers familiar with the comments of their own

---

[12] Cramer-Byng, in *Macartney*, p.343.

[13] 'О некоторых обыкновениях Китайских. Отрывок из путешествия в Китай Английского Посла Графа Макартнея' (Various customs of the Chinese. Excerpt from the journey to China of the English ambassador, lord Macartney), *Вестник Европы* 15 (1805), pp.195-206.

[14] Stonton (George Staunton), Makartnei (George Macartney), *Путешествие во внутренность Китая и в Татарию, учиненное в 1792, 1793, 1794 гг. лордом Макартнеем* (The Journey into the interior of China and Tartary, made in the years 1792-1794) (Moscow 1804-1805); translation of a French version of George Staunton, *An authentic account of an embassy from the king of Great Britain to the emperor of China.* Subsequent references will be to the second edition of the English original (London 1798), and will be included in the text.

envoys to Peking concerning their attempts to avoid the term 'tribute' would probably have taken particular note of this vignette (Staunton, ii.130-31). That Macartney was displaying diplomatic tact and not subservience in allowing this affront to pass unnoticed is evidenced by his very firm refusal soon afterward to perform the kowtow before the emperor. Staunton, discussing this situation, refers to the refusal of a former Russian ambassador to comply with Chinese protocol until certain agreements had been reached on the manner in which Chinese envoys would present themselves to the Russian tsar. He notes that this Russian envoy was said to be 'the only minister that had hitherto gained any point in negotiations with the Chinese court' (ii.131).

Macartney's visit to Canton differed in some respects from that of Anson in that as an official guest of the Manchu-Chinese government, he was formally received with honour (Staunton, ii.232). On the surface therefore the atmosphere surrounding the Macartney visit to Canton was considerably more pleasant than it had been for Anson (or would be some years later for Lisianskii and Krusenstern). But running throughout Staunton's account is the motif of failure, the realisation that the embassy has not achieved its objective. This theme, common to the reports of all four Western visitors to Canton, contributes to the sense of continuity to be found among them.

In their evaluation of Chinese society, the members of the Macartney mission did not fail to note certain positive features. The Staunton report praises the merit system of appointment for public officials, the limited amount of crime, the administration of the jails, and the closeness of family ties. It lauds the emperor for his skill in maintaining his vast Empire and for recently adding new acquisitions. The formality of Chinese ceremonies also made a pleasant impression on the English visitors. Commenting on the ambassador's audience with the emperor, Staunton writes: 'The commanding feature of the scene, was the calm dignity and sober pomp of Asiatic grandeur, which European refinements have not yet attained' (ii.237). The embassy's negative impressions, however, eventually crowd out the initial utopian vision. For example, while attempting characteristically to be objective, and pointing out the Chinese government's concern 'to maintain the general tranquillity and welfare', Staunton also suggests that the security of the individual seems to have been overlooked (ii.489). While acknowledging that through their skill in printing, which the Chinese have had for many centuries, they have spread the 'rules of moral rectitude' throughout the population, Staunton also stresses the propagandistic use of the press by the government for the preservation of the status quo (ii.301-302).

Many of Staunton's negative criticisms clearly reflect the cultural background of the travellers, and the moment in history at which they came to observe the Middle Kingdom. English tradition and practice are seen, for instance, when Staunton, commenting unfavourably on the Chinese system of justice, points out that there is no jury system. Speculation on the possibility of revolt by the populace is made by Staunton, in relation to recent European experience, the French Revolution. In questioning whether the 'Rights of Man', if translated into Chinese, would have any practical effect, Staunton writes: 'The general maxim of obedience to the prince, inculcated by the moralists of China, might not hold firm in every breast against the novel doctrine of the sacred right and duty of insurrection against oppression; tho it seems already to have been exploded as dangerous in practice, from the country where it first was propagated' (ii.300).

Staunton, like Krusenstern, points out the discrepancies between goals and practical realities in Chinese life, adding, moreover, a further dimension to the discussion by revealing why the Chinese ideals had so appealed to the eighteenth-century European mind. Rationalism and empiricism are the concepts against which Staunton measures Chinese practice. In connection with an account of certain burial customs, for instance, Staunton writes: 'Notwithstanding the philosophical doctrines of the learned Chinese, which exclude all notions unconsonant to reason, as well as the reality of all beings not referable to the senses; they often yield, in practice, to the current notions of the weak and vulgar' (ii.345). Again, in a statement concerning the custom of allowing a person convicted of a crime to provide a substitute to take the punishment, Staunton notes: 'The law, of which the maxims are rational and just, does certainly not warrant it, tho the dispensers of it may' (ii.492).

In another negative criticism of Chinese customs, Staunton refers to the popular eighteenth-century European concept of progress. Displaying more sophistication than many travellers, Staunton analyses the Chinese attitude of superiority toward foreigners in historical perspective. In the past, he explains, the Chinese were in fact superior both to their less civilised Asian neighbours, and at the time of Marco Polo's visit, even to Europeans; and they have maintained this attitude throughout the centuries. But, Staunton continues: 'not having since advanced, whilst the nations of Europe have been every day improving in manners, and in arts and knowledge of every kind, the Chinese are seen by the latter with less admiring eyes than they were by the first travellers who gave accounts of them' (ii.514).

The Staunton narrative, on the whole, in spite of its cumbersome syntax and lack of personal touches, is a fascinating document; it provided a dispassionate analysis of Chinese life, presenting the evidence not as a new discovery or as a contradiction of earlier views, but simply as a statement of fact. In so doing, it dispelled once and for all for Western Europeans the magnificent mirage of previous travellers. For Russian readers it added further touches to the unflattering side of the double image of China then taking shape in Russian literature.

Meanwhile a pair of multi-volume works translated from French, and a short work translated from French but written originally in Latin were providing Russian readers with a quite different set of impressions. The Latin work, appearing in Russia in 1795, was the account by the Franciscan friar, Giovanni de Plano Carpini, one of the first Europeans ever to describe Central and Eastern Asia.[15] Carpini was sent by pope Innocent IV in 1245 as a diplomatic emissary

---

[15] Karpini (Giovanni de Plano Carpini), *Любопытнейшее путешествие монаха францисканскаго ордена Жана дю План Карпина, посыланнаго в 1246 году в достойнстве легата и посла от папы Иннокентия IV к татарам* (Moscow 1795; 2nd ed. 1800) (The Very interesting journey of the Franciscan monk Giovanni de Plano Carpini, sent in 1246 as legate and consul to the Tatars by pope Innocent IV); *Contemporaries of Marco Polo*, ed. Manuel Komroff (London 1929). Subsequent references will be to the

to the Tartars. Of great historical importance, Carpini's work was undoubtedly of special interest to Russians because of friar John's description of his hospitable welcome by fellow Christians in the city of Kiev, which lay on his route to the East.

While Carpini visited the territory of the Mongols north of China rather than the Middle Kingdom proper, his discussion of the Mongols' wars with their neighbours brings him to a short description of the 'People of Cathay' (Carpini, p.36). Carpini's brief comments touch upon many of the same points that travellers to China five centuries later would include in their accounts, and his evaluations are quite favourable. Of the courage of the Chinese he states that they 'fought manfully' against the Mongols under Ghengis Khan (p.37). Regarding their skill, he writes, 'In all occupations which men practice, there are not better craftsmen in the whole world' (p.38). The Franciscan also views Chinese religious attitudes in a favourable way. As a prophetic foreshadowing of the complex and futile attempt on the part of the seventeenth- and eighteenth-century Jesuits to reconcile certain aspects of Chinese religious belief with Christianity, Carpini explains ambiguously that the Chinese are pagans, that they have many saints, but worship one God. They also have both the Old and New Testaments. Carpini continues: 'They adore and reverence Christ Jesus our Lord, and believe the article of eternal life, but are not baptised. They do also honourably esteem and reverence our Scriptures. They love Christians, and bestow much alms, and are a very courteous and gentle people' (p.37).

Nearly five hundred years later a similar approach taken by the Jesuits led eventually to the Rites Controversy within the Catholic Church. The resemblance between Carpini's remarks and the controversial statement made by the missionary Lecomte around the turn of the eighteenth century bears witness to the perceptive nature of the medieval traveller's observations. Lecomte stated: 'ce peuple a conservé près de deux mille ans la connaissance du véritable Dieu, et l'a honoré d'une manière qui peut servir d'exemple et d'instruction même aux Chrétiens'.[16]

Sharing Carpini's enthusiasm for the distant Cathay was the eighteenth-century French writer and compiler, Jean François de La Harpe, whose abridgement of abbé Prévost's *Histoire générale des voyages* (Paris 1746-1761) appeared in a twenty-two-volume Russian translation between 1782 and 1787.[17] The seventh and eighth volumes of La Harpe's *Abrégé* deal exclusively with China and Chinese Tartary (Manchuria). The materials dealing with China proper consist

English translation and will be included in the text.

[16] Louis Daniel Lecomte, *Nouveaux mémoires sur l'état présent de la Chine*, 3rd ed. (Paris 1701), ii.114.

[17] Lagarp (Jean François de La Harpe), *История о странствиях вообще по всем краям земнаго круга, сочинения господина Прево, сокращенная новейшим расположением чрез господина Ла-Гарпа* (A general history of voyages to all parts of the Earth by Prévost, abridged with a new arrangement by La Harpe) (Moscow 1782-1787). The work was translated in its entirety except for portions of volumes 9, 17, and 18 containing material on Siberia and Kamchatka, areas which had been thoroughly described in the works of S. P. Krasheninnikov and G. F. Müller. See *Union catalogue*, entry 5613, ii.465, note.

first of résumés and long quotations from the works of European travellers to China from the thirteenth to the eighteenth century, and second, of descriptive chapters on China's cities, institutions, history and art, based largely on the accounts of the Jesuit missionaries.

La Harpe's selection of résumés, which fortunately filled in many lacunae in the Russian repertory of travel literature, tends to present the idealists' concept of China. Marco Polo, for instance, is seen to praise the Chinese people – their disinclination toward jealousy and war, and their civility to foreigners. When Polo describes one city as 'a veritable paradise on earth', La Harpe notes that this gives us an idea of thirteenth-century China in general.[18] The travels of the Spanish Dominican, Dominique Navarette, which were quite influential in Western Europe, but which, to the best of my knowledge, had not been translated into Russian before the La Harpe *Abrégé* appeared, broaden Russia's acquaintance with missionary reports on China in terms of the national and denominational background of the writer. Navarette's evaluation of China, in the résumé presented here, however, is indistinguishable from that of the French Jesuits. The Chinese are praised for their many virtues, but above all for their humanity. Indeed when Navarette notes that the Chinese consider Europeans as barbarians, La Harpe, implying, it would seem, the moral superiority of the Chinese, adds the editorial comment that the Europeans have taken with them to China 'their discords, their anger, and their avarice' (La Harpe, vii.152).

La Harpe's *Abrégé* also adds considerable material to the Russian collection of Jesuit travels in China. While the account of Gerbillon's journey, taken from the fourth volume of Du Halde, had already appeared in Russian translation, the travels of father Gaubil were new to Russian readers. The treatment of the Rites Controversy within the Roman Catholic Church, presented in connection with the work of Gaubil, is especially important. Although La Harpe claims that 'all of Europe was inundated with writings pro or con the Chinese ceremonies' (vii.157), this is in fact one of the few eighteenth-century discussions of the controversy to appear in Russian literature. La Harpe's relation of the conversations between K'ang-hsi and the missionaries in regard to the dispute gives a valuable psychological portrait of the emperor, and at the same time provides a striking insight into the intensity of the feelings of those involved in the controversy. The emperor's questioning of such fierce disagreement among members of the same faith, his irritation at the idea of the pope pronouncing on Chinese affairs, and his perplexity at the European furor over which Chinese word should be used for 'God' may well have given the impression to Russian readers that the Chinese were as eminently reasonable as the Roman Catholics were disputatious (vii.184).

The account of another traveller, well-known in Western Europe but presented to Russian readers for the first time in the Prévost-La Harpe work, is that of John Nieuhof, who accompanied a Dutch embassy to China in 1655. The information about Nieuhof's experiences that reached Russian readers presents

---

[18] Jean François de La Harpe, *Abrégé de l'histoire générale des voyages* (Paris 1780), vii.10. Subsequent references will be to this original version of the work and will be included in the text.

a contrast to the generally favourable impressions seen in the other La Harpe résumés. The aggravations experienced by the embassy in gaining permission to travel from Canton to Peking, their difficulties in obtaining an audience with the emperor, and the ultimate failure of the embassy to establish regular trade relations with China present the Chinese as hardly congenial hosts (vii.99-134).

The chapter by Prévost-La Harpe entitled 'The Russian embassy' must have proved disappointing to Russian sinophiles, for only two accounts by persons connected with Russian missions, those by Ysbrants Ides and Lorents Lange, are discussed, and the treatment of both is quite superficial. A complete translation of one of Lange's journals had already appeared in Russian in 1776, but Ides' narrative was not to appear in full in Russian translation until 1789. The very brief résumés of these works presented in the *Abrégé* contain no references to the political tasks entrusted to the ambassadors, and give no indication of the unfavourable views of the Middle Kingdom which the travellers brought back to Russia with them.

The second section of the *Abrégé*, in which La Harpe undertakes a systematic description of China, achieves a somewhat greater degree of balance between complimentary and unfavourable appraisals. Since most of this material is drawn from Jesuit sources, the ideals and goals of Chinese society, it is true, receive more emphasis than the practical working out of the aims. La Harpe pays particular attention to such positive features of the system as the availability of justice for even the poorest, the existence of legal remedies against extortion by public officials, as well as such personal attributes of the people as the modesty of schoolchildren and respect for the elderly. The French writer does, however, occasionally qualify his praise, as in his opinion that there could hardly be a happier nation than China 'if all the Mandarins obeyed the laws of their country exactly'; but, La Harpe adds, with such a great number of officials, there are always those who will put their own interests first (viii.221). Also uncomplimentary are the descriptions of various forms of fraud, the practice of torture, and the vanity of the people.

As a whole, the two sections of the *Abrégé* made a valuable contribution to Russian knowledge about China and about Western European views of the Middle Kingdom. Judged as travel literature, the various accounts, abridged and joined together by an editor, certainly lack the freshness of the Anson, Krusenstern or Lisianskii journals. The value of the work, however, is in the broad coverage which its approach makes possible.

A second French work which also embellished the idealistic image of China was abbé Joseph de La Porte's *Le Voyageur français, ou la connaissance de l'ancien et du nouveau monde* (Paris 1768-1795). This work, appearing in a twenty-seven-volume Russian translation between 1778 and 1794, attempted a popularised presentation of geography through the medium of travel literature.[19] Its success in Russia is evidenced by the fact that it eventually went into three Russian editions.

[19] La Port (Joseph de La Porte), *Всемирный путешествователь, или Познание Стараго и Новаго света* (St Petersburg 1778-94). *Le Voyageur français ou la connaissance de l'ancien et du nouveau monde* (Paris 1768-1795). Subsequent references will be to the 2nd edition of the Russian translation, vol. v (1782), and will be included in the text.

The section of the work which deals with China, like the one by La Harpe, utilises a considerable amount of Jesuit material, but the style and format of the two compilations are entirely different. *Le Voyageur français* purports to present the impressions of an authentic traveller, but the universal scope of the journeys that is proclaimed by the title and supported by the great number of volumes in the work suggests that one is not to take the 'traveller' as more than a literary device. Nevertheless, La Porte makes a real enough personage out of the narrator-letter-writer, who as a tourist supposedly records his observations for a friend. Without citing sources, La Porte combines the impressions taken from the works of genuine travellers, and through various techniques achieves a unified and flowing style which the La Harpe volumes do not attempt. Readers who were familiar with the original works of travel literature which La Porte used, however, must have found the French *voyageur*, with his assimilated quotations from real travellers, somewhat disconcerting.

Among the borrowed quotations, for instance, is that from Prévost-La Harpe to the effect that no state could be happier than China if all governmental figures were to observe the laws of the land (La Porte, v.270). Another borrowed phrase is found in the 'traveller's' assertion that 'neither honour nor virtue, but the stick governs the Chinese' (v.340), a statement which parrots the much discussed words of Montesquieu, 'C'est le bâton qui gouverne la Chine.'[20] This sentiment of Montesquieu's had become a much discussed issue, and was commented upon by Voltaire, who was greatly incensed by the idea.[21] No reflection of the controversy is to be found in La Porte, however, the *voyageur* making the pronouncement as if it were his own.

La Porte uses various methods to make his *voyageur* credible, such as the popular eighteenth-century epistolary technique, combining the realistic elements of time and place with those of addressee and letter-writer, and also the introduction into his story of several well-known European missionaries, such as fathers Attiret and Gaubil (v.353-56). The latter supposedly even invites the *voyageur* to travel to the provinces with him. Father Da Rocha, another well-known missionary, whom the traveller supposedly meets at the outset of his journey, serves as guide, translator and interpreter of Chinese life throughout most of the book.

Among these 'China hands' whom La Porte mentions is one who would have been of special interest to Russian readers. He is a Swede named Bremend, who is described as a very old man who had come to Peking in 1720 with the Russian embassy sent by Peter the Great. We are told that he remained in China with the Russian Commercial Agent, Lange, after the embassy returned to Russia. The *voyageur*, who is introduced to Bremend by his missionary friends, is so fascinated by the story of the Russian embassy (which Bremend is said to have put in writing) that he includes some excerpts from it in his own narrative. A footnote (which turns out to be quite significant) in the Russian translation

---

[20] Charles de Secondat de Montesquieu, *Œuvres*, ed. Caillois (Paris 1951), ii.366. Montesquieu himself cites Du Halde as the source of this statement, but the actual phrase is not to be found in the volume of Du Halde which he cites. Guy, p.205.

[21] Voltaire, 'Commentaire sur l'*Esprit des lois*', M.xxx.430-31.

states that this Russian embassy was described in a work by John Bell, which was translated into Russian in 1774.

The *voyageur* explains that he will present to his readers the details from Bremend which can serve as an 'explanation' of the Chinese people (v.296). But no sooner does Bremend's tale begin – with a discussion of the Mongolian camels and pack horses which are to take the Russian party across the Gobi desert – than one becomes suspicious of the authenticity of the Swede's account. The detail about the horses refusing to co-operate because the riders do not smell like their usual masters is too striking for one who has encountered it elsewhere to forget. A few further comparisons confirm one's doubts. The real narrator is John Bell mentioned in the Russian footnote. The account by 'Bremend' has been assimilated almost word for word from Bell's *Travels from St Petersburg in Russia to diverse parts of Asia*.[22]

Bell's very readable narrative, which belongs to the story of the Russian diplomatic missions, will be discussed later. A few of La Porte's embellishments, however, are worthy of note, first because they provide an illustration of how La Porte manipulated authentic travel narratives, and second, because they probably made a considerable impression on Russian readers interested in Chinese attitudes toward Russia and her diplomatic envoys. 'Bremend' tells how the Russian ambassador, who was about to have an audience with the emperor, succeeded in exempting himself from the part of the ceremony which required one to approach the throne with a special running step. 'Bremend's' comment that during his stay at the Chinese court he had found it very amusing to watch the 'important' missionaries performing this ceremony and 'running like ducks across the entire hall' (v.308), a remark not found in Bell's more sober account, underscores the humiliating aspects of the Chinese ceremonial requirements.

Later, commenting on the Chinese view that all foreigners are barbarians, and that all foreign governments which send gifts to the emperor are to be considered as tributary states, 'Bremend' states: 'The Russians had considerable difficulty extricating them [the Chinese] from this misconception and forcing them to change for them [the Russians] this hateful appellation' (v.331). This sentence also is not to be found in Bell. It has, however, a history of its own in French works on China. A slightly different version of the same sentence appears in the description by father Bouvet of the Russian embassy's arrival in Peking, given by Du Halde in 1735: 'Quelque chose que fassent les Moscovites, ils auront bien de la peine à faire changer ce terme en leur faveur: quand même on le changerait, on ne laisserait pas de prendre l'ambassade comme un hommage qu'on vient rendre.'[23] In 1780 La Harpe, in his *Abrégé* of Prévost's work, presented the idea in the following form: 'Les Russes n'ont pas eu peu de

[22] John Bell, *Travels from St Petersburg in Russia to diverse parts of Asia* (Glasgow 1763); Bell (John Bell), *Белевы путешествия чрез Россию в разныя асиятския земли; а именно: в Испаган, в Пекин, в Дербент и Константинополь* (trans. of *Voyages depuis St Petersbourg en Russie, dans diverses contrées de l'Asie*), trans. M. Popov (St Petersburg 1776).

[23] Jean Baptiste Du Halde, *Description géographique, historique, chronologique, politique, et physique, de l'Empire de la Chine*, i.80.

peine à faire changer ce terme en leur faveur; et leur Ambassade n'en a pas moins été regardée comme un hommage.'[24]

The French writers Bouvet, La Harpe and La Porte were evidently quite impressed by the Russian attempt to overturn a fixed element of Chinese diplomacy. La Porte, it will be noted, at least in the Russian translation, gives the impression that the Russians were in fact successful in changing the attitude of the Chinese, while the others imply that they were not.[25] La Porte's Russian readers received on the one hand a vivid impression of how repulsive the Chinese protocol requirements were to the tsar's envoys, and on the other a sense of reassurance that the Russian representatives had managed to maintain their sovereign's honour.

The French *voyageur*'s overall view of the Middle Kingdom is a generally favourable one, although like Prévost-La Harpe, La Porte does not hesitate to mention certain shortcomings in the Celestial Empire. While the presentation is not a scholarly one, considerable factual information about the history, geography, and mores of China was made available to Russian readers in this work. That it was taken fairly seriously in Russia is indicated by the twelve-page index to the volume on China, and also by the translator's footnotes to Russian books, articles, and translations which could provide the more avid sinophiles with further information.

Le Voyageur français, like the other six travel accounts considered here, contributed to the Russian image of China through the presentation of a great deal of factual information, as well as the personal viewpoints of a considerable number of travellers. In these works we again find the two 'Chinas' that came to co-exist in Russian literature of the period. The French compilers Prévost-La Harpe and La Porte tend to present an idealistic picture of the Celestial Empire, even though they include some material that is unflattering to the Chinese. Carpini also compliments the Eastern state. The narratives by Anson, Macartney, Krusenstern and Lisianskii, on the other hand, present this supposedly ideal nation in a decidedly unfavourable light. In view of these varied attitudes one can conclude, incidentally, that the Russian translators and editors were not biased in their choices of narratives for publication. But the question again presents itself: why was the 'French China' generally a utopian kingdom, so unlike the realm visited by the Russians and the British?

To answer this question one might look again for psychological explanations. Are there in this group of narratives indications of the human tendency to react to a new environment in accordance with the success with which one's objectives there are fulfilled? The Prévost-La Harpe and La Porte volumes, composed mainly of missionary accounts, do certainly reflect the attitudes of men who felt that they had accomplished their mission, and this fact might be considered to be at least one of the reasons for their positive appraisal of the Chinese state. In the case of the medieval traveller Carpini, the papal ambassador's approval of the Chinese may result from the fact that the Chinese, like the Europeans,

---

[24] La Harpe, viii.166.
[25] I have not seen La Porte in the original French. Perhaps the Russian is a mistranslation, accidental or intentional.

considered themselves enemies of the Mongols, to whom Carpini's mission was *not* a success. The Chinese may therefore, in contrast, have seemed all the more congenial to Carpini. The Russian and British navigators, and the British ambassador to China, on the other hand, not only experienced great difficulties in their alien Chinese surroundings, but, more significantly, were not able to accomplish what they had set out to do, a fact which may then have coloured their outlooks.

This hypothesis concerning the divergent attitudes of European visitors to China might be kept in mind as we consider another group of travellers to China – the tsar's representatives at the Chinese court.

2. The embassies from Russia

'Every thing now appeared to us as if we had arrived in
another world.'
John Bell, with the Russian Embassy of
Lev Vasilevich Izmailov to Peking, 1720[26]

The first diplomatic mission to be sent to China by Russia – one of the first to be sent by any European nation in the modern period – arrived in Peking in 1618; in the following 187 years no less than nine official Russian embassies, not to mention numerous couriers and other representatives of the Russian government, were to visit the capital of Russia's neighbour to the east. The travel accounts written by members of these diplomatic parties did not become available to the Russian public in published form until roughly the last quarter of the eighteenth century. Then between 1772 and 1818 nine first-hand reports of the official embassies and other missions appeared in Russia in journals and in book form. That seven of these documents had been published by 1796 shows the intensity of public interest in China during this particular period.

The official account of the first mission sent to Peking, that headed by Ivan Petlin in 1618, was not to appear in published form in Russia during the eighteenth century.[27] But a vivid narration concerning the next delegation (the

[26] John Bell, *A journey from St Petersburg to Pekin, 1719-22*, ed. J. L. Stevenson (Edinburgh 1965), p.117.
[27] Petlin's account, of which fifteen Russian manuscript copies are extant, was written in 1619. An English translation entitled 'A Relation of two Russe Cossacks travailes out of Siberia to Cathay and other countries adjoining thereto' was included in *Purchas: his pilgrimes* in 1625. The account was again published in England by the poet John Milton in *A brief history of Moscovia and of other lessknown countries lying eastward of Rossia as far as Cathay* (London 1682). It also appeared in several other early European collections of travel accounts, including that of Pierre Bergeron, *Voyages faits principalement en Asie dans les XII, XIII, XIV, et XV siècles* (1634). The first Russian publication was in 1818: 'Роспись Китайскому государству и пообинскому и иным государствам, жилым и кочевым улусам и великой Обе реки и дорогам' (Description of the Chinese nation and other governments, towns and nomadic settlements along the Ob and the Great Ob River and routes), *Siberian herald*, no. 2 (1818), pp.211-46. J. F. Baddeley's modern English translation of the *Journal* is included in John Frederick Baddeley, *Russia, Mongolia, China* (London 1919), ii.73-84. See also N. F. Demidova and V. S. Miasnikov, *Первые русские дипломаты в Китае («Роспись» И. Петлина и статейный список Ф. И. Байкова)* (The First Russian

first to be officially designated an embassy) did become available to Russian readers in 1788. This was the mission of Fedor Isakovich Baikov, who was dispatched by tsar Aleksei Mikhailovich in 1654 and entrusted with the task of attempting to open trade negotiations between Russia and China. Baikov's *Статейный список*, the official daily record of the mission, appeared under the title of 'Путешествие российского посланника Федора Исаковича Байкова в Китай, 7162 (1654) года июня 25 дня' (Journey of the Russian envoy Fedor Isakovich Baikov to China, 25 June 1654) in a leading periodical published by the Russian intellectual leader Nikolai Novikov.[28]

By this time, 1788, the Russian public had, however, already become acquainted with the contents of Baikov's narrative through several scholarly works. The historian J. E. Fischer had given a summary of Baikov's account in his *Sibirische Geschichte* published in German in St Petersburg in 1768 and in Russian in 1774.[29] An even earlier discussion of Baikov's narrative is found in a lengthy article by G. F. Müller entitled 'The first Russian journeys and embassies to China', which appeared in the journal *Ежемесячныя сочинения* (Monthly compositions) in 1755, at the start of the period of active Russian interest in the Middle Kingdom. Here Müller discussed Baikov's journey and several other seventeenth-century Russian missions to China, including the first one, by Petlin.[30] Although Müller in 1755 did not have access to a Russian version of the Baikov journal, he provided a detailed analysis of the mission on the basis of a French translation and the Dutch version that was included by N. Witsen in his *Noord en Oost Tartarye* (Amsterdam 1692). Baikov's journal had in fact first appeared in part in certain copies of Thévenot's collection of travel accounts between 1663 and 1672, and had appeared in German and French, and in an English translation in Churchill's *Collection* in 1704. Parts of the narrative had therefore been available to Western European readers long before it was even commented upon in Baikov's own country.[31]

While the Müller article, as will be seen later, provided important historical documentation concerning the Baikov embassy, it did not attempt to reproduce the dramatic interest of Baikov's narrative itself, which must have been greatly appreciated by later Russian sinophiles who in 1788 were able to read the work in full. In his narrative Baikov emphasises the lively interchanges that took place between himself and the Chinese officials by placing the account of his experiences at Court first and giving incidental descriptive material separately.

diplomats in China [I. Petlin's *Description* and F. I. Baikov's *Journal*]) (Moscow 1966), and P. E. Skachkov, *Outline of the history of Russian sinology*, p.18 and note 24, p.295.

[28] *Древняя российская вивлиофика* (Ancient Russian library), no. 4 (1788), pp.120-42. The narrative was again published in the journal *Siberian Herald* in 1820.

[29] Fisher (Johann Eberhard Fischer), *Сибирская история с самаго открытия Сибири до завоевания сей земли российским оружием* (Siberian history from the actual discovery of Siberia to the conquest of this land by Russian arms) (St Petersburg 1774).

[30] G. F. Müller, 'О первых Российских путешествиях и посольствах в Китай' (The First Russian travellers and embassies to China), *Monthly compositions*, no. 2 (July 1755), pp.15-57. Müller later discussed Baikov's journey in his *Sammlung*, iv (1760), pp.473-548, which was published in German in St Petersburg. See Cahen, p.20.

[31] See Baddeley, ii.130-31 for complete citations to other translations.

The ambassador provides little personal commentary; the record of events at the Court, however, speak for themselves in setting the tone for the entire report.

From the time of his entry into China, Baikov encountered seemingly endless difficulties. After being kept waiting for ten days outside the frontier city while a letter was sent to the emperor for orders, the envoy was finally given an escort (but not the supplies which the Chinese usually provided for official travellers) and was ordered to proceed to Peking. From the start, Baikov's resolve and firmness are seen. When requested, for example, by Chinese dignitaries to show respect for the emperor by kneeling and bowing before a group of temples along the route, Baikov refused, explaining: 'It is not our custom to fall on our knees and bow, not having seen the tsar; with our own great sovereign the procedure is as follows: we bow to him standing, bare-headed.'[32]

Upon his arrival in Peking Baikov was requested to present the tsar's gifts for the emperor to representatives of the ruler, but the ambassador steadfastly refused to deliver the gifts before presenting his credentials. The Chinese dignitaries, incensed at his opposition to them, ironically suggested that he intended to trade the things he had brought, rather than present them as gifts. Responding to their threat to seize the articles, Baikov retorted that he had not come to China to have Chinese officials steal Russian government property. At last, according to one version of the narrative, the gifts were in fact taken from the ambassador by force.

Further difficulties ensued when the Chinese insisted that Baikov present his credentials to the Board, a governmental agency; the ambassador declared that he would present them only to the emperor himself. In addition, Baikov was told that he was to be instructed on how to kowtow, so that he would be prepared in the event that he should eventually attain an audience with the emperor. The envoy also refused to comply with this procedure, stating that his orders were to show respect to the emperor in the same way that he showed respect to the tsar himself. After numerous unpleasant encounters and arguments, the officials informed Baikov that he was to be executed for failure to comply with imperial commands. The ambassador was unmoved. He continued to insist upon presenting his credentials only to the emperor. Several days later the tsar's gifts to the emperor were returned to Baikov, and he was dismissed from Peking, in his own words, 'by no means politely' (Baddeley, ii.146).

Here Baikov interrupts the account of his aggravating experiences at the Court in order to give a very brief description of the city of Peking. The ambassador explains with some irony, it would seem, the limited nature of his material: 'Now, as to the city of Kanbalik, whether it is great or small is not certainly known; because the Russians were not allowed to leave the courtyard; they were locked in, as in prison; but why they were locked in is likewise not known.'[33] Baikov did succeed, however, in observing many outward character-

[32] F. I. Baikov, 'Статейный список' (Journal), trans. J. F. Baddeley, in Baddeley, ii.135-53 at p.144. Subsequent references will be to this English translation and will be included in the text.

[33] ii.147. By 'Kanbalik', Baikov means 'Peking'. It should be noted that the custom of confining foreign delegations to the embassy compound was also practised by Russia at this time. Baddeley, ii.384.

istics of the city and noted in particular such picturesque sights as the gold and silver, pearls and precious stones, unusual fruits and spices, elaborate ornamental inscriptions, decorative dragons, unfamiliar animals, such as goldfish in a red pond, and elephants, as well as shrines with gilded idols, candles and bells.

The information the ambassador gives about the more fundamental features of Chinese culture is considerably more limited than his description of the physical appearance of Peking. He does touch superficially on the religion of the country and notes that Europeans residing in China have been permitted to keep their own faith.

Baikov ends his description of Peking by mentioning briefly the arrival there of another foreign embassy. This group, the ambassador indicates, encountered difficulties similar to those which confronted the Russians. Baikov states only that they were Dutch, but Russian readers who were specialists on China would have known that this was the embassy of de Goyer and de Keyser. Contact between the Dutch and Russian embassies was prevented fairly successfully by the Chinese, Baikov reports. The fact that the members of the two embassies shared no common language, not even Latin, further impeded communication between the two groups. The Dutch did manage, however, to send out two letters in the care of the Russian embassy. The Dutch mission was soon to be described by one of its members, John Nieuhof, whose travel accounts were to become well-known in Western Europe and, as mentioned earlier, represented in Russia by at least one excerpt in translation. The existence of accounts by members of two foreign embassies who visited Peking at the same time prompted in Russia a noteworthy comparison which will soon be seen.

After commenting on the Dutch embassy, Baikov concludes the account of his unceremonious departure from Peking. His aggravating experiences with the Chinese Court did not end when he left the city, at least according to one version of his narrative which relates the following curious episode. Nine days after leaving the capital the ambassador is said to have dispatched a message to the emperor stating that if it was indeed the Chinese custom not to receive ambassadors personally, Baikov would, upon the emperor's order, return to Peking and follow Chinese protocol. A Chinese courier returned to Baikov with the report that the emperor, doubting the truth of the message, wanted Baikov's personal word that he would actually present his credentials to the Board and perform the kowtow. The ambassador reasserted his willingness to follow Chinese custom, and again waited for a reply from the emperor. The answer which at last arrived stated that because Baikov, after dispatching his first messenger, had moved on to a border town, the emperor and his officials had come to the following conclusion: 'he who behaves in such a manner cannot be in his right mind; he professes to have been sent from the Great Lord, from the orthodox tsar, but has not the slightest inkling how to show respect to a sovereign' (Baddeley, ii.152). Russian readers, it would seem, could only have viewed Baikov's experience as a great humiliation for the Russian government.

In spite of his final reported offer to come to terms with the Chinese, Baikov appears to have been extremely resolute in his determination to uphold the honour of the tsar. G. F. Müller, when analysing the account in his 1755 article on Russian embassies to China, praised the Russian highly for the stand he took, and expressed the opinion that the Chinese custom of requiring foreign envoys to appear before the Board as if they were representatives of vassal states was an example of the Chinese desire to appear superior to all other people.[34] It will be recalled that Müller presented similarly uncomplimentary views of the Chinese in his commentary on the journal of the Chinese ambassador Tulishen. In his article concerning embassies, however, Müller did not elaborate on his own opinions of the Chinese, but concentrated instead on a comparison between the Nieuhof account of China and Baikov's report on the Russian venture there. According to Nieuhof, from whom Müller gives extensive quotations, negotiations between the Dutch embassy and the Chinese were quite successful. Unlike the selection of excerpts from Nieuhof which La Harpe presented (and which Russian readers received in the 1780s at about the same time that Baikov's work was published), Müller's quotations from the Dutch ambassador reveal no adverse criticisms of the Chinese. Instead, the high degree of accord between the Dutch and their hosts is emphasised. Nieuhof tells how the Dutch had complied with a Chinese request to take part in a dedication ceremony for a new palace. The Russians, Nieuhof states, had refused to do this, and for this reason had been dismissed from Peking without obtaining an audience with the emperor. Müller, who proceeds here to make corrections on Nieuhof's commentary, implies that the Dutch did not comprehend the significance of the Chinese ceremonies. As they were interested only in commercial gain, Müller asserts, the Dutch simply complied with all Chinese requests. Baikov, on the other hand, rightly refused to do anything that would dishonour his own sovereign. Müller claims that Nieuhof was not only less principled than Baikov in this regard, but also less truthful in his account than was the Russian. For example, the Dutchman, Müller points out, fails to mention that his embassy was confined to its quarters as closely as was the Russian mission.

Müller's 1755 article, apparently the earliest published discussion in Russian on travel accounts about China, was in fact one of the very few such commentaries produced in Russia during the entire eighteenth century. While many original narratives of Russian and foreign travellers were to be published in the following decades, few Russian writers analysed the contents of these works. Müller's comparison of the Dutch and the Baikov embassies is especially significant because it brings out the fact that two foreign delegations could visit Peking at the same time and under relatively similar conditions, and could react to situations and problems, particularly the ceremonial requirements of the Chinese, very differently from each other. The publication of excerpts from a single writer by two different hands also illustrates quite strikingly the way two totally different sets of impressions can be made to emerge from an original work.

In 1675 a third Russian embassy was sent to Peking, this time with the aim of setting up regular diplomatic and trade relations between Russia and China, and also of locating the best routes between the two countries. The unsuccessful mission was later documented in detail by its leader, Nikolai Spafarii, in one of

[34] Müller, p.41.

the most spirited of the early Russian travel accounts. Unfortunately for eighteenth-century Russian, as well as Western European readers, the narrative remained unpublished until it was found in the Russian government archives in the latter part of the nineteenth century.[35] Several of Spafarii's other works concerning the Orient did, however, appear in print during the eighteenth century as will be seen later in connection with the intellectuals' views of China.[36]

Less than ten years after the return of the Spafarii mission from Peking, a fourth official Russian embassy, headed by Fedor Alekseevich Golovin, was entrusted with the difficult mission of negotiating a treaty concerning boundaries and commercial affairs with the Chinese. The resulting Treaty of Nerchinsk, the first international treaty signed by China in the modern period, which was concluded in August of 1689, was unfavourable to Russia in some respects, but did establish direct trade between Russia and Peking, which the Russian government very much wanted.[37] Eighteenth-century readers had little information about this diplomatic mission. Golovin's own account of the embassy has in fact only recently been made public.[38] The next Russian delegation to

[35] Iu. V. Arsenev, 'Статейный список посольства Н. Спафария в Китае 1675-1678 гг.' (Journal of the embassy of N. Spafarii in China 1675-1678), *Вестник археологии и истории* (Herald of archeology and history) 17 (1906). Also published separately in the same year. The English translation of Arsenev's edition of the manuscript is: 'Spathary: his embassy to China, 1675-1677', trans. J. F. Baddeley, in Baddeley, ii.242-422. Nikolai Gavrilovich Spathari Milescu (*c.*1636-*c.*1708) was Moldavian by birth. Although 'Spafarii' (in a variety of spellings) is generally given as his last name, the word 'spatar' is in fact in Romanian a title meaning 'commander of cavalry'. See Mark Mancall, *Russia and China: their diplomatic relations to 1728* (Cambridge, Mass. 1971), p.324, note 9.

[36] Spafarii's embassy was mentioned in 1757 in an article by G. F. Müller: 'История о странах при реке Амуре лежащих, когда оныя состояли под Российским владением' (History of the lands located on the Amur River, when they belonged to Russia), *Monthly compositions* (July-October 1757), at pp.200-201. The ambassador's lack of success was discussed briefly in a work by Ivan Pisarev in 1772. See Ivan Pisarev, 'Дополнение к историческому в сей книге, о Китайском государстве, описанию' (Supplement to the historical description in this book about the Chinese government) in Antonio Katiforo (Antonio Catiforo), *Житие Петра Великаго, императора и самодержца всероссийского* (The Life of Peter the Great, All-Russian emperor and ruler), trans. Ivan Pisarev (St Petersburg 1772), pp.481-511 at pp.484-85. The general lack of knowledge during the eighteenth century about Sparfarii's embassy, however, is demonstrated in a publication of 1787, a translation of five official letters written in Latin and sent to the Russian government in the seventeenth century by the emperor of China: *Старинныя письма китайскаго императора к российскому государю* (Old letters from the emperor of China to the Russian sovereign), ed. Matvei Komarov (Moscow 1787). Spafarii is mentioned in the letters, and the editor notes that he has no documents pertaining to this embassy, and asks readers to supply any material they may have. (See Viktor Shklovskii, *Матвей Комаров, житель города Москвы* (Matvei Komarov, Resident of Moscow) (Leningrad 1929), pp.146-51 at p.146.) The letters contain complaints that Russian subjects in the border area between China and Russia are harrassing the local population.

[37] Clifford M. Foust, *Muscovite and mandarin* (Chapel Hill 1969), pp.6-7.

[38] Müller and Pisarev, however, mention the embassy in their accounts. See notes 30 and 36 above. Golovin's account is now available in *Русско-китайские отношения в XVII веке: материалы и документы* (Russo-Chinese relations in the 17th century: materials and documents), comp. N. F. Demidova and V. S. Miasnikov, ii (Moscow 1972), pp.69-641.

China was, however, to be well documented for eighteenth-century Russian readers. This was the embassy of 1692-1795 led by Everard Ysbrants Ides, a Western European merchant in the service of Peter the Great. Ides' journal, originally written in Dutch, appeared in Amsterdam in 1704 and in London in 1706. In 1789 Müller made the work available in a Russian translation entitled, 'Путешествие и журнал [...] Ебергарда Избраннедеса' (The journey and journal [...] of Everard Ysbrants Ides).[39]

Ides' journal provides a contrast to the narratives of the previous Russian envoys in that it presents a generally favourable picture of the Middle Kingdom. While Ides did not, in fact, achieve the object of his mission, which was to conclude further commercial agreements with the Chinese, he was nevertheless treated respectfully, and accorded numerous favours by the emperor himself. Rigid stances such as those maintained at the time of the Baikov and Spafarii embassies are not to be seen in this account; the emperor appears to have been genuinely desirous of maintaining good relations with Russia, and the tsar's ambassador was willing to acquiesce in matters of Chinese protocol. Ides, striving for objectivity in his journal, generally refrains from making personal, subjective evaluations about most of what he saw and experienced, but his satisfaction with the treatment he was accorded can be felt throughout the entire narrative.

The Ides mission went well from the start. The ambassador was met respectfully outside the Chinese border, and enjoyed one pleasant reception after another in the towns he passed through en route to Peking. He was presented to the emperor, to whom he delivered his credentials, about a week after his arrival in the capital. During his stay, tours of the city and special entertainment were arranged for him, and before he departed he was again granted an imperial audience. Ides's account of this farewell audience with the emperor is particularly significant. In it one senses the ambassador's satisfaction with the proceedings;

[39] Evert Ysbrandszoon Ides, *Driejaarige Reise nach China* (Amsterdam 1704); English edition, E. Ysbrants Ides, *Three years travels from Moscow overland to China* (London 1706). Subsequent references are to this edition and will be included in the text. Ides's work also appeared in French in C. Le Brun, *Voyages de Corneille Le Brun*, i (Amsterdam 1718) and in *Recueil de voyages au nord*, viii (Amsterdam 1727). The original Russian translation was 'Путешествие и журнал [...] Ебергарда Избраннедеса', *Ancient Russian library*, no. 4, pt. 8 (1789), pp.360-475; pt. 9 (1789), pp.387-461. See also the recent Russian translation in M. I. Kazanin (comp.), *Записки о русском посольстве в Китаи (1692-1695)* (Notes on the Russian embassy to China (1692-1695) (Moscow 1967). Brief mention of the Ides embassy had appeared in Russian two years earlier with the publication of the Ambassador's official papers, in F. Tumanskii, *Собрание разных записок и сочинений [...] о жизни [...] Петра Великаго* (Collection of various notes and works on the life of Peter the Great), i, pt. 2 (St Petersburg 1787), pp.71ff. Cited in Cahen, p.clxxxi. (Ides was frequently cited in Russian by his second name Ysbrandszoon or Yzbrants; both of his names appeared in a variety of spellings.) A second account of the mission, written by Adam Brand, a secretary in the embassy, was published in Western Europe even before the authoritative one by Ides: Adam Brand, *Beschreibung der Chinesischen Reise* (Hamburg 1698); *A journal of the embassy from their majesties John and Peter Alexievitz emperors of Muscovy, etc. overland into China* (London 1698); and *Relation du voyage de M. Evert Isbrand, envoyé de sa majesté czarienne à l'empereur de la Chine en 1692, 1693, et 1694* (Amsterdam 1699). Brand's narrative was apparently not translated into Russian during the eighteenth century.

the contrast between Ides' complacent attitude and the puzzled, angered or outright belligerent attitudes of his predecessors is very apparent. The scene inside the 'Forbidden City' within the emperor's palace is also noteworthy because of its colourful details concerning the 'Bean Decoction or Coffee' (Ides, p.77) served for refreshment, and the bells, drums, lutes and pipes which were heard during the ceremonies. Whether or not Ides performed the kowtow during this particular audience is not clear from his account. He states cryptically that he paid 'a respectful compliment' to the emperor.[40] There is, in fact, no mention anywhere in Ides' account of Russian performance of the ceremony. In any case the Chinese ceremonial requirements did not seem to offend the ambassador or his party.

In regard to the realm of art and architecture Ides departs from his practice of not recording his own personal opinions. Here the ambassador praises the Chinese consistently, singling out for mention many things which appealed to him because of their beauty or novelty. His descriptions of the pretty villages he passed through, an attractive monastery, a marvelous arched bridge beautifully decorated with lions, the luxurious suburban houses in Peking, the imperial palace itself, are in fact very similar to the enthusiastic accounts of the journeys of fathers Bouvet and de Fontenay and the other Jesuit missionaries who travelled in China at approximately the same time that Ides did. The richly ornamented junks; porcelain, which Ides describes as the best in the world; exquisite flowers made of silk; the brocade uniforms of court dignitaries, embroidered with cranes, dragons, lions and tigers; the emperor's elephants (including one that was entirely white) with gilded harnesses mounted with silver, are only a few of the unusual sights which Ides notes. Unfamiliar food, including birds' nest soup, is also praised. Only a particular concert, where the music struck Ides' ear as 'a hideous confused noise' so that he would rather have been at a distance from it, seems to have appeared exotic in an unpleasing way to the ambassador (Ides, p.61).

Like his predecessor Baikov, Ides provides little real insight into the mores and institutions of his hosts. But like the previous ambassadors he includes a considerable amount of practical information in his account, such as commentary on the roads, descriptions of the security system, the drainage canals, a haberdashery that he visited, the emperor's pharmacy and even the medicines that were available there. Because Ides's opportunities to move about and observe Peking were greater than those of Baikov, the panorama which he presents to his readers is considerably broader than those given by the earlier envoy from the tsar. While Ides does not present Chinese institutions as models to be emulated by the West, most of the components of the picture he draws are very appealing. It is, incidentally, curious that this particular journal is one of the sources believed to have been used by Defoe for his quite negative portrayal of China in Part Two of *Robinson Crusoe*, which will be seen later.[41]

[40] Ides, p.77. Brand's narrative (note 39, above) indicates clearly, however, that at least on one occasion the entire Russian party did perform the full kowtow with nine bows: Brand, *A journal of the embassy*, p.92.

[41] Percy G. Adams, *Travelers and travel liars, 1660-1806* (Berkeley, Los Angeles 1962), p.236.

In the decades immediately following the return of the Ides embassy to Russia several important events of Sino-Russian relations took place, several of which were to be chronicled in literary accounts by those who participated in these events. The state-run trade operation began in 1689, an undertaking which was to send to Peking by mid-century twelve official caravans, staffed by around 3,000 persons;[42] the Chinese envoy Tulishen visited Russia, as we have seen, in 1714; and Peter the Great sent an emissary, Lorents Lange, to Peking in 1715. And it was in 1715 that the Russian Orthodox religious mission was officially established in Peking with the arrival there of the first Russian archimandrite. When by 1719 certain problems had arisen in the commercial affairs of the two countries, Peter the Great turned again to direct negotiations. An embassy headed by Lev Vasilevich Izmailov arrived in the Chinese capital in November of 1720. The ambassador's own report of his mission was kept secret, but fortunately for Russian readers, as well as for Western Europeans, the journey and the visit to Peking were carefully documented by the Scottish doctor, John Bell, mentioned earlier, who accompanied the Russian mission in the capacity of official physician. While he was not present at all of the official meetings between Izmailov and the emperor K'ang-hsi, and was not in a position to report on the negotiations themselves, Bell did present a very detailed, well-rounded and highly readable account of his own experiences in Peking.

Another account pertaining to the same embassy appeared in Western Europe long before that by Bell. It was written by the First Secretary of the embassy, Lorents Lange, a Swede by birth, who had been in the service of the Russian tsar at least since 1715 when he had first travelled to Peking as Peter the Great's emissary.[43] Altogether Lange made six journeys between the Russian and Chinese capitals. The Russian archives contain a great many of his official reports, and several narratives pertaining to his missions were published in Russia during the eighteenth century. His account of the Izmailov embassy, entitled *Journal de la résidence du sieur Lange [...] à la cour de la Chine*, first published in Leyden in 1726, complements rather than duplicates Bell's *Travels*, as it relates Lange's experiences from about the time Izmailov and Bell and the rest

[42] P. E. Skachkov, *Outline of the history of Russian sinology*, p.28 (note 27 above).

[43] Lange's name appears in a wide variety of spellings. In modern Russian it is Lorents Lang; in English, however, the last name has usually been spelled Lange. A journal by Lange concerning the caravan of 1715-1716 was published in part in F. C. Weber, *Das Veränderte Rußland* (Franckfurth 1721), pp.72-116, and in several other early Western European collections of travel accounts, including Prévost's *Histoire générale des voyages*, xx.288-314. See G. Cahen, *Histoire des relations de la Russie avec la Chine sous Pierre le Grand (1689-1730)*, p.clix. This journal was not published in Russia in the eighteenth century. The first part is now available in *Русско-китайские отношения в XVIII веке: материалы и документы* (Russo-Chinese relations in the 18th century: materials and documents), comp. N. F. Demidova and V. S. Miasnikov, i (Moscow 1978), pp.487-97; the second part is in T. K. Shafranovskaia, 'Путешествие Лоренца Ланга в 1715-1716 гг. в Пекин и его дневник' (The Journey of Lorents Lange in 1715-1716 to Peking and his journal), *Страны и народы востока* (Lands and peoples of the East), issue 2 (Moscow 1961), pp.188-205.

of the party began their return trip to Russia, leaving Lange in Peking as the resident Russian commercial agent.[44]

An English translation of Lange's work was included with Bell's narrative, published in Glasgow in 1763, forty-four years after the mission took place. A French edition of Bell's and Lange's narratives appeared in Paris in 1766, and it was from this edition that a Russian translation was done ten years later. The two narratives appeared together in St Petersburg in 1776 in a three-volume work entitled *Белевы путешествия чрез Россию в разныя асиятския земли; а именно: в Испаган, в Пекин, в Дербент и Константинополь* (Bell's travels through Russia into various Asiatic countries; namely: Isphagan, Peking, Derbent and Constantinople).[45]

Bell's narrative is characterised by the same sympathetic approach that was seen in the journal of his immediate predecessor, Ysbrants Ides. While the aims of the mission to which Bell was attached were not fully achieved, the embassy was, on the whole, a success, and a sense of accomplishment seems to be reflected in Bell's account. Like his predecessors Bell relates practical information and, for the most part, avoids generalisations regarding sociology or philosophy. Instead, a broad discussion of many facets of Chinese culture is presented. In addition, while many instances of the unusual and exotic are to be found in the account, they do not stand out as sharply as they did in the earlier journals because Bell has interwoven them with the many minute details of Chinese life which he records.

The Scottish doctor's report of Izmailov's first audience with the emperor illustrates his attempt to be objective in his evaluations. Bell's description of the event reflects a certain personal distaste, but at the same time conveys the impression that the ceremony was in general a success. Telling how the ambassador was invited to lay his credentials before the emperor, Bell notes how great an honour this was. Even when relating how the entire Russian party was later ordered to perform the full kowtow, the most disagreeable part of the ceremony, he describes the scene and his own feelings of displeasure with great restraint. He writes: 'Great pains were taken to avoid this piece of homage, but without success. The master of the ceremonies stood by, and delivered his orders in the Tartar language, by pronouncing the words *morgu* and *boss*; the first meaning to bow, and the other to stand; two words which I cannot soon forget.'[46]

Although Bell records some unfavourable criticisms of certain aspects of Chinese life, such as the tendency of many toward cheating, and the custom practiced by the very poor of abandoning newborn infants if they could not care for them, the Scottish observer's praise of the 'order and economy' of the Chinese people (p.120), their patience, hospitality, good manners, and the honesty of the majority of the populace are more typical of his evaluations. Bell also praises the artistic skill of the Chinese, particularly in the making of fine fabrics, paper

---

[44] Lange's journal for 1721-1722 also appeared in J. F. Bernard, *Recueil de voiages au nord* (Amsterdam 1727), viii.221-371.

[45] Note 22, above.

[46] Quotations are from the text of Bell (1965 ed.), p.134. Subsequent citations to Bell will be included in the text and will refer to this English edition or to the Russian translation, as indicated.

and lacquerware. (Here Russian readers of Bell's account are warned in a footnote, apparently supplied by the Russian translator, to take Bell's remarks with a grain of salt. Unlike most of the annotations, which consist of factual material, this note contains the comment that while many writers have 'praised to the skies the superiority' of the government, arts and sciences of China, all those who know the Chinese assert that they are inferior in all ways to the Europeans (*Bell's travels* [Russian translation], ii.177).)

Bell's generally friendly attitude toward the Chinese people is exemplified by his warm feeling toward the emperor K'ang-hsi. In addition to his eulogistic descriptions of the ruler, to whom he once refers as 'the good old Emperor' (1965 English ed., p.168), Bell provides a number of small appealing glimpses of K'ang-hsi. On one occasion, for instance, the emperor, concerned that the Europeans were not properly dressed for the cold Peking winter, sent word to Izmailov that he intended to give him a Chinese dress which would be warmer than the European style of clothing (p.138). Another time the emperor gave the ambassador what Bell terms a 'piece of friendly and wholesome advice' when he suggested that Izmailov advise Peter the Great not to 'hazard his life, by committing himself to the rage of the merciless waves and winds, where no valour could avail' (p.134). Russian readers of Bell's account would, one suspects, like Bell, have felt well disposed toward the kindly emperor.

Besides detailing the activities of the Izmailov mission, Bell provides information and commentary on certain other areas of Sino-Russian cultural and political contacts. The short history that he gives of the Russian Orthodox Church in Peking, for example, was one of the first published accounts of the religious mission to appear in Russia. Bell's assertion, in his comparison of the Jesuit and Orthodox missions, that the Russian priest 'minds chiefly his own small flock, and thinks very little of making converts' (p.140), provides a succinct evaluation of the mission's place in Chinese life.

A comment by Bell on the vulnerability of China to foreign attack could also have hardly escaped Russian notice. Bell writes: 'I know but one nation who could attempt the conquest of China, with any probability of success, and that is Russia; but the territories of that empire are so extensive, in this quarter of the world, as to exceed even the bounds of ambition itself; and the Russians seem to entertain no desire of extending them farther' (p.181). The topic of Chinese military strength, a recurrent one in the descriptions of China available to Russian readers reappears here. Bell credits the Chinese with greater strength than did admiral Anson, who had written in 1748 that the empire was 'exposed to the ravages of every petty invader' (Anson, p.545), but the Scotsman concludes that Russian power would probably be sufficient to conquer China.

The aspect of Bell's account that provides the greatest degree of continuity with the reports of the other diplomats is a recurring motif, the notion of strangeness. The theme is introduced by Bell when he describes the moment that the ambassadorial party, after a long and tedious month on the Gobi Desert, finally sighted the Great Wall of China in the distance (pp.116-17). Bell writes: 'One of our people cried out Land, as if we had been all this while at sea.' The simile, with its depiction of desert as sea, seems appropriate to describe the feeling of strangeness to which Bell alludes throughout his journal. The motif reappears when the doctor tells how, on the day following the sighting of the Great Wall, the Russian party paused to visit a small Chinese monastery. He relates: 'Every thing now appeared to us as if we had arrived in another world.'

In his usual objective way Bell reacted to the strange and unexpected with great equanimity. A quite different reaction is found in the second narrative pertaining to this mission, that written by Lorents Lange, and included in the 1763 publication of Bell's journal.[47] Lange's account, like Bell's, makes it clear that the traveller feels he has entered 'another world', but for him this world is far from enticing. For this reason the narratives by Lange and the Scottish doctor are curious companion pieces.[48]

One of the achievements of the Izmailov mission had been the concluding of an agreement with the Chinese Court that a Russian representative could remain in Peking, primarily to supervise Russo-Chinese commercial affairs. This agent was to be Lange. The arrangement, however, met with considerable opposition from certain circles at the Chinese Court, and consequently Lange's seventeen-month stay in Peking in 1721-22 was marked by obstacles raised at every turn by the officials who objected to his presence there. Lange's difficulties in obtaining a passport to accompany count Izmailov and the departing ambassa-dorial party as far as the Great Wall; his problems in getting his credentials accepted by the Court; friction because of an order which essentially prevented Chinese merchants from entering the Russian compound to purchase Russian goods; troubles in gaining permission from the governor of Peking for a visit to the royal summer quarters at Jehol, even though a personal invitation had been given by the emperor; a struggle with the Court to prevent an approaching Russian trade caravan from being forced to camp in the desert until the officials returned to Peking (a stratagem of the First Minister, Lange felt, to prevent the presents intended for him from being distributed in Peking before he returned from Jehol to the city) – these events constitute only some of the daily trials recorded by the tsar's Agent during his stay in Peking.

Even such rudimentary matters as food and housing presented problems for the Russian Agent. While these difficulties were undoubtedly insignificant to

[47] Lorents Lange, *Journal of the residence of Mr. de Lange, agent of His Imperial Majesty of All the Russias, Peter the First, at the Court of Pekin, during the years 1721 and 1722*, in Bell, *Travels from St Petersburgh in Russia to various parts of Asia* (Edinburgh 1788), ii.223-423; Lorents Lange, 'Ежедневная записка пребывания г. Ланга, агента [...] при дворе Пекинском, в 1721 и 1722 годе' (Daily notes on the stay of Mr Lange, Agent, at the Court of Peking in 1721-1722) in Bell (John Bell), *Белевы путешествия*, iii.i-viii, 1-150 (note 22, above). Subsequent citations to Lange will be to the English translation of 1788 and will be included in the text.

[48] The Jesuit compiler Du Halde, who, as we have seen, was quite sympathetic to the Chinese, suggested that Lange presented a distorted view of the Middle Kingdom. Commenting on the journal for 1721-22, Du Halde wrote, 'People will bring the charge against this Journal that it is replete with much passion against the Chinese, who were not satisfied with the behaviour of the author, hence it is that he describes them as the most vicious of people' (Du Halde, *Description [...] de la Chine* (Paris 1735), quoted by John Dudgeon, *Historical sketch of the ecclesiastical, political and commercial relations of Russia with China* (Peking 1872; 1940), Appendix, p.3. (The section of Du Halde concerning Lange's journal did not appear in the Russian Du Halde abridgement.)

the total course of Sino-Russian relations, Lange's account of them is engaging and memorable, and one suspects that Russian readers of Lange's journal in 1776 would have gained from it the impression that the Chinese were indeed difficult to deal with. On the day after his return from seeing Izmailov off for Russia, for instance, Lange states irately that a man with the 'appearance of a poor beggar' entered the Russian courtyard with 'some poor starved fowls, and salted cabbage' and some pots of a Chinese beverage (ii.236-42). Learning that this man had the contract with the Chinese government to provide his supplies, the Agent returned everything, stating firmly that he would accept whatever the emperor should provide, if it were sent 'in a proper manner'. Lange suspected that the emperor himself was not aware of the situation, but that the 'gentlemen Mandarins' had hoped to supply their own tables with his provisions. At last, upon receiving a list of what was to be regularly supplied him, Lange agreed that he would accept what was brought on one condition. He relates: 'I assured them, "I should make no objection, provided they did it in a decent manner, and not by unknown people that marched off as soon as they had thrown it down in my courtyard, as they had once done."'

Lange's housing problem was less easily solved. Notations on the matter of having repairs made on the building which had been assigned for his use are to be found throughout the Agent's journal. On 22 March Lange noted that the Russians' quarters were badly in need of repairs, and that he had informed the government that he would be willing to pay rent for another house while the work was being done. This suggestion was turned down (ii.253-57). Six weeks later there was a severe rain and wind storm. With admirable restraint the Agent noted in his journal: 'The old house where I was lodged could no longer stand the bad weather; all the wall of one side of my chamber fell, about midnight, into the court-yard, which made me very apprehensive for what remained.' Immediate repairs were, however, impossible, Lange was told, since everyone was completely occupied with the imminent departure of the emperor for his summer quarters at Jehol. Lange offered to pay for the work himself, but was told by the mandarins that they might be in serious trouble with the emperor if he were to learn that they had permitted such an arrangement. On 20 May Lange noted cryptically that the house 'remained still in the same condition' (ii.280-85).

At this point the brigadier of the Chinese guard at Lange's residence stepped in to issue a formal complaint and to demand that repairs be made at once. While the journal entry for 25 May states simply that the repairman did appear to put the apartment 'into an habitable state', the entries during the following autumn (ii.326-29) find Lange still trying desperately to have repairs finished before the Russian trade caravan arrived. His concern all along had been that the new merchandise would be damaged by exposure to the weather. The Agent was again promised that the work would be done, and was forbidden to arrange for it himself, but no action was taken. On 29 September the Russian caravan arrived. Lange states that it rained all day and that the baggage had to remain in the courtyard. He notes that there was no place for the Commissar or any of his people to be 'covered from the rain'. At last on 12 October repairs were made. Lange's final ironic commentary on the matter was as follows: 'It was done so negligently, that, when they made an end, there was little alteration for the better.'

Lange's journal does not present a rounded picture of Chinese life. There is little if any exoticism. It does, however, contain a great deal of practical information about Chinese commerce, the realm with which the Russian Agent was primarily concerned. One section of the account is in fact devoted to 'the present state of trade in the city of Peking'. In a statement reminiscent of Fedor Baikov, however, Lange notes that the material presented here could have been more complete 'if they had let me enjoy the means of informing myself thoroughly of things' (ii.287-88).

The Russian Agent makes no attempt to analyse or evaluate Chinese institutions, although he does comment specifically on one aspect of the governmental system. This is the procedure for the redress of grievances, a subject with which Lange was obviously quite preoccupied. Explaining that complaints cannot be made directly to the emperor, but must go through the ministers, Lange asserts with the voice of experience that it is impossible to receive satisfaction (ii.333-34).

While Lange does not generalise on Chinese national character, his descriptions of a number of individuals with whom he came in contact provide some insight into his impressions of his hosts. Lange has very high praise for the brigadier of the guard assigned to his quarters and for the Poyamba or Great Marshal of the Court, who helped him considerably. But he describes numerous incidents in which Chinese officials attempted to receive personal illegal gain through his presence, and he comments directly on the avarice of the subordinate members of the guard at his courtyard who attempted to extract bribes from those who came to do business with him (ii.276).

Just before his premature departure from Peking (he was unexpectedly dismissed, purportedly because of unresolved problems concerning deserters to Russian territory), Lange had a noteworthy conversation with the Allegamba, one of the chief officials of the Chinese Court (ii.421-22). The Agent was asked if he would have to report in writing to the Russian government on all that had transpired during his stay in Peking. On hearing that he would, the Allegamba advised Lange that in writing his report, he 'would do well not to insert a number of trifling things, which could answer no good end, but might embroil matters more'. The Allegamba went on to speak of the importance of good understanding between the empires. Lange reassured him as follows: 'I replied thereupon, that, not having been sent to the court of Pekin as an instrument for creating misunderstandings, I would make it my business, in my relation, not to touch upon any things but such as was necessary for our court to be informed of.' While Lange may have fulfilled this promise in his official secret reports for the Russian government, one has reason to suspect that his *Journal*, reaching the Russian public in 1776, did little to promote 'good understanding' between Russia and her neighbour to the east.

The *Journal* for 1721-1722 was the first of three accounts pertaining to Lange's official missions to China which were published in Russia during the eighteenth century. Lange's second journal appeared in Russia only in German and therefore can be assumed to have had less influence than the Russian accounts.[49] A third report, written evidently by someone other than Lange, but pertaining to Lange's mission of 1736, was published both in German and in Russian.[50] This last narrative, in its Russian form, was no doubt more widely read.

The journal for 1736 emphasises practical information, but a number of exotic touches are also to be found. Reminiscent of the account of Baikov, for instance, are the colourful sidelights given about the numerous shrines and idols (one, for example, with a thousand hands and an eye on each hand) to be seen along the route from the Russian border to Peking. The report also gives some description of the city of Peking, providing a list of the points of interest. Among these are the headquarters and churches of both the European and the Russian missionaries. Lange, who was particularly concerned with the affairs of the Russian Orthodox Mission on this journey, had brought a religious image from Siberia for the newly completed Russian Church. The consecration ceremony for the church is described, and an account is given of the Russians' discussions with the Chinese about where the Orthodox priests were to reside. (The journal does not, however, indicate that Lange had been ordered to escort back to Russia the archimandrite Anton Platkovskii, who had been recalled for improper conduct. According to Adoratskii's history of the mission, Lange took the archimandrite to St Petersburg in chains).[51]

As in the other narratives pertaining to Lange's journeys to China, the many difficulties encountered by the Russians in Peking are enumerated, but not commented upon at length. While this account seems somewhat less irritable in tone than either of the journals written by Lange himself, it, like Lange's own narratives, provided Russian readers with vivid examples of the unexpected and

[49] 'Tagebuch einer in den Jahren 1727 und 1728 über Kjachta nach Peking unter Anführung des Agenten Lorenz Lange gethanen Karawanenreise' in Peter Simon Pallas, *Neue nordische Beyträge zur physikalischen und geographischen Erd- und Völkerbeschreibung, Naturgeschichte und Oekonomie* (Leipzig, St Petersburg 1781-1796), ii (1781), ch. 7, at pp.83-159. An introductory comment in Pallas (p. 84) indicates that the German version is an abbreviated form of the Russian original. An English translation of part of Pallas's version of the journal is found in John Dudgeon, *Historical sketch* (note 48, above), Appendix, 'Journal of Lange's residence at Peking in 1727-28 (third journey)'.

[50] 'Дневные записки караванного пути через Наунскую дорогу от Цурухайту до Пекина в 1736 году' (Journal of the caravan route by way of the Naun Road from Tsurukhaitu to Peking in 1736), *Academic news* (April 1781), pp.466-505; (May 1781), pp.602-31. The German version also appeared in P. S. Pallas, *Neue nordische Beyträge* (note 49 above), ii, ch. 8, pp.160-207. Pallas states in a note that this journal was written by another member of Lange's party, not Lange himself. P. E. Skachkov in his *Bibliography of China*, lists the work as anonymous. T. K. Shafranovskaia (see note 43 above) indicates, however, that this is Lange's own diary, as does Clifford Foust in his bibliography. The journal is written in the third person, and in both style and tone seems to me significantly different from Lange's other works.

[51] Nikolai [Adoratskii], 'Православная миссия в Китае' (The Orthodox mission in China), *Православный собеседник* (The Orthodox companion), pt. 2 (May 1887), p.135, quoted in V. P. Petrov, *Российская Духовная миссия в Китае* (The Russian religious mission in China) (Washington, D.C., 1968), p.38, and I. Korostovets, 'Русская духовная миссия в Пекине' (The Russian religious mission in Peking), *Русский архив* (Russian archives) 3, issue 9 (1893), pp.57-86 at p.61.

the inscrutable aspects of the life of a foreign envoy in Peking at the beginning of the eighteenth century.

The commercial venture of 1726-1728, described by Lange in his second narrative, was connected with a Russian diplomatic mission to China under the leadership of Sava Lukich Vladislavich-Raguzinskii. The great achievement of the Vladislavich mission was the signing of the Treaty of Kiakhta (1727), which dealt with border delimitations and the problem of trespassers, set up new trade arrangements, and permitted the building of a Russian Orthodox Church in Peking. Some colourful notes on the practical difficulties encountered by the mission, including long delays caused by the exchange of grievances, were penned by the clerk of this mission, Stepan Pisarev. A short account of the embassy and Pisarev's personal appraisal of the Chinese are appended to Pisarev's 1772 translation of an Italian biography of Peter the Great. The Russian notes that the Chinese people are inclined toward the arts and sciences (studying moral philosophy, among other subjects, with great interest), but he finds the Chinese individual to be deceitful, sly and not faithful to his word.[52]

In the years following the 1726-1728 mission of Vladislavich, Russian trade caravans and couriers continued to make their way to Peking, but no further Russian embassies were to meet with the Chinese until the two Kropotov embassies of 1762 and 1768. The reports of both of these missions remained secret. A narrative relating to this approximate period, however, was written by a government courier, Vasilii Bratishchev, who arrived in Peking in 1757. Bratishchev's work, which appeared in 1783 in a publication of Moscow University, and which relates more to sinology than diplomacy, will be discussed in connection with the intellectuals and China.[53]

The last of the official Russian embassies that set out for Peking in the period between the early seventeenth century and the very early years of the nineteenth century was that headed by count Iurii Aleksandrovich Golovkin in 1805. Golovkin's mission, the purpose of which was primarily to negotiate further commercial agreements, was, in fact, an absolute failure. The Chinese kept the ambassador waiting at the border, parleying over the size of the party, for some weeks. Then, after the embassy had finally proceeded to the town of Urga (now Ulan Bator), a three-week journey into Mongolia, problems of protocol arose which were so complex that the entire Russian party turned around and returned to Siberia.

One of the members of the mission was a well-known German scholar, Julius Klaproth, who lived and worked in Russia. On his return to St Petersburg Klaproth published there a lengthy article entitled 'Bemerkungen über die

---

[52] Ivan Pisarev (note 36, above) in Antonio Katiforo, *Житие Петра Великаго*, trans. Ivan Pisarev, p.501.

[53] 'Осведомление или некоторое поверение Волтеровых о Китае примечаний собранное в краткую Братищева бытность в Пекине' (Information about or verification of Voltaire's remarks on China, made during Bratishchev's short stay in Peking), *Опыт трудов Вольнаго Российскаго собрания при Императорском Московском университете* (Essays of the Free Russian Assembly of Moscow University), pt. 6 (1783), pp.39-62.

chinesisch-russische Gränze'.[54] The Russian sinophiles who happened to read German would have found this article noteworthy. In addition to the historical material concerning Sino-Russian relations, which constitutes the main body of the work, Klaproth provides a short impressionistic sketch of the Chinese border town of Mai-mai-cheng, which he found quite attractive because of its unexpected architectural features. The German scholar also makes a few remarks about the inhabitants of the town, praising their 'order, exactness, good taste and shrewdness'. Giving them credit for having learned enough Russian to do business in this language, he comments, however, that in their commercial dealings, the Chinese are exceedingly crafty.[55]

Klaproth's brief observations on Chinese life and on the Golovkin embassy are complemented by the more detailed commentary of another member of the ill-fated mission, Filip Filipovich Vigel, who was to become a Russian governmental figure in the mid-nineteenth century, and who took part in the Golovkin embassy as a young man. Vigel's Записки (Memoirs) were not published until 1864-1865, but one surmises from his work that the members of the mission, returning to Russia in 1806, related their experiences and their views to the society gatherings of St Petersburg, and one can assume that the popular image of China was indeed affected by impressions such as those which Vigel later recorded in his *Memoirs*.[56]

Especially colourful is Vigel's account of how the Russian Ambassador was called in by the Chinese officials for a rehearsal of the ceremony to be performed should he have an audience with the emperor. Vigel, interjecting 'Believe it or not', tells how Golovkin, on all fours, with his credentials resting upon a pillow on his back, was to enter a room in which had been placed a likeness of the emperor (Vigel, pt. 2, p.210). (The memoirist, and the ambassador too, were evidently not familiar with the accounts of the previous Russian diplomats in China, particularly with Baikov's description of a similar attempt by the Chinese officials to give him a lesson on the kowtow etiquette.)

[54] Julius Klaproth, 'Bemerkungen über die chinesisch-russische Gränze gesammelt auf einer Reise an derselben, im Jahre 1806', *Archiv für asiatische Litteratur, Geschichte und Sprachkunde* (1810), pp.159-224. The article appeared in Russian translation in 1823 and was also published in Paris in 1824-1828. Iu. Klaproth, 'Заметки о китайско-русской границе, собранные Юлием Клапротом во время путешествия по оной в 1806 году' (Notes on the Chinese-Russian border, compiled by Julius Klaproth during a trip along it in 1806), *Северный архив* (Northern archives), no. 9 (1823), pp.184-204; no. 10 (1823), pp.253-77; no. 11 (1823), pp.328-46; no. 12 (1823), pp.413-34.

[55] Klaproth, *Northern archives*, no. 12 (1823), p.421.

[56] F. F. Vigel, *Записки (Издание ‹Русского архива›, дополненное с подлинной рукописи)* (Memoirs, 'Russian Archives' edition, supplemented from the original manuscript), 5 parts (Moscow 1891-1892). A further reason for including here a discussion of a work not published until late in the nineteenth century, is the fact that Vigel was an acquaintance of A. S. Pushkin, the great nineteenth-century Russian poet. It can almost certainly be assumed that in the discussions which Vigel and Pushkin are known to have had in Odessa in 1823, China and Vigel's experiences there were a topic of conversation. Pushkin's interest in China, and the use he was to make of Chinese motifs in his work must have been influenced by the stories Vigel related. See M. P. Alekseev, 'Pushkin and China', pp.114-21, for a valuable analysis of this subject and background concerning the theme of China in eighteenth-century Russian literature.

Golovkin informed his hosts that he could not participate in such a ceremony until he had received further instructions from the Russian Court. The following day the Chinese returned all of the chests and boxes of presents from the Russian government by throwing, not placing, them in front of the ambassador's quarters. Here again, the experiences of Baikov were repeated. Golovkin and his party, with limited provisions given them by the Chinese, immediately returned to Siberia to await further orders. Vigel (who was not with the group at this point) comments on his colleagues' plight: 'There were no unpleasantnesses that they did not experience from these barbarians' (pt. 2, p.211).

In his few impressionistic sketches of the Chinese and their customs Vigel reveals surprise, a keen awareness of the unfamiliar, and mixed feelings of approval and dislike of what he encountered in the distant land. The peripheral elements of Vigel's account – the sophisticated society circles in which he moved, the literary allusions, and the witty, urbane style bear witness to the fact the one hundred fifty years have passed since Vigel's seventeenth-century predecessor Baikov did his best to uphold in China the honour of the Russian tsar. But the reactions of both Russian travellers to the attractively exotic and the unfamiliar, disturbing aspects of life in that Eastern kingdom are surprisingly alike.

There is, in fact, a noticeable sense of continuity in the narratives pertaining to the Russian diplomatic missions from Baikov's to Vigel's. First there is in nearly all of them that feeling of strangeness which resulted partly from the peculiar and unexpected requirements of protocol, and partly from the exotic elements of the unknown land, which struck the travellers sometimes as beautiful, sometimes as awe-inspiring, and often as disagreeable.

The sense of continuity is also a result of the preoccupation in each account with practical political and commercial considerations. In discussions of the specific political objectives of each mission, of the actual dealings and negotiations with the Chinese Court, and also in the personal reflections of some of the writers on the relative military strengths of Russia and China, the theme of practical politics is constantly evident. The writers were, for the most part, interested in Chinese behaviour only in so far as it affected the way Europeans could or could not conduct their affairs in China; the way the Chinese organised their society and way of life was of less concern to the emissaries of the Russian tsar. The diplomatic chroniclers also paid little attention to previous accounts of China. Many of them, because they wrote at a time when the Jesuit works were unavailable in Russian translation, or because they were personally not well read were simply not familiar with the Jesuits' views. Moreover, the purpose of these writers was usually to provide a chronicle of a particular mission, rather than a comprehensive study of China which would include comparisons between their own observations and those of others.

The most important similarity in these accounts of Russian diplomatic missions is the overall impression they convey of the distant post to which their authors had been sent. While the tsars' representatives did not agree with each other on all matters, most of them saw China as a nation with more shortcomings than positive attributes. The most enthusiastic reporters among them were Ysbrants Ides and John Bell, who in fact appreciated many aspects of Chinese culture. Even they, however, ignored the theory that China was a model to be emulated by European nations. Applying here the test considered earlier of comparing a visitor's views of China with the success of his respective endeavour, one finds that Ides and Bell reported on embassies which were at least treated respectfully, even if the missions were not entirely successful; the other writers, who bestowed very little praise indeed on the Middle Kingdom, were chroniclers of less satisfactory embassies.

The envoys from Russia then were like the British diplomatic chronicler George Staunton, whose narrative of the Macartney expedition, coming late in the 1790s, was the century's only Western European diplomatic account of China. The tsars' representatives can likewise be compared to the Russian and British navigators, who expressed such displeasure with their Chinese hosts, as well as to the Russian missionaries who had so languished in Peking. Quite different are the views of this group of eighteenth-century travellers from those of the enthusiastic Jesuit proselytisers, and from the attitudes of the French writers Du Halde, La Harpe and La Porte, who made the Western European missionary accounts available, in differing formats, to all of Europe.

Curiously enough, while many of the accounts pertaining to the Russian diplomatic missions were also published in Western Europe, the dissident voices of these disgruntled travellers were lost in the continuing rounds of Western European praise for the Empire in the East. At least until the publication of Anson's hostile report in mid-century and even afterward, China was for the Western European reader an abstract and glorious concept. As Voltaire so insightfully pointed out, it was easy to admire a distant land with which one was not in competition. But what was the reaction of the reader in Russia, who, like his Western European counterpart, came upon reports of both 'Chinas', but for whom the diplomatic accounts of his own countrymen must have seemed particularly significant? We can only surmise that the perceptive Russian armchair traveller must indeed have been perplexed.

4. The land of the sage: China in the belletristic literature of eighteenth-century Russia

'This young man [...] sincerely loved virtue, and put it
into practice; but he was not considered a marvel because
of this, virtue being so common in Che-Kiang.'

Вторый Кандид, уроженец китайской
(Candide the Second, a Native of China)[1]

Two kinds of popular literature about China were to be found on the library shelves of the eighteenth-century Russian. One was the literature of travel, the work of missionaries, merchants, diplomats and others who had actually visited the Middle Kingdom, who depicted in minute detail the dust on the roads, the colour of the houses, the taste of the soup. From the pages of their journals emerged a real and almost tangible entity, Russia's immediate neighbour to the East. While the travellers, both Russians and Western Europeans, who had made these difficult journeys frequently disagreed with each other in their evaluations of what they had seen, they nevertheless tried to present a realistic picture supported by a wealth of descriptive detail.

The second literature of China, which coexisted with that of the travellers, was a body of fictional works produced in part by Chinese writers but mainly by Russian and Western Europeans who in most cases had seen China only in the works of others and in their own lively imaginations. Throughout the last half of the eighteenth-century, and especially between 1760 and 1800, Russian translators laboured diligently over works in French, English, Italian, German and Chinese, which portrayed this distant exotic land. At the same time Russian poets and prose writers joined in the vast endeavour to bring China to the Russian reader, contributing a smaller but significant number of works of their own.

The fictionalised China existed in many modes – from serious drama to comic opera, doggerel verse to sophisticated odes. The intentions of the creators of this mythical landscape ranged from pure entertainment to such Enlightenment purposes as general edification or pointed commentary, either by means of satire or through the portrayal of morally uplifting characters, on the Western world and on man himself. Sincere praise of the Chinese, as well as criticism or eulogies of other governments, were among the objectives of these writers.

But while the authors of these fictionalised works differed greatly from each other in their purposes and techniques, they were, with only a few exceptions, in general agreement about the main features of this intriguing land which most of them had never seen. A few writers and translators of fiction and poetry presented China in a supposedly realistic and sometimes unflattering way. The majority of them, however, did not attempt to delineate backgrounds and landscapes or to provide historical précis. Their China was a vaguely defined

---

[1] *Вторый Кандид, уроженец китайской, или друг истинны, южная повесть*, trans. Petr Vel'iaminov (St Petersburg 1774), p.6.

locale, hazy in atmosphere. Only the characters who moved in this world were sharply in focus. And they were not at all the same figures who peopled the China of the travellers – the intrepid voyagers from the West with their frustrations and successes, and the haughty and capricious emperors and their inscrutable government bureaucrats. Instead, in this imaginary world the stage was occupied by characters modelled upon a set of literary prototypes. This was the China of the Sage – the wise Confucius, the good emperor, the morally just individual, and the scholar. And as the protagonists of this literary world were standardised, so to a large extent were the themes which predominated in their world. The search for a wise man, the moral education of a prince, the journey for the purpose of enlightenment, the insistence upon the cultivation of such virtues as honesty, loyalty and fairness – these were the motifs touched upon again and again. While the theme of the Chinese Sage began to decline in popularity in French and other Western European literatures after the middle of the century, beginning shortly after Rousseau's attacks on China in *La Nouvelle Héloïse*, it was at about this point that the motif began to assert itself in the literature of Russia.[2]

To Russian readers who were concerned with the literary portrayal of China, it was probably not a matter of great importance whether a particular piece of fiction was an original work by a Russian writer or a translation from a foreign language. The cosmopolitanism of the eighteenth century fostered the acquaintanceship by readers with the literature of all countries, and at the same time encouraged writers to emulate current international literary trends. Consequently, the original Russian and the translated literature on China became closely intertwined. The influence of the 'French China' was especially important in the realm of artistic literature. The majority of the longer belletristic works concerning China that appeared in Russian were translations, and the greater part of these were done from the French. And it was, of course, the French and other Western European works of this type which provided inspiration for the Russian writers. Finally, French translations from the Chinese also served as intermediaries for three of the five original Chinese literary pieces that I have located in Russian literature.

In a survey of this literature then it seems appropriate not to separate the Russian from the translated literature, but to consider all of the works together, since the Russian reader of the period would most likely have done this. And in order to recreate the composite image of China and the Chinese which the Russian reader would have formed on the basis of this literature, it seems most useful to organise the survey primarily in accordance with the types of characters who were portrayed.

For the depiction of the imaginative China, the realm of wisdom and moral perfection, it was natural that the figure of Confucius should be a powerful source of poetic inspiration. The great philosopher was seen as the personal embodiment of the virtuous and contemplative approach to life which character-ised this land. Alexander Pope showed the position of honour which the great

[2] Basil Guy, 'Rousseau and China', *Revue de littérature comparée* 30 (1956), pp.531-36 at 536.

thinker held in the minds of Western Europeans in his poem *The Temple of Fame* (1715) with the lines:

> Superior, and alone, *Confucius* stood,
> Who taught that useful Science, to be *good*.

Pope's poem, translated into Russian in verse by the well-known poet Mikhail Kheraskov, appeared in 1761 at the beginning of the period when the *rêve chinois* began to flourish in Russian literature. The poem appeared again, this time in a prose translation, in 1790.[3] Meanwhile, in 1777, Voltaire's tribute to Confucius had appeared in the first Russian translation of the *Henriade*. In Heaven, to which the hero of the epic was transported in a vision, Henry saw the representatives of many nations and religions, including the 'последователей Конфуция велика', the followers of the great Confucius.[4] Voltaire also expressed his admiration for Confucius in a footnote to his *Poème sur la loi naturelle*, translated into Russian as *Естественный закон поема* in 1787. Noting the deceptions spread by the many world religions, Voltaire excepted Confucius from criticism since the Chinese philosopher was an adherent of natural religion without revelation.[5]

The translation of the biography of Confucius by the French missionary J. M. Amiot, published in St Petersburg in 1790, provided inspiration for the ode 'Памятник герою' (Monument to a hero) (1791) by Gavriil Romanovich Derzhavin, the greatest of eighteenth-century Russian poets. In his poem, a tribute to the Russian general N. V. Repnin, whose army had defeated the Turks, Derzhavin utilised some meditations by Confucius relating to battles; and building on a theme which would later receive further development in Western European and American literature – that of seeing Confucius as an artist, he presented the image of the Chinese thinker as a philosopher-poet-musician.[6] The meditations by Confucius are drawn from a passage in Amiot's biography in which the philosopher, mourning the death of his mother, 'took the kin [a stringed instrument] into his hands; with its gentle and sad sounds he nourished the weariness of his soul, which was still filled with sadness.'[7] The song of the philosopher, as presented by Amiot, concerned the transitory nature

---

[3] Alexander Pope, *The Poems of Alexander Pope*, ed. John Butt (New Haven 1966), p.176; Pop (Alexander Pope), *Храм славы* (The Temple of Fame), trans. M. M. Kheraskov (Moscow 1761); *Храм славы из творений славнаго Попе* (The Temple of Fame from the work of the famous Pope), trans. Pavel L'vov (St Petersburg 1790).

[4] Vol'ter (F. M. A. Voltaire), *Генрияда, героическая поема в десяти песнях*, trans. Iakov Kniazhnin (St Petersburg 1777), p.103; the poem or an excerpt from it also appeared in *Академическия известия*, pt. 5 (1780), p.85; *Генриада, героическая поэма г. Волтера, переведенная с французскаго языка стихами*, trans. A. I. Golitsyn (Moscow 1790).

[5] M.ix.444; 'Естественный закон поема,' trans. I. I. Vinogradov in *Жизнь славнейшаго г. Вольтера* (The Life of the most famous Voltaire) (St Petersburg 1787), at pp.77-120.

[6] Amio (J. M. Amiot), and others, *Vie de Koung-tsée, appellée vulgairement Confucius*, abridged Russian trans. by M. I. Verevkin (St Petersburg 1790); Gavriil Derzhavin, *Сочинения Державина* (Works), ed. Ia. Grot (St Petersburg 1864), i.428-35. On Confucius and Romanticism see David Wei-Yang Dai, 'Confucius and Confucianism in the European Enlightenment', Diss. Univ. of Illinois 1979, pp.7 and 218-19.

[7] Zh. M. Amio, quoted in *Сочинения* (Works), i.432, note.

of life on earth. Confucius sang: 'Nevertheless, heat and cold, spring and autumn, return again each year; the sun lets itself be seen again each day. Waters that have whirled away are replaced by other waters [...] The general who erected this edifice, his horse, upon which he sat on the day of bloody battle, his resounding exploits. [...] what has happened to them? Who has taken their place? [...] Alas! The monuments of human glory are: ruins, brambles, thorns' (*Сочинения Державина*, i.433, note).

Using this vignette, Derhzavin begins his ode with a classical invocation to the muse, eventually asking the Muse of Confucius to build a literary monument to the Russian hero. The poet then pursues the theme of Confucius's song concerning the transitoriness of life (incidentally a favourite concept of Derzhavin's), and reproduces the thoughts expressed by Confucius almost word for word in his sonorous verse. Derzhavin notes that the seasons return, but that men's deeds are not seen again, and even monuments erected to the memory of great exploits will be destroyed by time. He then asks (i.432-33):

> кто ж был полководец?
> Куда его прошли победы?
> Где меч его? где шлем? где образ?
> 　Увы! и честь сия героев,
> Приступов монументы, боев,
> Не суть ли знаки их свирепства?
> Развалины, могилы, пепел,
> Черепья, кости им подобных,
> Не суть ли их венец и слава?

> 　　who was the general?
> Where have his victories gone?
> Where is his sword? his helmet? his face?
> 　Alas! and this honor of heroes,
> The monuments of assaults, of battles,
> Are these not symbols of their fierceness?
> Ruins, graves, ashes,
> Skulls, bones of ones like them,
> Are these not their crown and glory?

Derzhavin's song, however, concludes optimistically by affirming that the memory of men's deeds will be passed down by posterity as legend. It is therefore the Muse, inspiring the creation of song, who can build a truly lasting monument.

A brief reference to Confucius is to be found in the unfinished poem 'Песнь историческая' (Song of history) (written in 1802, published 1807) by Alexander Radishchev, the well-known Russian radical of the late eighteenth century. Radishchev, describing the fame and accomplishments of various ancient peoples, including the Chinese, addresses Confucius as a 'heavenly mortal', and speaks of the philosopher's 'radiant word' which has shone throughout the centuries.[8]

By the end of the eighteenth century the figure of Confucius had also appeared in Russia in numerous factual descriptions of China, and was the subject of a

---

[8] A. N. Radishchev, *Избранные сочинения* (Selected works) (Moscow, Leningrad 1949), p. 351.

long non-fiction work in French entitled *Yu le Grand et Confucius* (Soissons 1769) which will be discussed below in connection with ideological uses of Chinese themes by intellectual leaders. While not in fact published in Russia, the book must have been known there as it was written by Nicolas Le Clerc, the French tutor of the Russian crown prince Pavel.[9] Frequent mention of Confucius was made by another French writer, Jean Castillon, in his collection of anecdotes and stories concerning the life of Asian people, translated into Russian in 1791 as *Китайские, японские, сиамские, тонквинские и прочие анекдоты* (Anecdotes chinoises, japonoises, siamoises, tonquinoises, etc., Paris 1774).[10]

Like the figure of Confucius, the character of the just ruler, the 'Enlightened Monarch' occupies a prominent position in the China of fiction. In Russia the Good Chinese Emperor was to be found in two literary genres which enjoyed considerable popularity. These were the anecdote concerning Chinese history and life, and the oriental tale. The Chinese anecdote, as it developed in France, was an attempt to present quasi-factual material about China in a pleasant, easy to read manner. Basil Guy, in his detailed survey of eighteenth-century French literature about China, finds the anecdote representative of the movement which gained momentum throughout the eighteenth century to present an accurate picture of Chinese life.[11] Jean Castillon's *Anecdotes chinoises* mentioned in connection with Confucius provides an example of this kind of fictionalised history which came into Russian literature.[12] After devoting a long introduction to a discussion of Chinese history, Castillon presents a series of short anecdotes concerning China's rulers. Stories of this type, the reader is told, were traditionally recorded by the Chinese in their yearly records of events. The anecdotes, going back to the year 2941 B. C. tend to glorify the virtuous leadership of most of the monarchs. The morality of the people as a whole becomes the subject of the second section of the book, entitled 'Moral Anecdotes, taken from various Chinese books', a compendium of appealing and well-told stories concerning individuals in all walks of life, from royalty to the most humble subjects of the realm.

The figure of the good Chinese ruler was also developed in another popular genre, the oriental tale. One original Russian work belongs to this category, and at least five short oriental tales with Chinese, as opposed to Near Eastern, themes were translated into Russian and appeared in periodicals or as parts of collections between 1785 and the turn of the century. Several longer translations of tales appeared as separate books.[13] Citing the tale and apologue as another

---

[9] Nicolas Gabriel Clerc, *Yu le Grand et Confucius, histoire chinoise* (Soissons 1769).

[10] Kastiion (Jean Castillon), *Китайские, японские, сиамские, тонквинские и прочие анекдоты* (Moscow 1791).

[11] Basil Guy, *The French image of China before and after Voltaire*, p.371.

[12] See footnote 10. *Chinese anecdotes* which appeared in the periodical *Друг юношества* (The Friend of youth), 1 (1810), pp.75-87; 10 (1810), pp.100-109; 11 (1810), pp.54-73, are evidently another example of this genre.

[13] I have not seen all of these tales. Citations are to be found in *Union catalogue*, and in A. N. Neustroev, *Index to Russian periodicals and collections of 1703 to 1802*. At least one oriental tale was published with a title that implied Chinese thematics even though the work had a Middle Eastern colouring. This was 'Чудное похождение Израда, китайскаго гражданина' (The Marvelous adventure of Izrad, a citizen of China) (Moscow 1790).

step toward a realistic portrayal of the Near and Far East, Basil Guy points to certain early translations and adaptations of tales which actually originated in the Orient. The term 'oriental tale' in a broader sense, however, has been used to describe many types of stories concerning the East. Some of these are indeed authentic tales, other imitations of authentic stories with realistic backgrounds, and others completely fanciful. Works with oriental characters set in non-oriental countries are sometimes included in the genre.[14]

As with other forms of imaginative literature about China, the tale was intended to serve various purposes. In Western Europe it was sometimes meant for pure entertainment, and at other times, in the spirit of the Enlightenment, as a vehicle for satire, or for a philosophic or moral lesson. (In Russia there was also another group of oriental tales which combined moral and ethical teachings with a religious background. The spirit of this kind of tale was exactly the opposite of that of the Enlightenment type. The religious oriental tale is not, however, represented among the Russian tales concerning China that I have found.) In Russia, following still another Western European line of development, the oriental tale served quite frequently as a means of propagandising enlightened absolutism. Discussing this function of the tale, V. N. Kubacheva in her excellent survey of the oriental tale in Russia points out that, not surprisingly, few works ever found fault with or satirised a ruler. Even if criticism of an individual monarch was voiced in a tale, the principle of absolute monarchy remained unchallenged.[15]

The Good Chinese Emperor appeared more than once in the oriental tales and other works of Voltaire, which in translation were highly popular with Russian readers. Voltaire presents a most complimentary picture of the Chinese monarch in the *conte*, *La Princesse de Babylone* (1768), first translated into Russian as *Принцесса Вавилонская* in 1770 and reprinted in at least three more editions by 1789. When Formosanta, the Princess of Babylon, is received by the Emperor of China, the monarch is described as the 'fairest, most courteous and most intelligent' of rulers.[16] The Emperor is praised particularly for his encouragement of agriculture, his attitude toward punishment for crime and for his opposition to the intolerance of foreign missionaries in China. (The last of these points is, incidentally, also the subject of Voltaire's *L'Empereur de la Chine et le frère Rigolet*, also known as *Relation du bannissement des jésuites de la Chine* (1768), entitled in a Russian manuscript translation of the second half of the eighteenth century,

---

The use of China in this title was no doubt intended to entice the reading public with whom China was then very much in vogue. See V. V. Sipovskii, *Из истории русского романа и повести* (The History of the Russian novel and short story) i, part 2 (St Petersburg 1903), pp.258-59, 265-69.

[14] Guy, pp.371-74; Martha Pike Conant, *The Oriental tale in England in the eighteenth century* (New York 1908).

[15] See Conant's classification of tales in four categories. See also V. N. Kubacheva, '«Восточная повесть» в русской литературе XVIII – начала XIX века' (The oriental tale in Russian literatre of the 18th and early 19th centuries), *XVIII век* (The Eighteenth century) v (Moscow, Leningrad 1962), pp.295-315 at 309.

[16] *Union catalogue*, i.184, entries 1134-37; [Vol'ter (Voltaire)] *Принцесса Вавилонская*, trans. F. Polunin (Moscow 1770), p.80.

'Разговор Иокт-шина, китайского императора с иезуитом Риголетом'.[17] Here Voltaire shows the emperor Yung-cheng (1723-1735) to be a perceptive and objective ruler.)

An original Russian contribution to the fictional portrait of the wise Chinese ruler appeared in 1783 in an oriental tale written by the empress Catherine the Great. The story, *Сказка о Царевиче Февее* (The Tale of Prince Fevei), which was intended for Catherine's grandsons, presenting them with a model of the enlightened monarch, played a not insignificant part in the cultural interchange between Western Europe and Russia. It was published in German in 1784, and appeared in French in Grimm's *Correspondance littéraire* for 1790.[18] The tale concerns a Siberian people who are governed by a wise and good ruler of Chinese ancestry. Considerable emphasis is placed on the intelligent, healthy and character-building upbringing which the ruler prescribes for his son, the future king. The prince's conduct in a variety of difficult situations shows that he is obedient, considerate, modest and concerned for prisoners and the poor.

While the work is stylistically undistinguished, it is noteworthy in that unlike the majority of the belletristic representations of China in Russian literature, the story is supplied with a considerable amount of realistic detail, incorporating Russian, Central Asian and Chinese elements. Intrigues among the Tatar and Mongol tribes, and the appearance of Kalmuk consuls are again reflections of what, as has been seen in the narratives of the authentic Russian and Chinese travellers, was actually taking place in this area during the eighteenth century. The empress, following the preromantic currents then reaching Russia, has also introduced into her story the folkloristic device of repetition, a stylistic touch which sets her work apart from the traditional oriental tale, which was quite polished in form.

The notion of the administrative wisdom and goodness of the enlightened Chinese monarch was also developed in a tale entitled *Благодетель и мудрец* (The Benefactor and the sage), translated into Russian from an unspecified foreign language. The story appeared as part of a collection entitled *Полезное и увеселительное чтение для юношества и для всякаго возраста [...] Собрано из лучших иностранных сочинителей* (Useful and entertaining reading for youth and all ages collected from the best foreign writers) in 1788, and was published a second time in the periodical *Чтение для вкуса, разума и чувствова-*

---

[17] Manuscript cited in P. R. Zaborov, 'Вольтер в русских переводах XVIII века' (Voltaire in Russian translations of the eighteenth century), *Эпоха просвещения: из истории международных связей русской литературы* (The Age of Enlightenment: from the history of the international ties of Russian literature) (Leningrad 1967), pp.110-207, at p.206.

[18] Catherine II, *Сказка о царевиче Февее* (St Petersburg 1783); *Märchen von Zarewitsch Fewei* (Berlin, Stettin 1784); 'Le Czarowitsch Feveh, second Conte russe', F. M. Grimm, *Correspondance littéraire, philosophique et critique par Grimm, Diderot, Raynal, Meister, etc.*, xvi (Paris 1882), pp.85-98. Catherine's comic opera *Fevei*, published in 1786, is based on this story, but contains virtually no Chinese colouring: Catherine II, *Опера комическая Февей, составлена из слов скаски, песней руских и иных сочинений* (The Comic opera Fevei, composed from the words of the tale, of Russian songs and from other works) (St Petersburg 1786). See Grigorii A. Gukovskii, 'The empress as writer', in *Catherine the Great: a profile*, Marc Raeff, ed. (New York 1972), pp.64-89 at pp.82 and 88.

ний (Reading for taste, intelligence and sensibility) in 1791. The tale depicts the Emperor, who is the Benefactor of the title, and the Sage, an old man who the Emperor finds fulfills the requirements for being called a 'wise man'. The old man, who is modest, loves people, and does good by helping the unfortunate, is eventually made First Minister by the monarch. The latter through his desire to find such a man, his discernment in rejecting other candidates such as arrogant, unfeeling and selfish scholars, and through his persistence in continuing his search even when advised that 'wisdom is a beautiful dream and looking for it is like chasing a shadow',[19] demonstrates his own qualities of judgement and intelligence.

Finally, the figure of the virtuous Chinese prince and his efforts to acquire enlightened statesmanship came to Russian readers in a tale of another kind, one which utilised the device of the 'oriental spectator'. The work, which was published first in shortened form in a periodical in 1778 and again in book form in 1782, was entitled *Путешествие добродетели, или Странствование по свету юнаго китайскаго царевича с философом предводительствовавшим и научившим онаго* (The Journey of Virtue, or travels around the World of a young Chinese prince with a philosopher who guides and teaches him). The story is said to be a translation, although the language of the original is not specified.[20]

The author of the story, leaning on a number of literary conventions and using the fictional travel account as the basic form for the tale, brings a visitor from the East to Europe. The Chinese prince's outlook, however, differs considerably from that of the traditional oriental spectator, made famous by Montesquieu in his *Lettres persanes* (1721) and Goldsmith in *The Citizen of the World* (1762). Unlike his literary predecessors, Usbek of the *Lettres persanes* and Goldsmith's Lien Chi Altangi, the prince of *The Journey of Virtue* goes to London and Paris to observe and learn, not to satirise. In Paris he acquires 'urban politeness', which is still needed for the development of his character (*Утренний свет*, pt. 3, p.234). In London he admires the laws, and the ability of the people to reason and to express their thoughts. At last, after ten years of worthwhile observations, the prince returns to China, better prepared to become a wise and just ruler. Perhaps this variation on the oriental spectator theme served as inspiration for an original Russian 'spectator' creation, which, as we will soon see, departed even further from the literary convention.

A third type of Chinese Sage which Russian readers were to meet in belletristic representations of China was the highly perceptive, common man, the morally just individual. The device of the oriental spectator was also used for the

---

[19] 'Благодетель и мудрец', *Полезное и увеселительное чтение для юношества и для всякаго возраста ... Собрано из лучших иностранных сочинителей* (Moscow 1788), pp.82-107 at p.94; also in *Чтение для вкуса, разума и чувствований* 1 (1791), pp.107-31.

[20] 'Путешествие добродетели', *Утренний свет* (The Morning light), pt. 2 (1778), pp.239-66; pt. 3 (1778), pp.97-184, 191-263; *Путешествие добродетели, или Странствование по свету юнаго китайскаго царевича с философом предводительствовавшим и научившим онаго; в новейшия времена случившееся*, trans. A. K., 2 pts. (Moscow 1782).

portrayal of this kind of character. One such figure was sketched out in a work entitled *Пильгрим* (The Pilgrim) by Charles Johnstone, which appeared in Russian translation in 1793.[21] Johnstone's oriental spectator follows rather closely in the steps of Goldsmith's *Citizen of the World*, in terms both of itinerary and outlook. *The Pilgrim* consists of a series of letters written by a certain Choang, who is visiting London, to his friend in China. Like Goldsmith's and Montesquieu's protagonists, Choang relates what he sees from a supposedly objective point of view, providing a satirical picture of European life. Condemning such abuses as the dishonesty of public officials and the lack of law enforcement, or poking fun at pedantic scholars or narrow-minded ecclesiastics, Choang, who is portrayed as an exemplary, moral, intelligent Chinese citizen, makes a number of comparisons between English and Chinese customs. He points out such good features of Chinese life and government as the Emperor's willingness to listen to grievances, and the intellectual qualifications required of those who write books. These details provide Choang with some credibility as a Chinese citizen (more than that of his counterpart traveller in the *Journey of Virtue*, which contained few Chinese elements). But the *The Pilgrim* does not make a serious attempt to give information about Chinese ways, aiming primarily at presenting a gentle satire on English life, and at entertaining through a series of maudlin, sentimentalised adventures.

Strangely enough, Goldsmith's *Citizen of the World*, the work which inspired such imitations as *The Pilgrim*, was apparently not translated in full into Russian during the eighteenth century. An excerpt from the book appeared in the periodical *Monthly compositions* in 1763, the year after *The Citizen of the World* was published in England in book form. The selection is entitled 'A Chinese story, from the English book: The Citizen of the World, or letters from a Chinese philosopher'.[22] (Goldsmith's name is not given.) The story, however, has nothing to do with the Chinese traveller. It concerns instead a Korean, and represents a satirical commentary, not on life in England, but on human nature in general.

A unique Russian contribution to the figure of the virtuous and sagacious Chinese citizen appeared in a poetic treatment of the oriental spectator theme. The work, 'Письмо Китайца к Татарскому Мурзе, живущему по делам своим в Петербурге' (Letter of a Chinese to a Tatar nobleman living in St Petersburg on business), published in the periodical *Собеседник любителей российскаго слова* (Colloquy of the amateurs of the Russian word) in 1783,[23] combines Far Eastern, Turkic and European elements. The purported author of the letter-

[21] Dzhonston (Charles Johnstone [Johnston]), *Пилгримъ, то есть по обещанию странствующии, или Картина жизни*, trans. by N. N. of *The Pilgrim : or, a picture of life*, 2 pts. (Moscow 1793); C. Johnstone [Johnston], *The Pilgrim: or, a picture of life. In a series of letters, written mostly from London, by a Chinese philosopher, to his friend at Quang-Tong. Containing remarks upon the laws, customs, and manners of the English and other nations* (London [1775]).

[22] [Goldsmith], '‹Китайская повесть› (из Англинской книги *The Citizen of the World, or letters from a Chinese philosopher*)', *Monthly compositions* (Oct. 1763), pp.348-53.

[23] M. S. (Maria Sushkova), 'Письмо Китайца к Татарскому Мурзе, живущему по делам своим в Петербурге', *Собеседник любителей российскаго слова*, pt. 5 (1783), pp.3-8.

poem is a good and virtuous Chinese individual; the recipient is a 'Tatar' traveller, a version of the oriental spectator. The 'Letter', shows some original innovations on the oriental spectator convention. The epistolary form of the work reflects the influence of Montesquieu's *Lettres persanes* (which were, however, written in prose). But the spirit of the poem is closer to that of the anonymous translation, *The Journey of Virtue*, in which the oriental spectator praises European culture rather than finding fault with it. While *The Journey of Virtue* stresses the usefulness of various European institutions for the education of the Chinese prince, the 'Letter', focuses attention on one particular institution which the spectator observes and admires, the government of Russia. The device of the oriental spectator becomes a means of presenting an extravagant eulogy of the empress Catherine the Great!

In the introduction preceding the poem the 'Tatar' (the name applied to the Turkic inhabitants of Central Asia and Northern China) to whom the letter is addressed is identified as the purported author of an ode which had been published in a previous edition of the *Colloquy*. In this first poem, supposedly translated from Arabic, the Tatar, in Russia for business reasons, had described his life in St Petersburg in the glorious reign of Catherine II.

The 'Letter', addressed to this 'Tatar Nobleman', opens on a favourite enlightenment theme (p.5):

> Дар разума сей луч всещедра божества,
> Соделал смертных род Царями естества:

> The gift of reason, this ray of the bounty of the deity,
> Made the human race the rulers of nature:

The 'Chinese' letter-writer discusses man's perfecting of reason, the development of the arts and sciences, and the spreading out of civilisation. He then picks up the theme of the achievements of Catherine, which the 'Tatar Nobleman' had previously developed at length in his ode. The 'Chinese' poet states ('Letter', p.6):

> Величество души, премудрость, кротость нрава,
> Благотворительны законы и дела,
> Которыми себя толико вознесла,
> Пример земных Владык, полночных стран Царица,
> И днесь тобой, Мурза, воспетая Фелица.

> Greatness of soul, wisdom, gentleness of disposition,
> Philanthropic laws and deeds,
> By which she has so elevated herself,
> A model of earthly rulers, Empress of the midnight lands,
> And today Felitsa [the name used by poets of the period
>   for Catherine] is sung by you, Nobleman.

Heaping extravagant praise on the empress, the poet conjures up the following incongruous image ('Letter', p.6):

> В Пекине, о Мурза, стихи твой читаем,
> И истинну любля, согласно говорим:
> На троне Северном Конфуция мы зрим.

In Peking, o Nobleman, we read your verses,
And loving truth, we say in agreement:
On the Northern throne, we see Confucius.

The 'Letter' has virtually no Chinese colouring, but the figure of the letter-writer, who describes his people in Peking as 'loving truth', is evidently intended to represent the sagacity and sound judgement of citizens of the East. When the 'Chinese' poet states that on the banks of the Neva, 'wisdom in the likeness of the empress holds the sceptre' ('Letter', p.7) the reader is, no doubt, supposed to assume that the Chinese commentator is knowledgeable on such matters.

The poem is followed by a note of thanks from the editors of the journal to M. S., the contributor of the letter, who supposedly acquired it from a Siberian merchant bringing back goods from China to Russia. M. S. has been identified as Maria Sushkova,[24] a writer and highly successful translator, who had been invited by Catherine to her court. Sushkova, using the realistic detail about the Siberian merchant returning from China, revealed, in the same way that the empress did in the *Tale of Prince Fevei*, the proximity of Russia's eastern province to China; China emerges as a nation contiguous to Russia rather than a land so remote as to be almost mythical.

The good man of Cathay, the ordinary citizen, is seen not only as he corresponds with travellers in Russia or visits Europe himself but also in his own surroundings, as in the oriental tale *Candide the second, a native of China, or the friend of truth, a southern story*, translated from French into Russian in 1774. This anonymous tale, a witty and amusing satire, is intended to entertain more than to instruct, but the moralistic element, inherent in the subtitle's description of Candide as the 'Friend of truth', is ever present. A short poem by V. Ruban, prefaced to the story, advises the reader:

> Кто любит истину, кто свято правду чтит,
> Тому китайский сей Кандид не досадит;
> Но для кого сия богиня не приятна
> И повесть оному сия не будет внятна.[25]

> He who loves the truth, who holds veracity to be holy,
> Will not be annoyed by this Chinese Candide;
> But he who does not find this goddess agreeable
> Will not find this story intelligible either.

The tale relates the adventures of a young virtuous representative of a very wise and good people in a 'southern' area of China. The China of the story happens to be a land of magic, but more important it is a realm of moral perfection. When Candide is born, a prophecy is made by a sorceress that at

---

[24] M. P. Alekseev, 'Pushkin and China', p.117.

[25] *Candide the second*, opposite p.1 (see note 1 above); a second translation of the story appeared in *Зимния вечеринки, Другой Кандид, или Друг истины* (Winter evenings, the other Candide, or the friend of truth), trans. I. N. Vodop'ianov (Moscow 1789). This is a translation of an anonymous work entitled 'L'Autre Candide ou l'ami de la vérité', in *Soirées d'hiver ou recueil de moralités mises en action* (Liége 1771) (Bibliothèque de l'Arsenal, B. L., 16932). See Daniel Mornet, 'Les imitations du *Candide* de Voltaire au dix-huitième siècle', *Mélanges offerts par ses amis et ses élèves à m. Gustave Lanson* (Paris 1922), pp.298-303.

the age of eighteen the boy will have to leave his native land, and will not be able to return to it until he has found a person who will accept a disagreeable truth from him without becoming indignant. To fulfil the prophecy Candide travels through various countries of the East. His love of the truth and insistence on saying what he thinks cause him constant difficulties, and serve as the means by which the author makes a wide variety of satirical thrusts. Shortcomings of human nature, such as vanity and hypocrisy, receive a large share of the criticism. In an entirely different vein, customs of the orient, such as the necessity to kowtow fifty-one times in a certain court (where Candide, unfortunately performed only fifty kowtows) are also poked fun at. On still another plane individuals, such as the creator of the first Candide, come under satirical attack.

Candide the second is introduced to 'El-rovt', the author of Raiza, Epid, Peroma, Zairla and Rengiade. ('El-rovt' is an anagram of the Russian spelling of Voltaire, and El-rovt's 'works' are, of course, anagrams of the Russian spellings of *Zaire*, *Œdipe*, *Merope*, *Alzire* and *La Henriade* respectively.) El-rovt, we are told, is well-known in China, and is in fact the most highly esteemed person there after Confucius. Candide, who has nothing but admiration for this great defender of truth, feels sure that anything he might say to El-rovt, even if it should be an unpleasant truth, will be graciously accepted by the famous writer. Candide will then be able to return to his native land. Unfortunately El-rovt asks Candide's opinion of a new manuscript which he had hoped to send to Peking. The young Chinese is forced to admit honestly that this work is far from that 'fair and forceful description' which the writer had given elsewhere about the Chinese and their conquerors. El-rovt, who has been accustomed to receiving praise rather than criticism from 'all Asia' for over forty years, cannot bear Candide's comments, and angrily sends the Chinese visitor away (*Candide the second*, pp.24-25). At last, however, Candide finds not only a virtuous person who can accept an unwelcome truth from him, but also a wife, and they return to China to live happily ever after.

The publication of this satire on Voltaire in Russian implies that the French writer enjoyed a considerable reputation in Russia, just as the story claimed he did in China. This was indeed the case. By the end of 1774, the year *Candide the second* was published, at least fourteen Russian translations of Voltaire's works had appeared in book form, not to mention translations that had appeared in periodicals of the day.[26]

The 'fair and forceful description' of the Chinese referred to in the story *Candide the second* was not, however, to appear in Russian literature for another fourteen years. This work, *L'Orphelin de la Chine* (1755), translated into Russian verse by Vasilii Nechaev in 1788, was Voltaire's most serious effort to illustrate in his fictional works the moral superiority of the Chinese people.[27] The inspiration for this work, as Voltaire explains in the dedication, was the fourteenth-century Chinese play, *The Orphan of the House of Chao*, which had been translated

---

[26] See *Union catalogue*, pp.177-86. See also P. R. Zaborov, 'Voltaire in Russian translations of the eighteenth century', note 17.

[27] Vol'ter (F. M. A. Voltaire), Китайский сирота – трагедия (The Chinese orphan – a tragedy), translated into Russian verse by Vasilii Nechaev (St Petersburg 1788).

into French by father Prémare, and had appeared in Du Halde's *Description de la Chine* in 1735.

The original Chinese play, one of a very small number of actual works of Chinese fiction to become available in Europe during the eighteenth century, was highly influential in Europe. The plot concerns the orphaned heir to the Chinese throne and the obstacles he had to overcome to avenge his father's death and become the ruler of his nation. This theme caught the imagination of numerous translators and writers who adapted it in a variety of ways, often using it to project their own widely varying philosophic or political ideas. Prémare's translation, originally published by Du Halde, appeared in French as a separate publication in 1755 and was translated into English, German, and Dutch. As early as 1741 an English adaptation entitled *The Chinese orphan* was worked out by William Hatchett, primarily as a political attack on sir Robert Walpole. A second English adaptation by Arthur Murphy, entitled *The Orphan of China*, appeared in 1759. In 1762 Thomas Percy included in his *Miscellaneous pieces relating to the Chinese* an English translation made from the French in Du Halde. In Italian literature Metastasio's opera *L'Eroe cinese* (1752) was based on a similar theme, while in Germany the original work served as the inspiration for the play by Friedrichs *Der Chineser, oder die Gerechtigkeit des Schicksals* (1774), for Wieland's *Der goldene Spiegel, oder die Könige von Scheschian* (1772), and for Goethe's fragment *Elpenor* (1783).[28]

Two works which embodied the *Orphan of the House of Chao* theme, but which presumably attracted less attention than Voltaire's *Orphelin*, had become available to Russian readers even before the French *philosophe*'s play appeared in Russian in 1788. The main emphasis in these other works is not, as in Voltaire's *Orphelin*, on China's admirable individual citizen, but rather on her virtuous royalty; nevertheless it seems appropriate to consider all three works of the cycle together.

Prémare's version of the *Orphan of the House of Chao*, contained in the third volume of Du Halde's *Description*, did not appear in Russian, since only an abridged version of the first two volumes of that work were translated. But in 1759 in the periodical *Трудолюбивая пчела* (The Diligent bee) there appeared a short poem entitled 'Монолог из китайской трагедии, называемой Сирота' (Monologue from the Chinese tragedy entitled The Orphan). The journal notes only that the poem is a translation by A. S. 'from a German translation', but the poet has since been identified as the well-known Russian classicist Aleksandr Petrovich Sumarokov, the editor of the periodical.[29] The monologue itself follows closely the first part of the speech of the Chinese princess in Act 1 Scene 2 of

---

[28] Appleton, *A cycle of Cathay*, pp.81-87. For a discussion of English versions of the *Orphan of the House of Chao* (as well as other Chinese themes in eighteenth-century English literature) see also Beverly Sprague Allen, *Tides in English taste (1619-1800)*, ii.17-42, especially pp.22-26.

[29] 'Монолог из китайской трагедии, называемой Сирота' (translated from the German by A. P. Sumarokov), in *Трудолюбивая пчела* (The Busy bee) (Sept. 1759), p.570. Alekseev, p.116, n.2.

Prémare's version of the play as it appeared in the German translation of Du Halde's *Description*.[30]

Prémare's version of the monologue, and the German translation of it, are written in simple, straightforward prose. In Sumarokov's poetic rendering of the speech the simplicity is retained. The mother of the 'orphan' recalls how her husband, before he was killed, instructed her to bring up the yet unborn child to avenge his father's death. Sumarokov's opening lines express the mother's anguish in this way:

> Мне кажеця, что всех нещастье человеков,
> На сердце ах мое едино устремилось.
>
> ('Monologue', p.570).

> Scheint es doch, als ob das Unglück aller Menschen
> auf mein Herz allein zustürme.
>
> (*Ausführliche Beschreibung*, iii.423)

In the following eleven lines the poet describes the situation concisely, following the spirit, and even to some extent, the wording of Prémare's translation in his presentation of the mother's plight.

The *Orphan of the House of Chao* theme reappeared in Russia in 1781 in the translation of C. M. Wieland's *Der goldene Spiegel, oder die Könige von Scheschian* (1772) (*Золотое зеркало, или Цари Шешианские*). Wieland's work has both the character of the rococo literary chinoiserie of the period, and of a political novel imbued with the spirit of the Enlightenment.[31] The concern of the novel is enlightened government, and in the second part of the work, using the *Orphan of the House of Chao* as a thematic framework for his story, Wieland tells of the life of the great emperor Tifan, who was regarded as the restorer of his nation. Noteworthy when Wieland's and Voltaire's versions of the Orphan theme are compared is the description in *Der Goldene Spiegel* of Tifan's youth and his superior upbringing, which took place far away from the court in a rustic atmosphere. Wieland concurs here with Rousseau's theory that simplicity is vital to the development of the virtuous individual, and that on the large scale a highly sophisticated civilisation is harmful for mankind.

Just the opposite point of view was presented in *Китайский сирота* (L'Orphelin de la Chine), Voltaire's adaptation of the Orphan theme. It was Voltaire's conviction, of course, that the strength of the moral fibre of a nation's citizenry is proportionate to the degree of sophistication of its arts, sciences and other aspects of civilisation. He illustrates this theory here by showing the moral superiority of the highly developed Chinese nation over its conqueror, Ghengis Khan and his wild Tatar hordes. Representative of the elite of the highly refined Chinese culture are the virtuous heroes of the drama, a mandarin Zamti and

---

[30] 'Tchao Chi cou ell', in Jean Baptiste Du Halde, *Ausführliche Beschreibung des chinesischen Reichs und der großen Tartarey*, trans. from the French, iii (Rostok 1749), pp.420-44.

[31] Viland (Christoph Martin Wieland), *Золотое зеркало, или Цари Шешианские, истинная повесть*, 4 pts. (Moscow 1781). For a discussion of Wieland's work see Eduard Horst von Tscharner, 'China in der deutschen Dichtung, II Aufklärung und Rokoko', *Sinica* 12, Heft 5/6 (1937), pp.181-207 especially 194-95, and Ursula Aurich, 'China im Spiegel der deutschen Literatur des 18. Jahrhunderts', pp.80-82.

his wife Idame. The efforts of the mandarin and his wife to preserve the life of the orphaned heir to the throne, whose care was entrusted to them when their country was overrun by Ghengis Khan, constitute the plot of the drama. The selflessness and devotion to duty and honour of Zamti and Idame eventually affect the previously unfeeling and uncivilised Khan so much that he, the 'conqueror', capitulates at last to the 'conquered'.[32]

Among the many virtuous Chinese individuals that are found in the pages of eighteenth-century Russian literature, Zamti and Idame are perhaps the most earnestly portrayed. The oriental colouring of the play, however, is extremely vague, and there is little to characterise Zamti and Idame as Chinese. Furthermore, while the mandarin and his wife are indeed shown to be virtuous people, the drama loses credibility in that the beneficial influence of their conduct on Ghengis Khan is effected too abruptly. The final speech of the Khan summarises the thesis of the play, but is not very convincing. In Nechaev's Russian verse translation the Khan says to Idame:

> Не думал, что б я был собою усмирен;
> Но днесь то познаю и вам сим одолжен,
> Вам честь та подлежит, меня что пременили,
> Из победителя Царя что учинили.
>
> (*The Chinese orphan*, p.72).

> J'ignorais qu'un mortel put se dompter lui-meme;
> Je l'apprends; je vous dois cette gloire suprême:
> Jouissez de l'honneur d'avoir pu me changer.
> [...]
> Je fus un conquérant, vous m'avez fait un roi.
>
> (M.v.355-56)

In the final analysis, Voltaire's noble Chinese figures are unfortunately not plausible characterisations of the virtuous Chinese individual.

Nechaev's translation of *L'Orphelin* was done in the manner traditional among Russian translators of the period, which was to follow the original very closely, without attempting to introduce new stylistic features. While the result of this method of translating has been termed somewhat 'cheerless and monotonous',[33] it seems likely that Voltaire's popularity in Russia at this time, and the Russian public's continuing interest in anything having to do with China must have attracted considerable attention to the play.

The discussion of the artistic presentation of the wise and virtuous Chinese citizen in Russian literature would be incomplete without mention of another group of works which can be described as moral treatises – some authentically Chinese and some pseudo-oriental – which present precepts for good living in poetry or poetic prose. This poetry complements ideologically the prose writings on morality translated from the Chinese by the Russian sinologists (which will be seen later in the discussion of China and the intellectuals). The first of the poetic works is, in the original, an English book which purports to be, but is not, of eastern origin, entitled *The Economy of human life, translated from an Indian*

---

[32] For a thorough discussion of this work see Guy, pp.221-31.
[33] Zaborov, p.169.

manuscript, written by an ancient Bramin.[34] The work is generally thought to have been written by Robert Dodsley, although it has also been variously attributed to lord Chesterfield, to whom it is dedicated, and to John Hill. The preface, dated 1749, Peking, explains that the manuscript, containing 'a small system of morality', was found in Tibet in the archive of the temple of the Dalai Lama by a Chinese scholar sent to Tibet by the emperor of China. The scholar translated the manuscript from the 'language [...] of the ancient Bramins' into Chinese, from which the writer of the preface translated it into English.

Surprisingly enough, after this colourful, contrived background there is little that is Chinese or Tibetan about the style or contents of the book. Even the supposed 'translator' of the 'Tibetan original' states that if it were not for the ancient language of the manuscript, one might think the work has been written by a European. He explains that in his translation he followed the stylistic pattern of such Biblical books as the *Song of Solomon* and the *Psalms*. The result is a work which, while attributed to an ancient Brahman, in fact presents a general Deistic approach to life, in the language, in the original English work, of the King James version of the Bible.

The appeal of this work in Russia must have been enormous. It appeared in four separate translations, the first in a periodical in 1762 with the title 'Устроение человеческой жизни' (The Arrangement of human life). The second translation, entitled *Экономия жизни человеческой* (The Economy of human life), appeared three years later and was reprinted in 1769, 1781 and 1791. Meanwhile in 1773 a translation entitled *Китайский мудрец* (The Chinese Sage) was published in St Petersburg, and reprinted in 1777 and 1785. The fourth translation, *Книга премудрости и добродетели* (The Book of wisdom and virtue) was first published in 1786 and reprinted in 1794.[35]

The Russian public evidently read with great enjoyment such purported wisdom of the East as the following opening paragraph concerning 'Hope and fear' in the chapter on the passions: 'The promises of hope are sweeter than roses in the bud, and far more flattering to expectation; but the threatenings of fear are a terror to the heart' (Dodsley, p.22).

A book review in 1777 concerning the Russian translation recommends the work to readers of all ages. The article discusses specifically the translation entitled *Китайский мудрец*, made from a French version of the English. Praising the philosophy of the Eastern world, the reviewer appears to accept the book as an authentic product of the Orient. The publishers of this particular translation

---

[34] Robert Dodsley (supposed author), *The Economy of human life, translated from an Indian manuscript written by an ancient Bramin*, 2 pts. in one volume (London 1807).

[35] 'Устроение человеческой жизни', *Полезное увеселение* (Useful entertainment) (Feb. 1762), pp.57-68; (April 1762), pp.147-73; *Экономия жизни человеческой, или сокращение индейскаго нравоучения* (The Economy of human life, or an abstract of Indian moral philosophy), trans. E. and P. Tsitsianov (Moscow 1765, 1769, 1781, 1791); Robert Dodsley (supposed author), *Китайский мудрец, или Наука жить благополучно в обществе* (The Chinese sage or the science of living successfully in society), trans. by S. P. Kolosov of *The Economy of human life* (St Petersburg 1773, 1777, 1785); *Книга премудрости и добродетели, или Состояние человеческой жизни* (The Book of wisdom and virtue, or the condition of human life) (Moscow 1786, 1794).

of *The Economy of human life* had certainly fostered this view; the introduction noted that included with the translation were three selections about 'Christian law' from the work *Esprit, maximes et principes* by that 'European sage' Rousseau, and it suggested that readers could therefore make a 'comparison of Asiatic thinking with European'.[36]

At the time that *The Chinese Sage* was enjoying such success in Russia, there appeared a translation by Aleksei Leontiev of an authentic Chinese children's reader entitled *Букварь китайской* (Chinese ABC book), an intriguing work (apparently unknown at this time in the Western world except in Russia) which provided authentic rather than imagined glimpses of Chinese ideas about human conduct. The book was published in 1779 and was not reprinted.[37]

The form as well as the content of the *Chinese ABC book* are quite appealing. The first part, 'Сань дзы гин. То есть Книга троесловная' (San Tzŭ Ching, or the three word book), the 'Three character classic', contains a series of rhymed verses, which in the original Chinese are each three characters in length.[38] Leontiev in his so-called 'prose translation' has followed the Chinese form closely, and has often succeeded in the Russian in producing lines consisting of only three words, or three important words. The number of stresses and of syllables differs from line to line, but a definite accentual rhythm results from the three word organisation of each line. Further poetic effects are achieved through devices of parallelism.

The same devices are used to some extent in Part Two of the *Chinese ABC book*, which is translated as 'Мин сянь дзи. То есть Речи славных мужей' (Min sian' dzi or Sayings of famous men). This is a collection of proverbs, composed in four to seven word verses. (In the longer lines the translator has not always attempted to make the number of Russian words correspond to the number in the original Chinese.) Examples of the effects achieved by Leontiev can be seen in the following 'four word verse' from the 'Sayings of famous men':

> Человека чужестраннаго, люди презирают,
> Вещь чужестранную, люди почитают.
>
> (*Chinese ABC book*, p.31).

> A foreign person, people despise.
> A foreign thing, people esteem.

---

[36] 'О книгах: Китайский мудрец или наука жить благополучно в обществе' (About books: The Chinese sage or the science of living successfully in society), *Санктпетербург-ския ученыя ведомости* (St Petersburg Scholarly news) 21 (1777), p.167; 22 (1777), pp.169-70; *Китайский мудрец* (1777) (note 35 above), p.viii.

[37] *Букварь китайской состоящей из двух китайских книжек, служит у китайцев для начальнаго обучения малолетных детей основанием* (A Chinese ABC book consisting of two Chinese booklets, which serves among the Chinese as a basis for primary education of young children), trans. Aleksei Leontiev (St Petersburg 1779). Leontiev had studied Chinese at the Russian Orthodox Mission in Peking.

[38] For a brief discussion of this work and other texts of this type see Kenneth Scott Latourette, *The Chinese: their history and culture*, 4th ed. (New York, London 1964), p.662. The basis of the metric pattern in Chinese poetry is the number of syllables (each syllable being expressed by one character) in a line. In some, but not all, types of Chinese poetry the number of characters is the same in each line. See James J. Y. Liu, *The Art of Chinese poetry* (Chicago 1962), p.21.

The first section of the *Chinese ABC book*, the 'San Tzǔ Ching', which is written in true primer fashion, was a standard text memorised by Chinese children in the primary school. The work emphasises the importance of learning and education, and at the same time presents factual material such as a simple description of the Chinese classics, and information about famous philosophers and rulers of China. Perhaps the most appealing segment of this section of the book, and the most valuable for readers really concerned with Chinese ideas, is a series of verses combining numbers and the basic Confucian outlook on the world and man's place in it. (See English translation in Appendix.)

Part two of the book, the proverbs, also reveals much about Chinese life. For example, the striving for calmness, and for control over the emotions, a characteristic Chinese theme, is reiterated throughout the proverbs. A 'four word verse' expresses this idea in the following way:

> Страсти наши должны мы пресекать,
> Справедливости небесной должны мы следовать.
> > (*Chinese ABC book*, p.31).

> We must suppress our passions,
> We must follow heavenly justice.

A number of the ideas expressed in the proverbs are of a universal nature, but they contain specifically Chinese colouring. Corresponding to the English proverb which recommends making hay while the sun shines, is the following saying:

> *Шуи Доу* чинить надобно, когда на небе чисто,
> А не в то время, когда сливной дождь придет.
> > (*Chinese ABC book*, p.36).
> One must make the canal on a clear day,[39]
> And not when it's pouring.

A comparison of a proverb concerning respect for parents from the *Chinese ABC book* with a passage on the same theme in the *Chinese sage*, the Russian translation of *The Economy of human life*, provides a good example of the two modes in which the real and imaginary moral precepts of the East were presented to Russian readers. The *Chinese ABC book* notes simply:

> Полезнее в доме воздавать почтение и повиновение своим родителям,
> Нежели ходить далеко на моление со свечами.
> > (*Chinese ABC book*, p.35).

> It is more wholesome to render respect and obedience to one's parents at home,
> Than to go a great distance to pray with candles.

The *Chinese sage* expresses the idea in this way: 'The piety of a child is sweeter than the incense of Persia offered to the sun; yea, more delicious than odours wafted from a field of Arabian spices by the western gales. Be grateful then to thy father, for he gave thee light; and to thy mother, for she sustained thee' (Dodsley, p.35).

---

[39] Leontiev uses the Chinese word 'Shui Dou' for canal, explaining in a note that it means 'a canal to drain water from a courtyard' (*Chinese ABC book*, p.36).

Judging by the fact that Leontiev's version of the *Chinese ABC book* was not reprinted, it would seem that the simplicity and subtle poetic effects of this 'prose' translation did not appeal to Russian readers' developing romantic tastes nearly as much as did the flowery imagery of *The Chinese sage*. Leontiev's work was nevertheless praised for its instructiveness in a review in 1780. The critic noted that readers could form some judgement about the literary style and modes of thinking of the Chinese from the excerpts from the *ABC book* which he included in the review. His own equivocal appraisal of the ideas contained in this work and in Leontiev's translation of a work by Confucius can be seen in the following statement: 'These translations can serve as new proof that in view of the present state of world enlightenment, the Chinese are entirely unfair in considering themselves to be the only people who can see straight, and all other nations to be blind, or one-eyed; but at the same time, Europeans would be entirely unfair if they were to completely disregard their learning.'[40]

The scepticism with which the reviewer eyed the concept of Chinese superiority may have reminded readers of the views expressed in many of the non-fictional accounts of China written by Russian merchants, missionaries and diplomats. In any case, the comment of the reviewer contrasted sharply with the belletristic illustrations of the outstanding moral philosophy of the Chinese.

Similar in intent to these moral treatises is a set of maxims included among the French writings of Catherine II, entitled 'Китайския мысли' (Chinese thoughts) and subtitled 'Sentences chinoises'. The style of Catherine's 'Sentences' is simple and seems to try to imitate the actual Chinese pattern as seen in the *Chinese ABC book*. Typical of the aphorisms are these lines:

> Le sage fait entrer tous les hommes dans son cœur,
> l'insensé en chasse ceux qui y sont.
> Le sage est grand dans les plus petites choses,
> l'insensé est petit dans les plus grandes.
> Le sage se perd en combattant ses pensées,
> l'insensé en les suivant.[41]

The behaviour of the wise man described here blends well with the archetype of the Chinese sage. Realistic Chinese colouring appears, however, only in the brief reference to two particular Chinese personages. ('Chinese thoughts', p.139).

In addition to the morally upright man, to whom these works of poetry allude, and to the literary stereotypes of the wise emperor, and the philosopher Confucius, there appeared in eighteenth-century Russsian literature one more version of the oriental sage – the Chinese man of letters. The learned man of Cathay was a favourite with Voltaire, and the figure appeared a number of

[40] 'Известие о новых книгах' (News of new books), *Санктпетербургский вестник* (St Petersburg herald) 6 (1780), pp.369-72, at pp.369-70.

[41] Catherine II, 'Китайския мысли', *Письма и бумаги императрицы Екатерины II хранящияся в императорской публичной библиотеке*, (Letters and papers of empress Catherine II, preserved in the Imperial Public Library), ed. A. F. Bychkov (St Petersburg 1873), pp.137-41, at p.137. I have been unable to locate any information about the date or background of the work. Since Catherine's collection of Russian proverbs is mainly of her own creation, it seems likely that these Chinese sayings are also her original work. See Gukovskii, note 18, p.82.

times in Russian translations of Voltaire's work. Voltaire frequently used the character as a satirical weapon. While appearing to belittle the scholar, Voltaire was in fact using him to cut Man, the rational being, down to size.

In the dialogue translated into Russian as *О славе. Разговор с китайцем* (*De la gloire, ou entretien avec un Chinois* (1738), later included in the *Dictionnaire philosophique* under 'Gloire')[42] the hero, a Chinese scholar visiting Holland, is presented with a copy of Bossuet's *Histoire universelle*. The scholar is incredulous to find that the work deals primarily not with China, about which Europeans are poorly informed, but with the ancient Hebrews, Egyptians, Greeks and Romans, about whom the Chinese scholar himself knows nothing. Voltaire is of course using the situation to point out the relative nature of glory and reputation.

A second of Voltaire's Chinese scholars appears in *Философическия речи о человеке* (*Discours en vers sur l'homme*, VI) (1737), which was translated into Russian in prose in 1788.[43] Here Voltaire relates a story which he states he found in a translation of a Chinese book. In the story various animals, man, and finally the angels are told by Tien, the God of the Chinese, that the world has not in fact been created for their benefit, as they flatter themselves it has, but rather that they have been created for God. A Chinese scholar then speaks up, protesting the limits of man's nature and abilities. Voltaire describes the scholar as being full of Confucius, with his logic in his head, combatting reason with beautiful arguments. But Voltaire puts the learned man in his place. The scholar is eventually forced to conclude that each being in the universe has its limitations and its measure. While Voltaire may to some extent be poking fun here at the Chinese scholar (or at the literary stereotype itself), he is primarily using the scholar, as a representative of the most learned and rational of human beings, to satirise Man in general.

In *Zadig* (1748), translated into Russian in 1765 as *Задиг или Судба*,[44] the hero encounters a Chinese who is not actually described as a scholar, but who is seen carrying on an intellectual discussion, putting up reasonable arguments in favour of his own religion over the faiths of several persons of other nationalities who are present. It takes Zadig to see the point that all of the disputants are in basic agreement because they all worship one superior being. The shortsightedness of such a reasoning man as the Chinese is used here to make sharper the criticism of man's intolerance.

The figure of the Chinese scholar served an entirely different function in an

---

[42] 'О славе. Разговор с китайцем', ('Gloire. III Entretien avec un Chinois'), trans. A. L. Dubrovskii, *Monthly compositions* 4 (Sept. 1756), pp.303-307. The dialogue also appeared in *Прохладные часы* (Cool hours) 2 (1793), p.71.

[43] Vol'ter (F. M. A. Voltaire), *Философическия речи о человеке*, trans. by I. G. Rakhmaninov of *Discours en vers sur l'homme*, VI (St Petersburg 1788). Excerpts were published as 'Отрывки из Разговор о человеке' (Excerpts from *Discours en vers sur l'homme*) in *Иртыш* (Irtysh) (Oct. 1789), p.34.

[44] *Задиг или Судба, восточная повесть; и Свет каков есть, видение Бабука, писанное им самим* (Zadig or Fate, an oriental tale; and The World as it is, the Vision of Babouc, written by Himself) (Moscow 1765, 1788, 1795). The tale also appeared in *Monthly compositions* 9 (1759).

original Russian work by the mathematician and philosopher Iakov Pavlovich Kozel'skii. The book, published anonymously in 1788, was entitled *Китайский философ или Ученые разговоры двух индийцов Калана и Ибрагима* ... (The Chinese philosopher or scholarly conversations of two Indians, Kalan and Ibrahim).[45] Kozel'skii, who was the translator of Diderot and d'Alembert, was also the author of several other works, including *Философическия предложения* (Philosophical propositions) (1768), in which he criticised serfdom and tyranny, and pointed to China as a model government. In the *Chinese philosopher* Kozel'skii discusses in a popularised way a wide range of scientific subjects, such as chemistry, physics and biology, taking issue, in passing, with the point of view expressed by Rousseau that the development of the sciences had a harmful effect on mankind.[46]

The full title of *The Chinese philosopher* is confusing, and the ambiguity concerning the native origin of the philosopher is far from being resolved by the preface, which explains that 'Once upon a time, or never, two Chinese or Indians, Kalan and Ibrahim', had a series of scholarly discussions about human knowledge. Apparently it was felt that the image of the 'Chinese philosopher' would enhance the book's appeal. But in the second, enlarged edition, also published in 1788 (but this time with Kozel'skii's name) the 'Chinese philosopher' of the title was omitted. (Kozel'skii's use of a dialogue format for introducing his material to nonspecialists is, incidentally, another popularising technique, one which may show further acquaintance with French literature, deriving perhaps from Fontenelle's *Entretiens sur la pluralité des mondes* (1686) in which scientific material is presented in the form of conversations with an inquiring lady.)

The frequent appearances of these four literary versions of the wise Chinese – Confucius, the good ruler, the just individual and the scholar – established firmly in Russian belletristic literature the image of China as the Land of the Sage. While the majority of the literary sketches of the Chinese sage were created by Western European, especially French writers, Russian authors, as has been shown, can be credited with significant contributions to the China of fiction. Russian writers utilised the same characters and themes as their Western European colleagues, while introducing such original variations as the use of

---

[45] [Iakov Pavloviy Kozel'skii], *Китайский философ или Ученые разговоры двух индийцов Калана и Ибрагима* (St Petersburg 1788). The second edition was entitled *Разсуждения двух индийцов Калана и Ибрагима о человеческом познании* (The Discussion of two Indians, Kalan and Ibrahim about human knowledge) (St Petersburg 1788). It has been suggested that the work was written jointly with N. M. Maksimovich-Ambodik, a well-known doctor, who published it after making various changes and abridgements. *Избранные произведения русских мыслителей второй половины XVIII века* (Selected works of Russian thinkers of the 18th century), ed. I. Ia. Shchipanov, i (Moscow 1952) contains excerpts from the second edition at pages 552-620.

[46] *The Discussion*, in *Selected works* (note 45 above), i.555 and annotation, i.688; M. M. Shtrange, '‹Энциклопедия› Дидро и ее русские переводчики' (Diderot's *Encyclopédie* and its Russian translators), *Французский ежегодник 1959* (French yearbook 1959) (Moscow 1961), pp.76-88 at p.79; Iu. Ia. Kogan, *Просветитель XVIII века Я. П. Козельский* (An Enlightenment figure of the eighteenth century, Ia. P. Kozel'skii) (Moscow 1958), pp.66-68; O. L. Fishman, *Китайский сатирический роман: эпоха Просвещения* (The Chinese satirical novel: the Enlightenment era) (Moscow 1966), p.166.

details that sometimes showed China to be a country bordering on Russia rather than a distant, legendary land, and the utilisation of the figure of the oriental spectator as a means of heaping lavish praise rather than satire on one's own government and ruler.

Among the fictional representations of China in Russian literature there were, in addition to those portraying the Chinese Sage, two somewhat different groups of writings; in this literature, exemplary characters and philosophic and moral lessons were not the centre of interest. In only a few cases, however, did these other materials fail to harmonise with the general belletristic conception of the Middle Kingdom as the land of goodness and truth. The first set of works depicted a remote corner, as it were, of the mythical China, a region where marvels and wonders occurred, and where amorous intrigues or comic situations determined the course of the narrative. In Russian literature of the eighteenth century this region was much less explored than were the other areas of the imaginary country. It first appeared in the translation of Thomas Simon Gueullette's *Les Mille et un quarts d'heure, contes tartares* (1712) (translated as *Тысяча и одна четверть часа, повести татарския*) in 1765-1766. This work, an imitation of the *Mille et une nuits*, contained stories with primarily Persian backgrounds. But Asian settings were also used, as in the tale 'L'Histoire d'Outzim-Ochantey, prince de la Chine'. There is no didacticism in the story. The plot moves forward through complex situations and stratagems involving an evil princess who tries to charm the prince, a beautiful princess of Tiflis with whom the Chinese prince falls in love, a magician, and a poisoning. In contrast to many of the heavy-handed oriental tales depicting the good which were translated into Russian, the 'Histoire d'Outzim-Ochantey' is extremely lively. The author's 'lightness of touch' and 'surety of manner' are especially singled out by Basil Guy, who feels Gueullette's chinoiseries are among the best of the period.[47]

Amorous intrigue, combined with humour rather than magic, predominates in another spirited version of the never-never land of China in the Italian comic opera *L'Idolo chinese* (*Идол Китайский*) by Giovanni Battista Lorenzi.[48] The opera was presented in the summer of 1779 at the new theatre at Tsarskoe Selo, the royal palace of Catherine the Great, located outside St Petersburg. Two editions of the text were published in that year, one containing both the translation and the Italian original.

[47] Gellet (Thomas Simon Gueullette), *Тысяча и одна четверть часа, повести татарския*, trans. from French, vols i-iv (Moscow 1765-1766; 2nd printing 1777-1778); Thomas Simon Gueullette, 'L'histoire d'Outzim-Ouchantey, Prince de la Chine', *Les Milles et un quarts d'heure, contes tartares*, in *Le Cabinet des fées ou collection choisie des contes de fées, et autres contes merveilleux*, ed. C. S. Mayer (Genève, Paris 1785-1789), xxi.198-339; Guy, p.190.

[48] Lorentsi (Giovanni Battista Lorenzi), *Идол китайский, шутливая музыкальная драмма, представленная на новом Сарскосельском театре июля дня 1779 года* (The Chinese idol, a musical comedy, presented at the New Tsarskoe Selo Theatre in July 1779), trans. V. A. Levshin (St Petersburg 1779). An edition containing both the Russian translation and the Italian original also appeared in 1779: *Идол китайский, шутливая музыкальная драмма представленная на новом Сарскосельском театре августа дня 1779 года – L'Idolo chinese, dramma giocoso per musica da rappresentarse nel nuovo teatro di Sarsco Selo il giorno d'agosto 1779*, trans. V. A. Levshin (St Petersburg 1779).

The work is an example of a literary chinoiserie, as well as a representative of classical comedy. The action is set in a certain Chinese province by the sea. But Chinese costumes and the idol in a temple are practically the only oriental features of the production. The complications of ill-fated lovers, deception and attempted murder are played out against the whimsical background of the Chinese 'Festival of the Egg', during which the pagan god Kam is expected to descend from heaven. Mistaken identities, including that of a European sailor who is taken for the god and escorted in honour to the temple, are finally resolved, and all of the major characters leave the country on the ship of a French captain who has been involved in the confusion.

Even greater deviations from the stereotype of the Chinese sage are to be found here and there in the small number of translated and original Russian works which treat the Middle Kingdom in a realistic or purportedly realistic manner. Among these is a section of the translation of *The Farther adventures of Robinson Crusoe* (1719), part two of Daniel Defoe's novel entitled in Russian *Жизнь и приключения Робинзона Круза природнаго агличанина.*[49] Defoe, like Lorenzi, reverses the 'oriental spectator' theme, presenting instead the European visitor in China. He places Robinson Crusoe in Nanking, and then develops a fictional travel account in the pattern of the real travel narratives of the period.

Defoe utilised authentic accounts for his background material, but the question of exactly which sources he used is a complex one. Authorities point variously to Dampier, Lecomte, and Nieuhof, from whom Defoe apparently borrowed many descriptions, as well as Ysbrants Ides and Adam Brand, whose itinerary across Siberia is closely paralleled by Crusoe's.[50] The question of the origin of Defoe's point of view about China poses as many problems as does the source of the details which he used. The travellers just mentioned were either favourably inclined or at worst indifferent to China. But Defoe's attitude is one of open hostility. Crusoe comments critically on the pride of the Chinese, on the level of their knowledge, on the Great Wall, the food, soldiers, poverty, and many other aspects of Chinese life. His attitude is summed up in this scathing comment: 'I must confess, it seem'd strange to me, when I came home, and heard our people say such fine things of the power, riches, glory, magnificence, and trade of the Chinese; because I saw, and knew that they were a contemptible herd or crowd of ignorant sordid slaves, subjected to a government qualified only to rule such a people.'[51] The attractive appearance of Nanking, some well paved roads, and the 'prudence and impartiality' of a Chinese judge are practically all Crusoe finds commendable in China (*Farther adventures*, p.288). The latter rare

[49] Defo (Daniel Defoe), *Жизнь и приключения Робинзона Круза природнаго агличанина* (The Life and adventures of Robinson Crusoe, an Englishman by nationality), trans. Iakov Trusov (St Petersburg, 1st ed. 1762-1764; 3rd ed. 1787; 4th ed. 1797).

[50] Appleton, p.58; Paul Dottin, *Daniel Defoe et ses romans*, vol. ii, *Robinson Crusoe: étude historique et critique* (Paris 1924), pp.340-42; R. M. Bridges, 'A possible source for Daniel Defoe's *The Farther adventures of Robinson Crusoe*', *British journal for eighteenth-century studies* 2 (1979), pp.231-36; A. G. Cross, 'Don't shoot your Russianists; or, Defoe and Adam Brand', *British journal for eighteenth-century studies* 3 (1980), pp.230-33.

[51] Daniel Defoe, *The Farther adventures of Robinson Crusoe* (London 1790; reprinted 1925), p.267; Defo, pt. 2, p.212.

instance of praise emerged in the Russian translation, however, in considerably attenuated form. The words 'prudence and impartiality' were omitted, and Crusoe's approval appeared only in the phrase, 'I could not contradict the opinion of this judge' (*The Life and adventures of Robinson Crusoe*, ii.235-36).

The most plausible explanations suggested by scholars for Defoe's attitude seem to be that as an English patriot and supporter of trade, he objected to China's exclusive commercial policies and her hostility toward British merchants. It may also be that since intense admiration for China was already firmly established in England by 1719, Defoe the publicist chose to present a controversial point of view with the aim of making his book original. Whatever Defoe's motivation may have been, the resultant attack on China has been acknowledged as one of the important sources of the anti-Chinese feeling which eventually developed in Western Europe.[52]

Defoe's comments on China could not, however, have been as startling in Russia as they were in Western Europe. First of all, there had not existed in Russia a long tradition of admiration for the Chinese; the translation, appearing in the early 1760s, came near the beginning of the period of intense Russian interest in China. Second, hostile views of the Chinese such as those presented by admiral Anson were already known to Russian readers, the *Voyage round the World* having been translated about a decade earlier. Furthermore, both Anson's and Defoe's works were soon followed by the publication of the narratives of such Russian diplomats and merchants as Baikov and Lange, who in fact concurred with many of the opinions expressed by Defoe.[53]

Among the other belletristic works which purported to present a realistic description of China were a number of authentic Chinese poems which made their way into Russia in translation, some directly from the Chinese and others by way of French intermediaries. The original works of Chinese belles-lettres which were known at this time in Western Europe had become available almost entirely through the translating efforts of the Jesuit missionaries. These translations, however, were very few in number, and only some of them became available in Russia. Several selections, for example, from the Chinese canonical book, the *Shih Ching or book of odes*, were contained in the second volume of Du

[52] Appleton, p.58; Dottin, ii.341; Guy, p.207.

[53] A second purportedly realistic (and also uncomplimentary) reference to the Chinese that was scheduled to appear in a translated work of fiction in Russian was that by Jean-Jacques Rousseau in *La Nouvelle Héloïse* (1761). Since, however, only two parts of the novel were actually published in Russia during the eighteenth century, Rousseau's hostile comments on China, which occur near the end of the work, were evidently known only to those Russian readers who happened to be able to read the novel in the original French. Other comments by Rousseau on China, did, however, reach the Russian public, a matter that will be discussed in a later chapter. Russo (Jean Jacques Rousseau), *Новая Елоиза*, trans. Pavel Potemkin (Moscow 1769), pt. I; Russo (Jean Jacques Rousseau), *Новая Елоиза*, trans. Petr Andreev (St Petersburg 1792), pt. II; Russo (Jean Jacques Rousseau), *Новая Елоиза* (St Petersburg 1792-1793), pts. 1-2. See *Union catalogue*, iii (Moscow 1966), pp.75-76, entries 6219-6221. Jean-Jacques Rousseau, *Julie, ou La Nouvelle Héloïse*, *Œuvres complètes*, ed. Bernard Gagnebin and Marcel Raymond, ii (Paris 1964), pp.413-14. Rousseau here bases his description on Walter's edition of George Anson's *Voyage autour du monde*. See *Julie*, note 1 to page 414 on 1583.

Halde's *Description de la Chine* (1735), but Du Halde's work appeared in abridged form in Russian, and the poetry was not included. On the other hand, the first three volumes of Amiot's *Mémoires concernant ... les Chinois* which had been translated into Russian between 1786 and 1788, did acquaint Russian readers at least briefly with Chinese poetry, through prose translation. In the poem entitled in Russian translation, 'Сад Сеэ-Ма Куанга' ('Le Jardin de See ma-Kouang') the author, Ssŭ-ma Kuang, who was the First Minister of China in 1086, presented a picturesque description of his garden with its rocks, waterfalls, bamboo trees, and ancient cedars; he praised the peacefulness he enjoyed there. In addition, in the second volume of the Russian version of Amiot's work there appeared a poetic work by the eighteenth-century emperor, Ch'ien-lung. Amiot translated in prose the emperor's long narrative poem *Monument de la conquête des Eleuths* which told of the military action taken by him against the 'rebel' Eleuth peoples (*Mémoires*, i.329-400).[54] The *Chinese anecdotes* of Castillon, discussed above, contained excerpts in prose from another poem by the emperor Ch'ien-lung, praising the city of Mukden.[55] Informative in intent, it presented a considerable amount of factual material about the city.

While these poems gave Russian readers some idea of Chinese verse, the form in which the works appeared – Russian translations of French translations of the original – was undoubtedly quite different from the form used by actual poets. Contemporary specialists on China tried to describe the nature of this poetry. In his account of the Macartney mission to China, George Staunton, for instance, commented on the poems of the emperor Ch'ien-lung with these words: 'They are less remarkable for invention, than for philosophical and moral truths; and resemble more the epics of Voltaire, than those of Milton.'[56]

A somewhat closer view of Chinese poetry was made possible for Russian sinophiles by the sinologist Aleksei Leontiev, the translator of the *Chinese ABC book*. In the translation *Уведомление о чае и о шелке. Из китайской книги Вань Боу Кюань называемой* (Information about tea and silk. From the Chinese book entitled Van' Bou Kiuan'), a description of the hard realities of the daily life of the Chinese peasant,[57] Leontiev brought to the public a set of simple Chinese verses quite unlike the formal poetry of the emperor. The first part of the *Information* consists of a description in prose of the growing of tea and the

[54] 'Сад Сеэ-Ма-Куанга. Поэма', translation of 'Le Jardin de See-ma-Kouang', *Mémoires concernant les Chinois*, ii (1777), pp.643-50. In *Записки, надлежащия* ..., iv (1787), pp.339-45. A short biographical sketch of Ssŭ-ma Kuang was to appear in Russia ten years later: 'Зсе-ма-коанг, или испытанная верность' (Ssŭ-ma Kuang, or fidelity put to the test), trans. P. L'vov, *Приятное и полезное препровождение времени* (Pleasant and useful pastime), pt. 16 (1797), pp.257-70, 273-80; Ch'ien-lung, 'Памятник завоевания Орды Елеутов', *Mémoires*, ii (1786), pp.72-164.

[55] Kastiion (Castillon), i.217-21.

[56] Stonton (George Leonard Staunton), Makartnei (George Macartney), *Путешествие во внутренность Китая и в Татарию, учиненное в 1792, 1793, 1794 гг. лордом Макартнеем* (The Journey into the interior of China and Tartaria made by lord Macartney in 1792, 1793, and 1794). George Staunton, *An authentic account of an embassy from the king of Great Britain to the emperor of China*, ii.266.

[57] *Уведомление о чае и о шелке. Из китайской книги Вань Боу Кюань называемой*, trans. A. Leontiev (St Petersburg 1775).

cultivation of silk worms. The final section is a translation from a Chinese medical book entitled *Byn tsou* which discusses the use of foods and herbs in connection with various illnesses. Of special literary significance is the second section comprising the translations of forty-six small poems. Leontiev notes that originally the verses were printed on a series of pictures that illustrated the sowing of grain and the making of silk by Chinese peasants. Leontiev's publication contains only the poems. Explaining that he is not a poet and does not know the rules of versification, Leontiev states that he nevertheless has translated the poems in verse rather than in prose in order 'to better convey the ideas of the original verses' (p.16).

Typical of the small realistic pictures of Chinese peasant life which emerge from the verses is the following poem, the first of the series, entitled 'Мочит хлебныя семена' (He soaks the grain seeds) (pp.16-17):

> Спокойная весна готовит все плоды,
> Я рано стал вставать принявшись за труды.
> Снес курицу сперва, на жертву обещал
> Чтоб хлебной урожай, весь осенью собрал.
>
> Теперь иду к реке, плетюшку становить;
> Я с неба жду дождя, повлажить, покропить,
> Мне надобны ростки, надежны семена,
> С сохой пойду на луг, в пристойны времена.

> The quiet spring prepares all of the fruits,
> I began to rise early, having set to work.
> First I took a hen; I promised it as a sacrifice
> So that I might gather the grain harvest all autumn.

> Now I go to the river, to place the stalk;
> And I await rain from heaven, to moisten, to sprinkle
> My necessary shoots, trustworthy seeds,
> I will go with the plough to the meadow at the proper time.

Some of the poems deal with more technical aspects of the peasants' work. These are supplied with numerous footnotes by Leontiev, who explains the meaning of Chinese terms and sometimes refers the reader to the prose descriptions of the first half of the book.

From a stylistic point of view Leontiev's verse translations are perhaps less effective than his so-called 'prose' translation of the *Chinese ABC book*. The latter is especially pleasing because of the subtlety of its stylistic devices; in contrast, the very regular metrical patterns, combined with the obvious rhyming schemes of the small poems of the *Information* tend to produce a rather sing-song effect in Russian. It must be admitted, however, that Leontiev's task was a difficult one – to translate into poetry the technical descriptions of various processes, the terminology for which was often lacking in Russian. If Leontiev's poems are somewhat weak from an artistic point of view, they nevertheless provided Russian readers with a large number of authentic samples of Chinese verse, and a unique series of glimpses into Chinese peasant life. (See Appendix for other selections.)[58]

---

[58] Another original work of Chinese belles-lettres available to Russian readers was

The realistic touches which embellished the Russian literary portrait of China were provided not only by original Chinese poetry, but also by the incidental allusions of Russian poets to their neighbour in the East. These poetic references dealt with the contacts Russia had with China and with the manifestations of Russian *chinoiserie* in art and architecture. The well-known satirist, Antiokh Kantemir, for instance, touched upon the trade relations of the two countries. Describing a wealthy nobleman as he began his day, Kantemir showed the protagonist of the poem awaiting the 'пойло, что шлет Индия иль везут с Китая' (the drink that India sends or which they bring from China).[59] Mikhail Lomonosov, the well-known scientist and poet, in his didactic poem 'Письмо о пользе стекла' (1752) (Letter on the use of glass), makes a somewhat technical reference to Chinese porcelain-making. Lomonosov relates that the 'ingenious Chinese' devised a way of making vessels out of pure clay instead of glass. He states:

> Огромность тяжкую плода лишенных гор
> Художеством своим преобратив в Фарфор,
> Красой его к себе народы привлекают,
> Что, плавая, морей свирепость презирают,

> Having transformed into Porcelain with their artistry
> The heavy enormity of the fruit of emptied hills,
> They attract to themselves, with its beauty,
> Peoples who sail there, despising the fierceness of the seas,[60]

Lomonosov adds that it is in fact glass, which through the glazing process renders this porcelain non-porous and strong, and makes possible a unique kind of decoration. He describes the ornamentation of porcelain, a delight to the eye, in this way (p.511):

> Сады, гульбы, пиры и все, что есть прекрасно,
> Стекло являет нам приятно, чисто, ясно.

> Gardens, diversions, feasts and everything beautiful,
> Glass reveals to us agreeably, purely, clearly.

Gavriil Derzhavin too mentions 'precious Chinese porcelain', including it among

contained in the book *Тшуанг-Тзе и Тиена, или Открытая неверность повесть китайская, с приобщением трех повестей из книги, называемой Превраты щастия* (Chuang Tzu and Tiena (?) or open infidelity, a Chinese story, with three stories from the book, Reversals of fortune), trans. from the French by A. V. K. P. A.: P. Tr. P. P. V. (St Petersburg 1785). See Skachkov, 'History of the study of China in Russia', p.179. This Chinese work, which I have been unable to locate in Russian, French or any other translation, is in all likelihood, an anecdote relating to the Taoist philosopher, Chuang Tzu, who lived in the fourth century B.C.

[59] Antiokh Kantemir, 'Сатира II. На зависть и гордость дворян злонравных. Филарет и Евгений' (Satire II. On the envy and pride of wicked nobles. Filaret and Evgenii.) *Поэты XVIII века, Библиотека поэта, Малая серия* (Poets of the eighteenth century, The Poet's library, Little series), 3rd ed. (Leningrad 1958), i.137-50 at p.142. The satire was written in 1729 but was not published in Russia until 1762.

[60] M. V. Lomonosov, 'Письмо о пользе стекла', *Полное собрание сочинений* (Complete works), viii (Moscow, Leningrad 1959), pp.508-522, at p.511.

the luxuries to be found at the opulent banquets described in his ode 'К первому соседу' (1780) (To the first neighbour).[61]

The empress Catherine the Great, who as a writer as well as a ruler was very much concerned with China, has already been shown to have used the Middle Kingdom in her own artistic works, *The Tale of Prince Fevei* and 'Sentences chinoises', and also to have provided inspiration for Sushkova's poem, 'The Letter of a Chinese'. Catherine's attitude toward her eastern neighbour was not, however, one of unalloyed admiration. While attracted by Western European *chinoiserie*, the tsarina had at the same time to deal with the political reality of an expanding empire at her eastern border. Consequently her writings and remarks about this empire ranged from praise to humour to outright antagonism.

The empress, who frequently mentioned China in her correspondence with Voltaire, Grimm, and the prince de Ligne, sometimes took a very lighthearted approach to the ruler of her neighbouring state. In a letter to the prince de Ligne she once referred to the emperor as 'mon voisin chinois aux petits yeux'.[62] On another occasion she composed the following verse about the monarch:

> Le roi de la Chi-i-i-i-ne
> Quand il a bien bu-u-u-u-u
> Fait une plaisante mi-i-i-ne.[63]

The empress did not, however, take lightly a reference to Ch'ien-lung's own poetic gifts, made in a letter to her by Voltaire. Catherine replied to her French correspondent: 'Si le destin veut que près de Vous j'aye un rival, au nom de la Vierge Marie, que ce ne soit point ce Roy de la Chine contre qui j'ai une dents.'[64] (Voltaire attempted to soothe the empress's ruffled feelings with the reply: 'En vérité, Madame, vous voilà la première personne de l'univers sans contredit; je n'en excepte pas vôtre voisin Kien-long, tout poète qu'il est.')[65]

Catherine's 'old grudge' toward her neighbouring monarch at times took the form of aggressive political posturing. The poet Gavriil Derzhavin states in his *Memoirs* that Catherine once told him: 'I shall not die until I have ejected the Turks from Europe, have suppressed the pride of China, and have established trade with India.'[66] It was these sentiments that inspired Derzhavin to compose the following militant lines:

> Доступим мира мы средины,
> С Гангеса злато соберем,
> Гордыню усмирим Китая,

[61] Gavriil Derzhavin, 'К первому соседу', *Сочинения* (Works), i (St Petersburg 1864), pp.102-06 at p.103.

[62] Letter of 6 November 1790 to the prince de Ligne, *Les Lettres de Catherine II au prince de Ligne*, ed. la princesse Charles de Ligne (Bruxelles, Paris 1924), p.134.

[63] Quoted in Alekseev, pp.115-16. The footnote to *Сборник русскаго историческаго общества* (Collection of the Russian Historical Society) 17, pp.188-463; 13, pp.349-50; 125 appears garbled, and I have been unable to locate the passage cited.

[64] Catherine II, Best.D16999.

[65] Best.D17283.

[66] Gavriil Derzhavin, *Записки* (Notes) in *Сочинения* (Works), vi (St Petersburg 1871), pp.405-842 at p.632.

Как кедр наш корень утверждая ...[67]

We will gain access to the centre of the world,
We will gather gold from the Ganges,
We will suppress the arrogance of China,
Like the cedar establishing our root ...

Lomonosov too had expressed this theme in his 'Ода ... императору Петру Феодоровичу' (Ode to the emperor Peter Feodorovich), written in 1761 upon the accession to the throne of Catherine's husband, Peter III. In the poem Lomonosov proposes to the new tsar an expansionistic policy in the East. He suggests that the frozen northern seas will open for Peter, providing a 'путь в восток' (route to the East), and he continues:

Чтоб Хины, Инды, и Яппоны
Подверглись под Твои законы.[68]

So that the Chinese, Indians and Japanese
May become subject to Your laws.

Russian political designs on the Far East are reflected again in a work by Derzhavin, 'На взятие Измаила' (The Taking of Izmaila) (1790), in which the poet, perhaps envisaging the future conquest of China, apostrophises Russia with these words:

Лишь ты, простря твои победы,
Умел щедроты расточать;
Поляк, Турк, Перс, Прусс, Хин и Шведы
Тому примеры могут дать.
На тех ты зришь спокойно стены,
Тем паки отдал грады пленны;[69]

Only you, viewing your victories,
Could lavish generosity;
The Pole, Turk, Persian, Prussian, Chinese and Swedes
Can give examples of this.
You look calmly upon their walls,
You gave back to them conquered cities.

But in spite of the realities of politics, Russian fascination with *chinoiserie* persisted. It was Derzhavin who preserved for posterity a poetic glimpse of the result of the empress Catherine's love of Chinese art and architecture, the Chinese buildings which she had constructed on the grounds of the palace at Tsarskoe Selo. Actually Catherine II was not the first Russian monarch who, emulating the sovereigns of Western Europe, had rooms and even entire palaces constructed and decorated in Chinese style. Early in the century a Chinese room, resembling the Porzellankammer in Berlin's Charlottenburg Palace, was constructed in 'Monplaisir' at the palace of Peterhof outside St Petersburg.

---

[67] Quoted in Alekseev, p.117, who cites Derzhavin, Ak. izd. i.430. I have been unable to locate the passage cited.

[68] M. V. Lomonosov, 'Ода [...] Императору Петру Феодоровичу', *Полное собрание сочинении* (Complete works), viii (Moscow, Leningrad 1959), pp.751-60, at p.757.

[69] Derzhavin, 'На взятие Измаила', *Works*, i (1864), pp.341-61 at p.353.

Catherine the Great followed this example, introducing Chinese decor designed by the Italian architect A. Rinaldi into the palace at Oranienbaum (now called Lomonosov), another of the royal residences near Petersburg. Later, in the 1760s, she ordered the construction there of a larger elaborately decorated Chinese palace. D. Barozzi of Bologna was commissioned to paint on the ceiling of its ornate 'Большой китайский кабинет' (Great Chinese room) the 'Китайская свадьба' (The Chinese wedding). (This palace can still be visited today.)[70]

Tsarskoe Selo (now called Pushkin), Catherine the Great's favourite palace, was the third imperial residence to be graced with Western European *chinoiserie*. In 1777 work was begun under the direction of the architect V. I. Neelov on the construction of a three-storey Chinese theatre or opera house. This building was evidently the 'new theatre' in which the comic opera *The Chinese idol* was first staged in 1779. Also in the 1770s the Scottish architect Charles Cameron designed for the grounds of the palace an entire 'Chinese village', which was to consist of a number of little houses surrounding a pagoda. The project, which was drawn up in accordance with the descriptions by sir William Chambers of Chinese architecture and landscape design, was not completed until the nineteenth century, and it differed considerably from the original plan. But lithographs of the grounds made in 1820 show numerous little summer houses and pavilions in Chinese style, arranged among attractive cascades and ponds. Some of these Chinese buildings have been restored and can still be seen. Among them are Neelov's 'Большой каприз' (Great caprice) – an artificial hill surmounted by an exquisite Chinese pavilion, and the so-called 'Chinese or squeaking summer house' ('Китайская, или скрипучая беседка').[71]

These are the buildings that Derzhavin memorialised in his poem 'Развалины' (The Ruins) (1797). During the reign of Catherine the Great's son, Pavel I, Tsarskoe Selo had been allowed to fall into ruin. In the poem Derzhavin provides an allegorical depiction of the palace and its grounds, lamenting their deserted state. Describing the partly empty park, Derzhavin writes:

> Здесь был театр, а тут качели,
> Тут азиатских домик нег;
> Тут на Парнассе Музы пели;
> Тут звери жили для утех;[72]

> Here was the theatre, and here the swing,
> Here the little house of Asiatic pleasures;

---

[70] Hugh Honour in *Chinoiserie: the vision of Cathay*, p.117, states that the room in Monplaisir was made for Catherine I (1725-1727); Tamara Talbot Rice in 'The conflux of influences in eighteenth-century Russian art and architecture: a journey from the spiritual to the realistic', *The Eighteenth century in Russia*, ed. J. G. Garrard (Oxford 1973), pp.267-99 at p.282, states that a room at Monplaisir, as well as one perhaps at the Summer Palace, was panelled in red Chinese lacquer by Peter the Great (1682-1725); V. Shvarts, *Пригороды Ленинграда* (The Suburbs of Leningrad) (Leningrad 1961), pp.95-119.

[71] Alekseev, pp.118-20; Shvarts, pp.151-52; see also A. Ikonnikov, *Китайский театр и ‹китайщина› в Детском селе* (The Chinese theatre and chinoiserie at Detskoe Selo) (Moscow, Leningrad 1931).

[72] Derzhavin, 'Развалины', *Works*, ii (1865), pp.92-101 at pp.96-97.

Here on Parnasse the Muses sang,
Here lived the entertaining animals.

The 'house of Asiatic pleasures' refers to a Chinese summer house, also known as the 'Turkish kiosk', while 'Parnasse' was the name given to a little hill opposite the theatre. A giant swing, a menagerie and other amusements had been part of the park.[73]

A footnote to the history of eighteenth-century *chinoiserie* in Russia appears in the poetry of the early part of the nineteenth century. The character of Tsarskoe Selo had changed by this time, but its elegance continued to inspire poetic descriptions. The palace figured in the work of V. A. Zhukovskii, and also in the poetry of A. S. Pushkin, the greatest of all Russian poets. As a boy Pushkin attended a lyceum at Tsarskoe Selo, and he was very fond of the park and the surroundings. The lyric 'Надпись к беседке' (Inscription to a summer house) (1814-1816), written during his lyceum days, is thought to refer to Neelov's pavilion, the 'Great caprice'.[74] The young poet wrote:

> С благоговейною душой
> Приближься, путник молодой,
> Любви к пустынному приюту.
> Здесь ею счастлив был я раз –
> В восторге пламенном погас,
> И время самое для нас
> Остановилось на минуту.[75]

> With a respectful heart
> Approach, young traveller,
> The deserted shelter of love.
> Here once I was happy with her –
> Expired in ardent rapture,
> And time itself
> Stood still for us for a moment.

The influence of the eighteenth-century *chinoiserie* of Tsarskoe Selo on the poetry of Pushkin has been traced in the valuable chapter 'Pushkin and China' in the work by M. P. Alekseev cited above.

The brief but illuminating references to China in the work of the eighteenth-century Russian poets add significant realistic touches to the fictionalised image of China in Russian literature. In these poetic allusions the duality of approach to the Celestial Empire which existed in Russia during this period can be detected. While the poetic descriptions of *chinoiserie* at Tsarskoe Selo reveal Russia's admiration of the fanciful China – the land of the sage, of magic and intrigue, Derzhavin's poetic formulation of Catherine's antagonistic feelings

[73] Derzhavin, ii.96. Huge swings, similar to Ferris wheels, were also to be found at eighteenth-century Russian fairs. See the article by Malcolm Burgess, 'Fairs and entertainers in 18th-century Russia', *Slavonic and East European review* 38 (1959), pp.95-113 at p.97. Burgess also mentions a popular fair display called 'The Chinese shades', a shadow-show presenting landscapes, storms and realistic puppet performances (p.110).

[74] Alekseev, p.121.

[75] Aleksandr Sergeevich Pushkin, *Полное собрание сочинений* (Complete works), i (Moscow, Leningrad 1937), p.289.

toward her political neighbour mirror the hostility which also emerged in nonfiction describing the Middle Kingdom to Russian readers. But neither the writers nor contemporary critics seem to have remarked upon this fact, or to have made comparisons between the two attitudes. The predominant Western European, particularly the French fashion of idealising China was generally emulated and in any case not questioned. In fact, among all of the belletristic works about China that I have found in the literature of eighteenth-century Russia – including those by Russian, Western European, and Chinese writers, only the two poems by Derzhavin, the lines by Lomonosov, and the views expressed in *The Farther adventures of Robinson Crusoe* reflect unfavourably on the Middle Kingdom. In general, these, as part of the small group of works that are realistic in intent, along with the few fairy-tale creations, blend into and are overshadowed by the main group of belletristic works, the portrayals of the Chinese Sage, to produce an image of China as the unique happy land where wisdom and virtue prevail.

5. China and the intellectuals

'If there is, or ever was, any government in the world
that deserved to be noticed by the philosopher and known
by the minister, it is without doubt the government of
the vast Chinese Empire.'
  О китайском правлении. Взято из ‹Энциклопедии›
(The Chinese Government. Taken from the *Encyclopédie*
  [of Diderot and d'Alembert]) (Moscow 1789)[1]

WHILE the missionaries, diplomats and other travellers who had actually journeyed to China penned their first-hand accounts about remote Cathay, and
writers of oriental tales, inspired by the travellers (as well as by each other),
spun their exotic fabrications about the utopia to the east, two other groups of
writers in Russia, as in Western Europe, became intensely involved with the
Middle Kingdom. One of these was made up of the true scholars, who dealt
with China as a historical and political entity, and who approached their subject
as specialists in the areas of the Chinese language, and of history, economics
and political relations. The other group was composed of the *philosophes*, that is,
those intellectuals who were primarily concerned with ideas and their history,
who came to hold very decided opinions about China and who frequently used
their interpretations of the Middle Kingdom to propagate their own philosophic
views.

1. The scholars

Among the Russian scholarly works, and those translated into Russian from
French and other languages, there were many of sufficiently general interest to
appeal to the reading public. Certain translations, for instance, by the Russian
sinologists, as well as a number of the scholarly writings of the French
missionaries, and various periodical articles by China specialists, all of which
included considerable human interest material, must have influenced public
opinion about Russia's eastern neighbour. A large proportion of the periodical
articles concerned Chinese economic and trade policies, and political and
diplomatic affairs. A limited number of other articles, some of them quite
lengthy, dealt with Chinese art, crafts, medicine and science, language and
various aspects of Chinese social life.[2]

Many of the other scholarly works, however, were presumably not of concern
or were not easily accessible to non-specialists. Several of the Russian studies,
for instance, appeared only in manuscript form; some were included in lengthy

[1] *О китайском правлении. Взято из Энциклопедии, сочиненной собранием ученых
мужей* (On the Chinese government. Taken from the *Encyclopédie* composed by a society
of learned men [by Diderot and d'Alembert]), trans. Ivan Zhdanovskii (Moscow 1789),
p. A.
[2] Articles cited in P. E. Skachkov, *Bibliography of China*. See also 'Китай' (China) in A.
N. Neustroev, *Index to Russian periodicals and collections for 1703 to 1802*.

multi-volume works on broad subjects such as Russian trade or Siberian history, and many took up rather technical issues. The influence of this body of material on the Russian image of China can be assumed to have been less significant that that of the more colourful travel narratives or the entertaining fiction, but a brief survey of the scholarly work that was being done is important to show the depth of Russian interest in the Middle Kingdom.

A translation of an early Western European geographic work, appearing at a time when Russian secular publishing was indeed limited, contains what was possibly the first information on China to be printed in Russia. The *География или краткое земнаго Круга описание* (Geography or short description of the Earth) (Moscow 1710), which is thought to be a reworking of the seventeenth-century Dutch atlas of Van Keulen, included China among the various countries for which brief factual discussions were provided.[3]

Translations of Chinese materials and of Western European sinological studies began to appear in Russia some thirty years later. Perhaps the earliest was a translation in 1740 of a work by the emperor Yung-cheng, 'Духовная, или завещательное письмо' (Last will or testamentary letter).[4] A number of the important studies made by the French missionaries to China were to follow. These included Gerbillon's work on the 'Grand Tartary', which appeared in 1744; the abridged version of the first two volumes of Du Halde's monumental work; and the first three volumes and the twelfth volume (containing the life of Confucius) of Amiot's highly influential *Mémoires concernant les Chinois*. These have been cited earlier in various connections.[5] Also discussed were Bouvet's life of K'ang-hsi,[6] extracts from Couplet's *Confucius Sinarum philosophus*[7] and an excerpt from Grosier's *Description générale de la Chine*.[8]

[3] *География или краткое земнаго круга описание* (Geography or short description of the Earth) (Moscow 1710); Van Keulen, *De groote Nieuwe vermeerdende Zee-Atlas* (Amsterdam 1697). See T. A. Bykova, M. M. Gurevich, and others, *Описание изданий напечатанных при Петре I. Сводный каталог. I. Описание изданий гражданской печати 1708 – январь 1725г.* (Description of publications printed during the reign of Peter I. Union catalogue. i. Description of publications of the secular press 1708 – January 1725) (Moscow, Leningrad 1955), pp.108-10.

[4] 'Духовная, или завещательное письмо китайскаго богдыхана Юншинг' (Last will or testamentary letter of the Chinese emperor Yung-cheng), *Календарь* (Calendar) (1740), pp.80-88.

[5] Gerbillon (Jean François Gerbillon), 'Описание и известие о Великой Татарии' (Description and news of the Grand Tartary), *Календарь* (Calendar) (1744), pp.76-92; *Собрание сочинений, выбранных из месяцословов* (Collection of compositions selected from calendars) 1 (1785), pp.227-50. Commentary by G. F. Müller; Diu Gal'd (Jean Baptiste Du Halde), *Description géographique*; *Mémoires*. Amio (Joseph Marie Amiot), *Vie de Koung-tsée*.

[6] Joachim Bouvet, 'Histoire de l'empereur de la Chine', trans. in *The Present condition of the Muscovite empire* (London 1699). The Russian translation is in F. O. Tumanskii, *Собрание разных записок и сочинений ... о жизни ... Петра Великаго* (Collection of various notes and works on the life of Peter the Great) (St Petersburg 1787-1788), i (1787).

[7] *Confucius sinarum philosophus, sive scientia sinensis latine exposita. Studio et opera Prosperi Intorcetta*, ed. Philippe Couplet (Paris 1687); Russian translation: *Описание жизни Конфуция, китайских философов начальника* (Description of the life of Confucius, the leading Chinese philosopher), corrected by Shcheglov (Moscow 1780).

[8] Groz'er (Jean Baptiste Grosier), 'Описание китайских войск и военного их порядка' (Description of the armed forces of the Chinese and their military organisation), *New monthly compositions* 28 (Oct. 1788), pp.47-55.

Among the other French contributors to Russia's knowledge of China was the geographer Louis Lacroix. A chapter of his important *Géographie moderne* (1747) was translated as *Географическое описание Азии* (Geographic description of Asia) and published in Moscow in 1789.[9] The well-known historical study by Joseph Jouve, *Histoire de la conquête de la Chine par les Tartares mancheoux* (1754), appeared in Russian as *История о завоевании Китая манжурскими татарами* in 1788.[10] Also known to Russian readers was Claude Pastoret's *Зороастр, Конфуций и Магомет* (*Zoroastre, Confucius et Mahomet comparés comme sectaires, législateurs et moralistes*, 1787), a truly scholarly study in comparative religion.[11]

German scholarship was represented by a work of Johann Gotthelf Stritter, entitled in Russian translation *Историческое и географическое описание города Пекина* (Historical and geographic description of the City of Peking), which appeared in a Russian periodical in 1781 and was reprinted in 1790.[12]

Russian scholars, like their Western European counterparts, provided sophisticated, serious studies of Chinese subjects (their publications, incidentally, far outnumbering the tendentious works of the Russian *philosophes*). Unlike the Western European scholarly works about China, which generally dealt with that nation as an isolated entity, these Russian studies placed particular emphasis on the political, cultural and economic relations between China and Russia; while Western scholarship consisted to a large extent of Jesuit writings and books based upon them, Russian specialists more often based their studies on their own experiences or on the oral or written reports (sometimes those found in official archives) of governmental employees who had had a personal role in these Sino-Russian relations.

One of the earliest scholarly studies of China presented by a Russian specialist was Nikolai Spafarii's *Описание первые части вселенныя, именуемой Азии, в ней же состоит Китайское государство* (Description of the first part of the Universe called Asia, in which is located the Chinese State),[13] the manuscript of which Spafarii presented to the Russian government after his return from his diplomatic embassy to China in the late 1670s. Spafarii's *Description* was not published until 1910, but it is known to have circulated widely in manuscript

[9] Lakrua (Louis Antoine Nicolle de Lacroix), *Географическое описание Азии, с присовокуплением к главным местам оныя политической и естественной истории* (A geographic description of Asia with a supplement of political and natural history for its main places) (Moscow 1789).

[10] Zhuv (Joseph Jouve), *История о завоевании Китая манжурскими татарами* (History of the conquest of China by the Manchurian Tatars) (Moscow 1788).

[11] Pastore (Claude Emanuel Joseph Pierre Pastoret), *Зороастр, Конфуций и Магомет, сравненные как основатели вер, законодатели и нравоучители, с приобщением табелей их догматов, законов и нравственности* (Moscow 1793). Guy, pp.378-80.

[12] Shtritter (Johann Gotthelf Stritter), 'Историческое и географическое описание г. Пекина', *Исторический и географический месяцослов* (Historical and geographic monthly) 20 (1781), pp.151-87; *Собрание сочинений выбранных из месяцословов* (Collection of compositions selected from calendars) 5 (1790), pp.1-33.

[13] N. G. Spafarii, *Описание первые части вселенныя, именуемой Азии, в ней же состоит Китайское государство с прочими его городы и провинции* (Kazan' 1910).

form. More than 40 copies from the seventeenth and eighteenth centuries have been found.[14] The work discusses Chinese geography, including the routes from Russia to China, governmental organisation and various aspects of social life in China. Spafarii's work is not, however, entirely original. J. F. Baddeley in his *Russia, Mongolia, China* relates his discovery that the *Description* is, with a few exceptions, a translation of the Italian Jesuit Martino Martini's monumental *Novus atlas sinensis*, published in Latin in 1655. Martini's work, the first scientific atlas of China, later appeared in many translations and editions. Spafarii, or perhaps another person, changed Martini's text so that there was nothing to indicate that the author was a Jesuit missionary, instead of a Russian official. One manuscript copy of the work does, however, acknowledge Spafarii's indebtedness to previous accounts of China. (Martini's *De bello tartarico historia* (1654) was also translated by Spafarii.)[15]

Spafarii's book was not only of importance to Russian readers, but was also used by the French Jesuit Philippe Avril, who travelled to Moscow in 1685 to request permission of the Russian government to follow the overland route through Siberia to China. Avril's request was refused, but he was permitted to study materials from the Moscow Chancellery concerning the various routes from Russia to China. In his *Voyages en divers états d'Europe et d'Asie entrepris pour découvrir un nouveau chemin à la Chine* (Paris 1692) Avril presents descriptions which follow closely those in Spafarii's work.[16]

Another seventeenth-century manuscript work on China was written by Iurii Krizhanich, the Croatian panslavist who spent many years in Russia. Krizhanich wrote in Latin a work later translated into Russian as 'Повествование о Сибири' (Report on Siberia) and a supplement devoted to China in which he discussed the establishment of Sino-Russian trade.[17] In his writings Krizhanich opposed the militant ideas which many Moscovites entertained against China after Fedor Baikov's unsuccessful mission to Peking in 1654.[18]

A seventeenth-century descriptive work about China which was eventually

[14] Iu. V. Arsen'ev, 'О происхождении ‹Сказания о великой реке Амуре›' (On the origin of the 'Tale of the Great River Amur'), *Известия Русского географического общества* (News of the Imperial Russian Geographic Society) 18, issue 4 (1882), pp.245-54 at p.246; P. E. Skachkov, *Outline of the history of Russian sinology*, p.25.

[15] John Frederick Baddeley, *Russia, Mongolia, China* (London 1919), ii.208-12.

[16] V. M. Florinskii, Appendix to Nikolai Bantysh-Kamenskii, *Дипломатическое собрание дел между Российским и Китайским государствами с 1619 по 1792-й год* (Diplomatic collection of affairs between the Russian and Chinese States from 1619 to 1792) (Kazan 1882), pp.513-44, at p.530.

[17] Iurii Krizhanich, 'Повествование о Сибири', *Сибирский вестник* (Siberian herald) 17 (1822), pp.1-24, 25-46, 47-68; 18 (1822), pp.69-92. The supplement is not contained in this translation, and I have been unable to locate it. See Baddeley, ii.212-13.

[18] V. E. Val'denberg (Waldenberg), *Государственные идеи Крижанича* (Krizhanich's ideas about the State) (St Petersburg 1912), p.313. Krizhanich was exiled by the Russian tsar Alexei Mikhailovich to Siberia, and he was there when Nikolai Spafarii travelled through Siberia on his diplomatic mission to China. According to Krizhanich's account, the exile helped Spafarii prepare for his journey, and allowed the diplomat to copy his book about China (probably the supplement to the 'Report on Siberia'). Baddeley, ii.212-13.

published in the late eighteenth century was the *Ведомость о китайском государстве* (Information about the Chinese government). The report, written in the late 1660s, evidently by the Siberian governor (voevoda) Petr Ivanovich Godunov and his associates, contained information gathered by Russian merchants and government officials. Although the material is presented in an unsophisticated style similar to that of the seventeenth-century Russian diplomats, and arranged in a haphazard manner, the work is nevertheless an encyclopedia dealing with many facets of Chinese life. Practical matters such as government, economics and the military are given particular coverage. At least seven manuscript copies of the *Information* are known to have circulated in the seventeenth century, and in 1791 it was published by G. F. Müller in the *Продолжение Древней российской вивлиофики* (Continuation of the Old Russian library.)[19]

Throughout the eighteenth century many outstanding historians in Russia, particularly those concerned with Siberia, touched upon China in their writings. One of the most influential of these scholars was the German-born Gerhard Friedrich Müller (1705-1783), mentioned frequently above, who came to Russia in 1725. Müller became a member of the Russian Academy of Sciences as a teacher in the Academy's gymnasium, and continued his research in Russian history. As the editor of *Monthly compositions*, Müller published numerous articles dealing with Russo-Chinese diplomatic relations, for instance, the narrative of the Chinese consul Tulishen, and many articles of his own, such as 'Изъяснение сумнительств находящихся при постановлении границ между Российским и Китайским Государствами 7197 года' (An explanation of the ambiguities involved in the establishment of the boundaries between the Russian and Chinese States in the year 7197 [1689]).[20] Müller's articles were among the few news accounts that Russian periodical readers received concerning the current state of political relations between their own government and that of China. Müller also published in 1750 a long work on Siberian history entitled *Описание Сибирскаго царства* (Description of the Siberian realm) which discussed Russo-Chinese relations.[21]

The well-known Russian scholar Mikhail Lomonosov, a historian as well as a scientist and poet, was also concerned with sinology. In addition to making suggestions about the development of cultural and economic relations with China, Lomonosov was involved in a project of the Academy of Sciences

[19] [Petr Ivanovich Godunov], 'Ведомость о Китайском государстве' (Information about the Chinese government), *Продолжение древней российской вивлиофики* 7 (1791), pp.198-224; P. E. Skachkov, 'Ведомость о китайской земле' (Information about the Land of China), *Страны и народы Востока* (Lands and peoples of the East), Issue 2 (Moscow 1961), pp.206-19, at pp.207-208.

[20] 'Изъяснение сумнительств находящихся при постановлении границ между Российским и Китайским Государствами 7187 года', *Monthly compositions* (April 1757), pp.305-21.

[21] G. F. Müller, *Описание Сибирскаго царства и всех произшедших в нем дел, от начала а особливо от покорения его Российской державе по сии времена* (Description of the Siberian realm and all that has taken place there, from the beginning but especially from its conquest by Russian arms to the present time), Bk. 1, trans. V. Lebedev and I. Golubstov (St Petersburg 1750).

to translate into Russian a lengthy work by contemporary Chinese scholars concerning Chinese history, geography and economics. The original had been brought to Russia from China by a trade caravan in the mid 1750s, and in 1756 the Russian government had asked the Academy to have it translated. The sinologist I. K. Rossokhin began the work and was joined by A. L. Leontiev, who finished the translation in 1782 after Rossokhin's death. Publication, however, was delayed for many years. Eventually, through the efforts of Lomonosov, the plan of several German members of the Academy to have the work printed in abridged form in Germany, rather than in Russia in the longer form prepared by the translator, was foiled, and at last in 1784 the highly significant seventeen-volume *Обстоятельное описание происхождения и состояния маньджурскаго народа и войска, в осми знаменах состоящаго* (Detailed description of the origin and state of the Manchu people and their army, consisting of eight banners) was published in St Petersburg.[22] The undertaking of so lengthy a translation project shows the intensity of the Russian government's interest in China, and also the competence of the Russian sinologists. It is worth noting by way of comparison that Western Europe, which produced so many scholarly works on China during the eighteenth century, had only one translation on general Chinese history during this period, De Mailla's version of the multi-volume *T'ung Chien Kang Mu*.[23]

One of the most valuable (though long unpublished) Russian works about China of the late eighteenth century is the *Дипломатическое собрание дел* (Diplomatic collection of affairs) by the historian Nikolai Bantysh-Kamenskii.[24] This work, cited earlier in connection with the narratives of the Russian missionaries and diplomats, represents a careful compilation of the government archival papers concerning the relations between Russia and China throughout the seventeenth and eighteenth centuries. Although Bantysh-Kamenskii com-

---

[22] *Обстоятельное описание происхождения и состояния маньджурскаго народа и войска, в осми знаменах состоящаго*, trans. I. K. Rossokhin and A. L. Leontiev (St Petersburg 1784); V. L. Chenakal, 'М. В. Ломоносов о странах Востока' (M. V. Lomonosov on the countries of the East), in *Из истории науки и техники в странах Востока: Сборник статей* (From the history of science and technology in the countries of the East: Collection of articles), Issue 2 (Moscow 1961), pp.190-94; R. V. Ovchinnikov, '‹Рапорт› М. В. Ломоносова и других академиков в Сенат о переводе ‹Истории Китайского государства›' (The 'Report' of M. V. Lomonosov and other academicians to the Senate on the translation of the 'History of the Chinese State'), *Исторический архив* (Historical archive) 6 (1961), pp.234-35.

[23] Joseph Anne Marie Moyriac de Mailla, *Histoire générale de la Chine, ou Annales de cet Empire traduites du Tong-Kien-Kang Mou* (Paris 1777-1785). Ilarion Rossokhin deserves the credit for producing the first translation of this work in a European language. His 2,900 page Russian manuscript, finished in the 1750s, was not, however, published by the Russian government. See Skachkov, 'History of the study of China', p.165. De Mailla's French translation served in turn as the basis for the modern work by Cordier, *Histoire générale de la Chine* (Paris 1920). Arnold H. Rowbotham, 'A brief account of the early development of sinology', *Chinese social and political science review* 7, no. 2 (1921-1923), pp.113-38 at pp.133-34.

[24] Nikolai Bantysh-Kamenskii, *Diplomatc collection of affairs between the Russian and the Chinese States from 1619 to 1792*.

pleted his work at the end of the eighteenth century, it was not approved for publication for about a hundred years.

Political relations between Russia and China were also discussed by the German-born historian J. E. Fischer, who utilised documents collected by G. F. Müller for his work. Fischer's book, originally published in German in St Petersburg, was translated into Russian in 1774 as *Сибирская история* (Siberian history). As early as 1756 Fischer had also published an article concerning Chinese titles.[25]

The history of Russo-Chinese trade as it had developed throughout the eighteenth century was covered in considerable detail by M. D. Chulkov in the third volume of his *Историческое описание российской коммерции* (A historical description of Russian commerce) which appeared in 1785.[26] Seven years after the publication of this work an analysis of the merits and problems of the border trade through the city of Kiakhta became the subject of a study entitled *Письмо о китайском торге* (1792) (Letter on the Chinese trade [1792]) by Alexander Radishchev.[27] Radishchev, one of the most outspoken of the Russian *philosophes*, had been exiled to Siberia because of the scathing attack he had made on the Russian government in his *Путешествие, из Петербурга в Москву* (1790) (Journey from Petersburg to Moscow). But unlike the other philosophic opponents of the Russian regime, Radishchev does not seem to have been attracted to Chinese principles.[28] In his *Letter on the Chinese trade* he is strictly concerned with the practicalities of economic policy and not at all with the ideological aspects of either the Russian or the Chinese governmental system.

Sinological scholarship was encouraged by the Russian government in various ways during the eighteenth century. As early as 1725 Peter the Great invited a German sinologist, T. Z. Baier, to continue his scholarly activities in St Petersburg. It was Baier's book *Museum sinicum, in quo sinicae linguae et litteraturae ratio explicatur* (St Petersburg 1730) which was given to the Chinese diplomats who visited Russia in 1732.[29] In 1730 the Russian Academy of Sciences began its acquisition of Chinese books, starting the collection with a group of works which

[25] Fisher (Johann Eberhard Fischer), *Сибирская история с самаго открытия Сибири до завоевания сей земли российским оружием* (Siberian history from the actual discovery of Siberia to the conquest of this land by Russian arms) (St Petersburg 1774); Fisher (Johann Eberhard Fischer), 'Рассуждение о разных именах китайского государства и о ханских титулах' (Discussion of the various names of the Chinese State and imperial titles), *Monthly compositions* (Oct. 1756), pp.311-27.

[26] Mikhail Chulkov, *Историческое описание российской коммерции при всех портах и границах от древних времян до ныне настоящаго и всех преимущественных узаконений* (Historical description of Russian commerce at all ports and borders from early times to the present and of all preferential legislation) (St Petersburg 1781-1788).

[27] Alexander Radishchev, 'Письмо о китайском торге (1792)', *Полное собрание сочинений А. Н. Радищева* (Complete collection of the works of A. N. Radishchev), ed. A. K. Borozdin and others (St Petersburg 1907), ii.201-42.

[28] Allen McConnell, *A Russian philosophe, Alexander Radishchev, 1749-1802* (The Hague 1964), p.128.

[29] T. Z. Baier, *Museum sinicum, in quo sinicae linguae et litteraturae ratio explicatur* (St Petersburg 1730). Baier's work, however, had no influence on the development of Russian sinological studies. See Skachkov, 'History of the study of China' p.163.

Lorents Lange had been commissioned to bring back from Peking.[30] The work by I. Bakmeister, *Опыт о Библиотеке и Кабинете редкостей и истории натуральной Санктпетербургской императорской Академий наук* (1779) (Essay on the Library and the Rare Objects and Natural History Room of the St Petersburg Imperial Academy of Sciences), describing the collections of the library, stated that in 1730 the library's Chinese holdings consisted of 82 books of notes. By about 1775 the collection contained approximately 2800 books of notes. Parts of Rossokhin's private collection were also eventually acquired by the library.[31]

The most successful measure taken by the Russian government to further sinological studies was the inclusion of students in the religious missions sent by the Orthodox Church to Peking. Upon their return to Russia these Peking-trained sinologist-manchurianists provided valuable service to the government. In addition they made highly significant contributions to the scientific study of China as well as to the formation of the popular image of China in Russia. In this respect their role was similar in effect if not in scope to that of the French missionaries who had lived in Peking. The translations provided by these specialists, which gave readers direct insights into Chinese thought and life, enriched many different aspects of the picture of China as it emerged throughout the eighteenth century in Russia; their translations were instrumental in projecting the image of the early Chinese visitors in Russia, in creating the imaginary China of belles-lettres, and, as we will see, in developing the 'philosophic' China of the Russian intellectuals. The translated texts were also of importance to the work of other Russian scholars. Ironically, the sinologists' academic contributions were not fully appreciated by the Russian government, which often failed to give support for their publication.[32]

While Iakinf Bichurin, the head of the ninth religious mission to Peking (1807-1820) is customarily considered the first great Russian sinologist, the important accomplishments of his eighteenth-century predecessors at the Orthodox Mission cannot be denied. The most outstanding among the early Russian sinologists

---

[30] K. I. Shafranovskii and T. K. Shafranovskaia, 'Сведения о китайских книгах в библиотеке Академии Наук в XVIII в.' (Report on Chinese books in the Library of the Academy of Sciences in the eighteenth century), in Akademiia nauk SSSR, Biblioteka (Academy of Sciences of the USSR, Library), *Научные и культурные связи библиотеки А. Н. СССР со странами зарубежного Востока* (Scholarly and cultural ties of the library of the Academy of Sciences of the USSR with foreign countries of the East) (Leningrad, Moscow 1957), pp. 83-93, at p.84.

[31] I. Bakmeister, *Опыт о Библиотеке и Кабинете редкостей и истории натуральной Санктпетербургской императорской Академии наук* (St Petersburg 1779); T. K. Shafranovskaia and K. I. Shafranovskii, 'Приобретение в начале XVIII в. китайских книг российским резидентом в Китае Лоренцом Лангом' (The acquisition, at the start of the 18th century, of Chinese books by the Russian Agent in China, Lorents Lange), in *Lands and peoples of the East* Issue 1 (Moscow 1959), pp.295-301, at p.300.

[32] Eric Widmer, *The Russian ecclesiastical mission in Peking during the eighteenth century*, pp.160-67.

were Ilarion Rossokhin and second to him, Aleksei Leontiev.[33] Rossokhin accompanied the second Orthodox Mission to China in 1729. Upon returning to Russia in 1740 he was appointed to serve at the Academy of Sciences to translate and work with Chinese and Manchu materials, many of which were later used by the historian Müller. Rossokhin translated and annotated over thirty works, but none of these was published during his lifetime. The most important of his translations was the multi-volume *Обстоятельное описание* (Detailed description of the origin and state of the Manchu people), referred to earlier, on which Rossokhin and Leontiev worked together.[34]

Aleksei Leontiev, who began his study of Chinese in Russia with a Chinese teacher, was sent to Peking in 1742 where he became a part of the third religious mission. Upon his return to Russia he was appointed translator at the Ministry of Foreign Affairs, and in 1757 was sent to the Academy of Sciences to assist Rossokhin. The works translated by Leontiev pertained to history, law, travel, moral teachings, and also Chinese philosophy. In addition Leontiev provided Russian versions of two parts of the Chinese classic *Ssu Shu* (The Four books). These were the Chung Yung (Doctrine of the mean) supposedly by a grandson of Confucius, and the Ta Hsüeh (The Great learning). To Leontiev also belongs part of the I Ching (Classic of changes), one of the Five Classics.[35] In an entirely different vein were Leontiev's translations relating to Chinese customs and social life, such as the 'Описание китайской шахматной игры' (Description of the Chinese chess game).[36] Leontiev's translations were accurate, stylistically pleas-

---

[33] For accounts of the early Russian sinologists see Skachkov, *Outline of the history of Russian sinology*, pp.28-88; Eric Widmer, *The Russian ecclesiastical mission*; Skachkov, 'History of the study of China'.

[34] A. V. Strenina, 'У истоков русского и мирового китаеведения (Россохин и Леонтьев и их труд ‹Обстоятельное описание происхождения и состояния маньчжурского народа и войска, в осьми знаменах состоящего›)' (At the sources of Russian and world sinology [Rossokhin and Leontiev and their work 'Detailed description of the origin and state of the Manchu people and their army consisting of eight banners']), *Советская этнография* (Soviet ethnography) 1 (1950), pp.170-77; V. P. Taranovich, 'Иларион Россохин и его труды по китаеведению' (Ilarion Rossokhin and his sinological works), *Советское востоковедение* (Soviet studies of the East) 3 (1945), pp.225-41. *Detailed description*, note 22, above. See Skachkov, 'History of the study of China', pp.164-66; Widmer, pp.160-62.

[35] *Сы шу гей, то есть четыре книги с толкованиями* (Ssu Shu, i.e., the Four books with interpretations), trans. A. Leontiev (St Petersburg 1780-1784). Another Russian version of the *Ta Hsüeh*, translated from the French, had appeared the previous year: 'Та-Гио, или Великая наука' (Ta Hsüeh, or the great learning), trans. D. I. Fonvizin, *Academic news* (1779), part 2, pp.59-101. Leontiev's partial translation of the *I Ching* appeared as an appendix to his translation *Тайцин гурунь и Ухери коли, то есть все законы и установления китайскаго (а ныне манжурскаго) правительства* (Taitsin gurun' i Ukheri koli, or all of the laws and regulations of the Chinese (now Manchu) government), trans. A. Leontiev (St Petersburg 1781-1783); Leontiev's *Депей китаец* (Depei the Chinese), trans. A. Leontiev (St Petersburg 1771), which also appeared as a chapter in his *Китайския мысли* (Chinese thought), trans. A. Leontiev (St Petersburg 1786), a translation of a commentary on the work of Mencius, acquainted Russian readers with another important branch of Confucian thought.

[36] A. Leontiev, *Описание китайской шахматной игры* (St Petersburg 1775).

ing, and his commentary showed a broad knowledge of Chinese life and literature.[37] According to P. E. Skachkov, the compiler of the invaluable bibliography of all Russian works on China that were published between 1730 and 1957, 120 books and articles pertaining to China were published in Russia during the eighteenth century, and of this number twenty books and two articles were contributed by Leontiev. Leontiev's work was also retranslated into French and German. The Russian sinologist was, incidentally, personally acquainted with the French Jesuit Antoine Gaubil, who had been elected a member of the Russian Academy of Sciences in 1739. The two sinologists met several times during Gaubil's visit to St Petersburg.[38]

Another Peking-trained sinologist was Aleksei Agafonov, a member of the sixth religious mission to China. Agafonov's translations of texts presenting a picture of the ideal monarch will be discussed later in connection with the *philosophes*. To him also belongs the *Краткое хронологическое росписание китайских ханов* (A short chronological list of the Chinese emperors), which was published in 1788.[39] Other students attached to the sixth mission were Fedor Baksheev, who compiled a Manchu-Russian dictionary (which, however, was not published), and Aleksei Paryshev, who left numerous unpublished manuscripts. All three of these men served as interpreters for the Russian government after their return from China.[40]

A member of the seventh mission, Anton Vladykin, became a specialist in the Manchu language, publishing several translations and leaving other manuscripts, including a Manchu grammar, a Manchu-Chinese dictionary, and other pedagogical materials which he used in the school founded in 1798 by the Ministry of Foreign Affairs for the teaching of oriental languages. To the student Lipovtsov of the eighth mission belonged a translation of the legal code of the Li-fan-yuan, the Chinese Colonial Office, as well as a Manchu translation of part of the New Testament, which was sold to the British and Foreign Bible Society.[41]

The success of the efforts on the part of the Russian government to train specialists in the Chinese and Manchu languages, and to lay the groundwork for scholarly sinological studies, while not fully appreciated by the government itself, was quite considerable. By the end of the eighteenth century the work of

---

[37] Skachkov, 'History of the study of China'.

[38] *Chinesische Gedanken, nach der von Alexei Leontieff aus der manschurischen Sprache verfertigten russischen Übersetzung. Ins Deutsche Übersetzt* (Weimar 1776; 1778; 1796); *Pensées morales de divers auteurs chinois, recueillies et traduites du latin et du russe [de Leontieff] par Levesque* (Paris 1782); *Chinese thought*, trans. A. Leontiev. See Skachkov 'History of the study of China', pp.167-73.

[39] *Краткое хронологическое росписание китайских ханов; из книги Всеобщаго зерцала, с показанием летощисления китайскаго и римскаго, от начала китайской империи по 1786 год* (A short chronological list of the Chinese emperors from the book, The Universal mirror, with an indication of the Chinese and Roman dates, from the beginning of the Chinese empire to 1786), trans. A. Agafonov (Moscow 1788).

[40] Skachkov, 'History of the study of China', pp.173-74.

[41] Skachkov, 'History of the study of China', pp.174-76; Skachkov, *Outline of the history of Russian sinology*, pp.182-83; John Dudgeon, *Historical sketch of the ecclesiastical, political and commercial relations of Russia with China*, p.46.

the Russian sinologists, combined with the writings of Russian and Western European scholars, provided in Russia a substantial body of factual information about China. The subjects studied by the Russian scholars and the choices made by the Russian translators of Western European sinological works demonstrate Russia's very practical interest in China's geography, her economic and military organisation and her commercial and political relations with Russia. If the influence of many of the China specialists was confined to academic circles, that of the mission-trained Russian sinologists, whose translations from the Chinese and Manchu pertained to so many aspects of life and culture, was undoubtedly more widely felt; both practically and figuratively speaking, these early sinologists became interpreters of the Chinese to the Russian people.

2. The *Philosophes*

Quite different in its intent from the writings of the China scholars was the work of the Russian *philosophes*, and, in translation, that of their French and other Western European counterparts. These moulders of ideas, while pursuing their own goals, received much of their inspiration and source material from the publications of the scholars, as well as from the narratives of the seventeenth and eighteenth-century travellers. The literature of travel was of particular importance to the *philosophes*; in fact this genre of literature has been shown to have helped determine many of the distinct philosophic currents of the eighteenth-century Enlightenment in Europe, particularly the cosmopolitanism of that movement, and the willingness to compare social systems and make evaluations from an objective point of view. China, in particular, of all the distant nations that were described by the travellers of this period, had a powerful impact on the development of social, political and philosophic thought.[42]

Throughout Western Europe *philosophes* used the Chinese to illustrate their own ideas and to bolster their own positions in the great controversies of the day. While most of them greatly admired China, others, finding that the Chinese example served to disprove their favourite theories, took violent issue with China's supporters. Often a single factual matter, as presented in the travellers' narratives, was used by these intellectuals to illustrate opposing points of view.

China's influence in Western Europe was particularly great in the area of religious thought. The Chinese concept of religious tolerance, for instance, made a significant contribution to the development of liberal thought. Moreover, the Chinese were used to support the positions of both religious and anti-religious groups. Many of the important descriptions of Chinese religious beliefs had been written by the Jesuits, who, as we have seen, claimed that the religion of the Chinese, since it honoured one Supreme Deity, was not unlike Christianity. The Deists, however, on the basis of these accounts, asserted that the Chinese were in fact adherents of the same 'natural religion' which they themselves professed,

---

[42] Geoffroy Atkinson, *Les Relations de voyages du dix-septième siècle et l'évolution des idées* (Paris [1924]); Arnold H. Rowbotham, 'China and the Age of Enlightenment in Europe', *Chinese social and political science review* 19 (1935-1936), pp.176-201.

a system in which belief in God, based not on revelation but on reason, without the elaborate apparatus of the Church, was the essential point. Meanwhile, the free-thinkers, using the same Jesuit material, claimed that the Chinese were not only not Christian, but were for the most part, atheistic. The fact that they were obviously a very virtuous people proved, according to this group, that religion is completely separable from morality.

Political philosophy in the West also became indebted to travellers' accounts of China; especially significant was the depiction of the Chinese emperor as an ideal 'benevolent despot', the personification of the theory which in France, at least, held the greatest appeal for political reformers. The Chinese judicial system and the examination system for civil servants were likewise given much attention. In economic thought the agrarian orientation of the Chinese economy served as an important source of inspiration for the Western European physiocrats.

In the Russian Enlightenment China's role was similarly influential. The broadening effect of the literature of travel, which underlay the Western European Enlightenment, was absorbed by the intellectual leaders of Russia, who followed and emulated their Western contemporaries, especially the French *philosophes*, adapting their methods to conform to the needs of Russian society.[43] Like the Western Europeans, Russian intellectuals in the last half of the eighteenth century used China in their publications. At the same time, many of the works on China by the French *philosophes*, and a smaller number by their English and German counterparts, were translated into Russian, acquainting Russian readers with at least some of the ideological and literary controversies of Western Europe in which the 'philosophic' China played a part.

The value of the work of the translators, as well as the publishers, who made these Western European writings about China available to Russian readers cannot be overestimated. Not only did these literary specialists keep the Russian public informed of contemporary intellectual developments in Europe, but they were also directly responsible for introducing ideas which, because of the political controls of the time, could not have been openly discussed by Russian writers, but which, in the form of a translation of a work by a foreign writer concerning still another foreign country, could often pass the censor's scrutiny.

The censorship conditions in Russia in the last part of the eighteenth century are of course highly relevant to the history of both the translations of the Western European writings and the original works of the Russian *philosophes*. From the early 1760s through the end of the century, the Russian government became increasingly sensitive about the importation of Western European ideas.[44] In 1763 the empress Catherine II ordered the Academy of Sciences and Moscow

---

[43] François de Labriolle, 'Le *Prosvescenie* russe et les "lumières" en France' (1760-1798)', *Revue des études slaves* 45 (1966), pp.75-92.

[44] The following material is based on the article by I. Aizenshtok, 'Французские писатели в оценках царской цензуры' (French writers in the evaluations of the tsarist censorship), *Литературное наследство* (Literary heritage), vols. xxxiii-xxxiv (Moscow 1939), pp.769-858 at pp.770-75. See also P. R. Zaborov, 'Voltaire in Russian translations of the eighteenth century', Appendix II, pp.200-207, and *Union catalogue*, entry 1086, note, p.178.

University to supervise the control of books being imported from abroad, as well as translations of foreign works. As the empress received little co-operation, however, in this effort, her first attempt at censorship had little effect. After the French Revolution the empress took firmer measures for the control of imported and translated literature. For instance, while originally a great admirer of Voltaire, Catherine eventually ordered that the new Russian edition of Voltaire's work not be printed without censoring and without approval of the Moscow Metropolitan, and in 1794 she forbade publication of the 1791 complete edition of Voltaire in Russian. Finally in 1796 censors were set up in various cities to review both imported and domestically printed books. Foreign works found to be in opposition to 'God's law and supreme authority' and those which were thought likely to corrupt morals were to be burned.[45] In 1798 the importation of foreign books was further limited by the emperor Pavel I, who then in 1800 forbade their importation altogether. In spite of these restrictions Western European ideas not approved of by the government continued to enter Russia. Forbidden works were smuggled in and manuscript translations circulated widely. Several works pertaining to China were, as will be seen, in the category of suspect literature.

The major concerns in Russia's translated 'philosophic' literature about China were government and religion. An example of the latter which on Russian soil proved quite controversial was *Les Voyages de Cyrus, avec un discours sur la mythologie* (1727) by Andrew Ramsay, a French writer of Scottish origin. The work, entitled in Russian *Новое Киронаставление,*[46] is actually a study in comparative religion. In the *Discourse* appended to the work Ramsay compares the beliefs contained in the Chinese classics with those of the Persians, Egyptians, Greeks, and Indians, and finds them similar in many respects. In effect the work is a plea for natural religion found among all people, and an attack on revelation and formal religion. Ramsay's work first appeared in Russian translation in 1765. A second, corrected edition was published by Nikolai Novikov in 1785. A significant note to the history of the importation of ideas into Russia in this period is provided by the fact that in 1787, 177 copies of the second edition of Ramsay's work were confiscated in the Moscow book stores.[47] The author's scepticism in regard to formal religion was evidently considered too outspoken by Russian authorities who were zealously seeking to suppress works 'in opposition to God's law and supreme authority'. The faculty of theology in Paris had

---

[45] *Сборник постановлений и распоряжений по цензуре с 1720 по 1862 год* (Collection of decrees and decisions on censorship from 1720 to 1862) (St Petersburg 1862), pp.33-34, cited in I. Aizenshtok, p.774.

[46] E. M. Ramzai (Andrew Michael Ramsay), *Новое Киронаставление, или путешествия Кировы с приложенными разговорами о богословии и баснотворстве древних,* trans. by A. Volkov of *Les Voyages de Cyrus, avec un discours sur la mythologie* (Moscow 1765); Ramzai (Andrew Michael Ramsay), *Новое Киропедия, или Путешествия Кировы, с приложенными разговорами о богословии и баснотворстве древних,* 2nd ed. corr. from the English original (Moscow 1785). Andrew Michael Ramsay, *The Travels of Cyrus. To which is annexed, a discourse upon the theology and mythology of the pagans* (London 1757). See also William W. Appleton, *A cycle of Cathay,* p.49.

[47] Bibliographic note in *Union catalogue,* iii.13, entry 5835.

reacted similarly nearly a century earlier by condemning a work by the Jesuit missionary Lecomte who suggested that the Chinese had preserved a pure worship of God for two thousand years. During the course of the eighteenth century works by the proponents of natural religion, such as the Deists, and by admirers of the 'rational' religions of pagan peoples had, of course, become very numerous in Western Europe. But acceptance of expressions of this point of view was still problematical. In 1721, for instance, Christian Wolff's praise of Confucius, which was interpreted by some as a defence of atheism, had caused him to lose his professorship at the University of Halle.

A work by Wolff's student Georg Bernhard Bilfinger, which also praised the Chinese philosophic system, surprisingly, met a fate in Russia quite different from that of Ramsay's *Les Voyages de Cyrus*. Bilfinger's *Specimen doctrinae veterum Sinarum moralis et politicae* (1724), which especially commended the Chinese for carrying their ethical precepts into their political and social lives, was translated as *Опыт древней китайцов философии о их нравоучении и правлении* (Essay on the ancient philosophy of the Chinese regarding their moral teachings and government) at the Alexander Nevskii Seminary. It was published by the Corps of Foreign Co-Believers (Корпус чужестранных единоверцов) in 1794. Bilfinger's essay was evidently interpreted in Russia not as a demonstration of Chinese atheism but rather as evidence of the closeness of Chinese beliefs to those of Christianity, for with it was published a translation from the Chinese concerning the earliest important record of Christianity in China. This work, a translation by the Russian sinologist Leontiev, entitled *Проповедь о Христе Спасителе в Китайском царстве, изображенная китайским письмом в 781 году по рождестве Христове на камне* (A sermon about Christ the Saviour in the Chinese empire inscribed on stone in Chinese characters in the year 781 A.D.),[48] describes the inscription on a Nestorian monument in China dating from the eighth century and discovered about the year 1625. The stele relates the coming of Nestorian priests to China in the year 635 and their activities in the empire.

A curious work concerned with both the religion and government of the Chinese was written by Nicolas Le Clerc, the French tutor of Catherine's son, crown prince Pavel. Like Fénelon, who almost a century earlier had written *Les Aventures de Télémaque*, showing among other things, his ideas about the ideal state for the benefit of his pupil the duke of Burgundy, Le Clerc composed for his student a long treatise entitled *Yu le Grand et Confucius, histoire chinoise*.[49] The

---

[48] G. B. Bil'finger (Georg Bernhard Bilfinger), *Опыт древней китайцов философии о их нравоучении и правлении, с приложением Проповеди* (Essay on the ancient philosophy of the Chinese regarding their moral teachings and government supplemented with a sermon) (St Petersburg 1794). Leontiev's translation had also appeared as a separate publication: *Проповедь о Христе спасителе в Китайском царстве, изображенная китайским письмом в 781 году по рождестве Христове на камне*, trans. A. Leontiev (St Petersburg 1784); and as 'Переводы с китайского языка. I Перевод с китайскои печатной копии, снятой с наиденного в земле камня' (Translations from the Chinese. I Translation from a Chinese printed copy taken from a stone found in the earth), *Monthly compositions* (Dec. 1764), pp.516-27. See Arnold H. Rowbotham, *Missionary and mandarin*, p.253 and pp.6-7.

[49] Nicolas Gabriel Le Clerc, *Yu le grand et Confucius, histoire chinoise* (Soissons 1769).

book, published in Soissons in 1769, was not in fact translated into Russian but was probably known to Le Clerc's associates in Russia. The stated object of the study is to show the accomplishments both of the outstanding Chinese ruler, Yu, and of Confucius. But in his consideration of Chinese history and Confucian philosophy, Le Clerc intermingles both his own ideas, such as a plan for setting up model educational institutions for young people, and certain theories then current in Europe, particularly those of the physiocrats. He even ascribes some of these contemporary notions to Confucius. To encourage Pavel to modernise Russia, for instance, he makes Confucius a 'physician' who is familiar with the experimental sciences.[50] To all of this he adds advice to the prince in regard to the duties he will have when he becomes tsar. The royal tutor also makes some digressions on Russian history. In view of Le Clerc's position, it is not surprising that he praises the accomplishments of Catherine the Great and notes that while the power of the Russian rulers is absolute, it is just (Le Clerc, p.436).

Among the Western European intellectuals who were intensely concerned with China, the best known to eighteenth-century Russians was Voltaire.[51] Russian readers, as has been shown, were familiar with a number of Voltaire's belletristic works in which China was used as a background, for instance, *L'Orphelin de la Chine*, in which Voltaire argued for the salutary effect on society of the development of the arts and sciences. They also knew several of his oriental tales. The portrait of the enlightened monarch as presented in *La Princesse de Babylone*, the concept of religious toleration seen briefly in *Zadig*, and incidental and implied praise for the natural religion of Confucius in the *Henriade* and the *Poème sur la loi naturelle* are examples of the philosophic convictions which Voltaire embedded in his belletristic works concerning China.

Several of Voltaire's more strictly philosophic writings relating to China were also translated into Russian. Here Chinese religion and government were of special concern. In the *Nouveau plan d'une histoire de l'esprit humain* (1745), which later became part of the *Essai sur les mœurs*, Voltaire praised the great antiquity of the Chinese nation, whose laws, manners and language were so durable as to have remained unchanged for four thousand years. The rational religious thought of Confucius, and various policies of the government are also commended. This work, entitled in Russian translation *Новое расположение истории человеческаго разума*, was published by Nikolai Novikov, one of the leaders of the Russian Enlightenment, in 1775.[52] Of this work more will be said shortly.

Voltaire's insistence on the Chinese emperor as an example of a benevolent monarch, and his praise of Chinese religious toleration appear again in the *Relation du bannissement des jésuites de la Chine* ('L'Empereur de la Chine et le frère

---

[50] See Lewis A. Maverick, *China a model for Europe* (San Antonio, Texas 1946), pp.59-60, and René Etiemble, 'De la pensée chinoise aux "philosophes" français', *Revue de littérature comparée* 30 (1956), pp.465-78 at p.468.

[51] For discussions of Voltaire's views on China see Basil Guy, *The French image of China before and after Voltaire*; Arnold Rowbotham, 'Voltaire sinophile', *PMLA* 47 (1932), pp.1050-65, and A. O. Aldridge, 'Voltaire and the cult of China', *Tamkang review* 2, no. 2, and 3, no. 1 (Oct. 1971 - April 1972), pp.25-49.

[52] V[oltaire], *Новое расположение истории человеческаго разума* (St Petersburg 1775).

Rigolet') (1768). The anti-clerical sentiments expressed in the work made it suspect, if not actually on the list of works forbidden to be imported or published in Russia. It appeared in a manuscript translation entitled *Разговор Иокт-шина, китайского императора, с иезуитом Риголетом* during the second half of the eighteenth century.[53] Voltaire portrays the Jesuit missionaries in China in a highly uncomplimentary way, and has the emperor Yung-cheng order them out of his kingdom with these words: 'Je suis tolérant, et je vous chasse tous, parce que vous êtes intolérants' (M.xxvii.16).

While Russian readers did not have available to them all of Voltaire's philosophic works praising Chinese society, they were at least acquainted with the points which Voltaire the sinophile stressed most. They were equally familiar with the opposing viewpoints on China, and especially on her government and society, expressed by Voltaire's philosophical adversary, Jean-Jacques Rousseau. In his *Discours sur les sciences et les arts* (1750) (first translated into Russian in 1768 as *Рассуждение, удостоенное награждения от Академии Дижонской в 1750 году*),[54] Rousseau took the position that if the development of the sciences and arts does indeed refine the mores of a society, the Chinese would theoretically be 'wise, free and unconquerable'. Instead, Rousseau implies, they are slaves and wretched people.[55]

A few years later Rousseau modified his stand somewhat, and in the article 'Economie (morale et politique)', which he contributed to Diderot's *Encyclopédie*, he praised the Chinese for such things as their method of solving differences between the people and government officials, and for certain aspects of their tax system. This article was one of many extracts from the *Encyclopédie* which became available in Russian translation. It first appeared in 1767 in a three-volume work entitled *Переводы из Энциклопедии* (Translations from the *Encyclopédie*),

[53] Manuscript cited in P. R. Zaborov, 'Voltaire in Russian translations of the eighteenth century'. See also Iu. Ia. Kogan, 'Из истории распространения антихристианских памфлетов Вол'тера в России в XVIII веке' (From the history of the distribution of anti-Christian pamphlets of Voltaire in eighteenth-century Russia), *Вопросы истории религии и атеизма: Сборник статей* (Questions in the history of religion and atheism: Collection of articles) 3 (Moscow 1955), pp.261-69, for an interesting account of the court proceedings against several persons found with manuscripts of Voltaire's forbidden works. Also published in Russian were excerpts from the correspondence of Voltaire with Jean Sylvain Bailly entitled 'Письма о начале наук и народов азииских', evidently a translation of *Lettres sur l'origine des sciences et sur celle des peuples de l'Asie, adressées a M. de Voltaire* [London 1777], *Растущий виноград* (The Growing grapevine) (June 1785 - Dec. 1786).

[54] Russo (Jean-Jacques Rousseau), *Рассуждение, удостоенное награждения от Академии Дижонской в 1750 году* ... (Discourse, awarded the prize from the Academy of Dijon in 1750), trans. Pavel Potemkin (Moscow 1768; 2nd ed. 1787); *Речь Ж. Ж. Руссо, удостоенная в 1750 году от Дижонской академии награждения* (The Speech of Jean-Jacques Rousseau, awarded the prize in 1750 from the Dijon Academy), trans. M. Iudin (St Petersburg 1792).

[55] Jean-Jacques Rousseau, *Discours sur les sciences et les arts*, ed. G. R. Havens (New York, London 1946), p.113. For a discussion of Rousseau's views of China see Basil Guy, *The French image of China*, pp.338-40, and also 'Rousseau and China', *Revue de littérature comparée* 30 (1956), pp.531-36.

edited by M. M. Kheraskov, the rector of Moscow University. The article appeared twice again in the following decades.[56]

Rousseau's basic outlook, however, his antagonism toward overly sophisticated culture, and his attraction to the virtues he saw in society when it was less complexly ordered, made it impossible for him to be a thoroughgoing admirer of the Chinese. In 1761 he described the Chinese in *La Nouvelle Héloïse* as an enslaved people lacking courage and ideas, hypocritical and distinguished only in matters of etiquette. While the part of the novel containing this attack, as we have seen, was apparently not translated into Russian in the eighteenth century, a new Russian version of the *Discours sur les sciences et les arts* in 1792 kept the Russian public aware of Rousseau's scepticism concerning the virtues of the Middle Kingdom.[57]

The government of China received adverse criticism from another French *philosophe*, Montesquieu, in his monumental *L'Esprit des lois* (1748). Montesquieu's classification of the Chinese empire as a despotism, a point made in the first part of his work, reached Russian readers in 1775 when volume one of *L'Esprit des lois* appeared in Russian translation. Montesquieu states that in spite of the admiration which certain missionaries expressed for China's political system, the nation nevertheless falls within his definition of the least desirable form of government. The principle upon which this form of government rests, he asserts, is fear.[58]

Russian readers also had some inkling, through the translations of several other French works, of the controversy which had arisen in Europe in regard to Montesquieu's theory. The abbé Millot, for instance, a Jesuit historian whose

---

[56] Jean-Jacques Rousseau, 'Economie (morale et politique)', *Encyclopédie, ou Dictionnaire raisonné des sciences, des arts et des métiers*, ed. D. Diderot and J. d'Alembert, xi (Lausanne, Berne 1779), pp.782 and 794; *Переводы из Энциклопедии* (Translations from the *Encyclopédie*) (Moscow 1767); Zhan Zhak Russo (Jean-Jacques Rousseau), *Гражданин, или разсуждение о политической экономии* (The Citizen, or discourse on political economy), trans. by V. Medvedev of the article 'Economie (morale et politique)' from Diderot's *Encyclopédie* (St Petersburg 1787); *Статья о политической экономии, или государственном благоучреждении* (Article on political economy, or good state institutions), trans. by A. I. Luzhkov of the preceding article (St Petersburg 1777). See P. N. Berkov, 'Histoire de l'*Encyclopédie* dans la Russie du dix-huitième siècle', *Revue des études slaves* 44 (1965), pp.47-58. Berkov notes that between 1767 and 1804 material translated from the *Encyclopédie* into Russian constituted approximately 500 articles and notices and 24 separate publications (p.52).

[57] Jean-Jacques Rousseau, *Julie, ou la nouvelle Héloïse*, *Œuvres complètes*, ed. Bernard Gagnebin and Marcel Raymond, ii (Paris 1964), pp.413-14; Russo (Jean-Jacques Rousseau), *Новая Елоиза*, trans. Pavel Potemkin (Moscow 1769), pt. i; Zhan Zhak Russo (Jean-Jacques Rousseau), *Новая Елоиза*, trans. Petr Andreev (St Petersburg 1792), pt. ii; Russo (Jean-Jacques Rousseau), *Новая Елоиза* (St Petersburg 1792-93), pts. 1-2. See *Union catalogue*, iii.75-76; see also note 54, above.

[58] Montesk'e (Charles de Secondat de Montesquieu), *О разуме законов* (On the spirit of the law), trans. Vasilii Kramarenkov, i (St Petersburg 1775), pp.254-59; see also A. P. Primakovskii, 'О русских переводах произведений Монтескье' (On Russian translations of works by Montesquieu), *Вопросы философии* (Problems of philosophy) 3 (1955), pp.138-39; Charles de Secondat de Montesquieu, *De l'esprit des lois*, *Œuvres*, ed. Caillois, ii (Paris 1951), pp.227-1037, at pp.365-68.

multi-volume world history *Histoire générale* (1772-1783) was translated in part into Russian in 1784, presented a comparison of Voltaire's and Montesquieu's views. One of the Millot selections translated was entitled *О состоянии Асии и новейших переменах Китая, Японии, Персии, и Мунгалии в последния времена* (Part of Volume 7 of the original, entitled 'De l'état et des principales révolutions de l'Asie dans les derniers siècles'). Millot, concurring with Montesquieu's opinion that the Chinese government was despotic, expressed his own conviction that it was only natural for a monarch who was revered as the father of his empire and treated almost like a god to become a despot. Millot asserted though, that the power of tradition among the Chinese militated against possible tyranny, thus making China one of the happiest of nations.[59]

Montesquieu's criticisms of the Chinese government were also discussed at some length in a work consisting of translated material from Diderot's *Encyclopédie* entitled *О китайском правлении. Взято из Энциклопедии, сочиненной собранием ученых мужей* (1789) (On the Chinese government. Taken from the *Encyclopédie*, composed by a society of learned men).[60] The volume, over two hundred pages in length, describes many facets of Chinese culture, government, science, religion, agriculture and trade. The compilation of material from the *Encyclopédie* appears to present an objective point of view, but praise of the fact that Chinese government is based on natural law, and commendation of the unique ability of the Chinese to unite moral teachings with politics suggest true admiration for the Chinese governmental system. It is therefore not surprising that a section concerning the alleged shortcomings of the Chinese government refutes the criticisms levelled at China, especially those of Montesquieu. Stating that political observers of the Western world have completely exaggerated the unlimited power of the Chinese government, the writer of this section quotes Montesquieu at some length and gives reasoned answers to a number of Montesquieu's criticisms. The assertion that China is ruled by the stick, for instance, is met with the reply that the use of the bastinade has nothing to do with the quality of government; each nation has its own form of punishment (*On the Chinese government*, pp.151-53).

Objections to the unqualified use of the term 'despotic' to describe the government of China appear again in the highly influential book by the abbé Raynal, *Histoire philosophique et politique des deux Indes* (1770). Raynal, who presents a fierce attack on the European monarchical system, does not, in fact, express wholehearted approval of the Chinese government, but he does point out the importance of law, and the rational basis of this law in China. An excerpt from

[59] Millo (Claude François Xavier Millot), *О состоянии Асии и новейших переменах Китая, Японии, Персии, и Мунгалии в последния времена* (On the condition of Asia and of the latest changes in China, Japan, Persia and Mongolia in recent times), trans. Ivan Ikonnikov (St Petersburg 1784); Claude François Xavier Millot, *Histoire moderne*, pt. 4 of *Histoire générale*, *Œuvres*, vii (Paris 1820), pp.115-26.

[60] *О китайском правлении. Взято из Энциклопедии, сочиненной собранием ученых мужей* (On the Chinese government. Taken from the *Encyclopédie* composed by a society of learned men [by Diderot and d'Alembert]), trans. Ivan Zhdanovskii (Moscow 1789). (The translated material was taken from various parts of the *Encyclopédie* of Diderot and d'Alembert.)

the *Histoire philosophique* concerning the Chinese constituted, to the best of my knowledge, the first selection from the work to be translated into Russian. A long article entitled 'Политическия разсуждения о китайцах' (Political considerations about the Chinese) appeared in instalments in a periodical throughout 1785-1786. In the following years Raynal's controversial work attracted considerable attention in Russia. Although the book had been forbidden in France and was burned by the public executioner, Raynal himself was cordially received by Catherine II in St Petersburg, and Russian translators evidently felt that the entire work could be published in Russia. A public announcement was made in 1787 that the translation was in progress. The introduction from the work appeared in 1799, but the book was not published in full in Russia until 1805-1811.[61]

Finally, among the translated works by Western European *philosophes* were those of a British intellectual, sir William Temple, whose admiration for the concepts of Chinese government was represented in Russian literature in two translations. A supporter of the 'Ancients' in their philosophical argument with the 'Moderns', Temple used the Chinese example to demonstrate the superiority of the civilisation of past ages. The essay 'Of popular discontents' (1701), which expresses Temple's approval of several of the basic principles of Chinese government, such as the avoidance of innovation, was translated in 1778. With it was published a translation of another of Temple's essays, 'Of health and long life' (1701), which commended various aspects of Chinese medical science.[62]

It can be seen from this survey that a fairly broad selection of writings on China by Western European, especially French, intellectuals appeared in Russian translation during the latter part of the eighteenth century. With the exceptions of Rousseau, Montesquieu and, in part, Raynal, the authors of these works admired China, particularly her religion and form of government. Many of these writings were, in all likelihood, chosen for translation because of the fame and popularity of their authors, as in the cases, for instance, of Voltaire, Rousseau, Montesquieu and Temple. Other selections, such as the excerpts from Raynal and from the *Encyclopédie*, may have been translated not only because the works they were taken from were considered important in Western Europe, but also because of Russia's political and economic interest in China. But Russian readers may well have been intrigued by these translations for other reasons. Adept at reading between the lines, they could have considered several points that were brought out repeatedly in these works to be implied criticisms of their own

---

[61] [Reinal] (G. T. F. Raynal), 'Политическия разсуждения о китайцах', trans. Vasilii Zuev, *Растущий виноград* (The Growing grapevine) (Dec. 1785), pp.46-64; (Feb. 1786), pp.54-74; (March 1786), pp.60-74 (April 1786), pp.86-95; (May 1786), pp.90-98; (June 1786), pp.78-84; (July 1786), pp.60-76; (August 1786), pp.84-92; (Sept. 1786), pp.69-86. See 'Bibliographic note' in *Union catalogue*, iii.24, Entry 5914. For commentary on Raynal's views of China see Guy, *The French image of China*, pp.328-29.

[62] Templ (William Temple), 'О народных недовольствах' (Of popular discontents), in *Опыт о народных недовольствах* (Essay on popular discontents), trans. P. P. Kurbatov (St Petersburg 1778); Templ (William Temple), 'О здравии и о жизни долголетней' (On health and long life), in *Опыт о народных недовольствах* (Essay on popular discontents), trans. P. P. Kurbatov (St Petersburg 1778).

government. Voltaire's 'enlightened' Chinese monarch, for instance, might in fact have been compared by Russian readers with their own 'enlightened' ruler, Catherine II. Such a comparison would not have failed to point up the shortcomings of the latter, especially her arbitrariness and her reliance on the advice of favourites rather than on reason. Montesquieu's warnings against despotic monarchs in nations 'ruled by the stick' could not have gone unheeded by educated readers who were all too well aware of the restrictions imposed by Catherine's regime. The emphasis placed by the *Encyclopédie* and Raynal on the importance of natural law in China could well have drawn attention to the status of justice in Russia.

The Russian tradition of interpreting works about China in this way is alluded to briefly by P. N. Berkov in his remarks about the social role of the material on China that was translated from the *Encyclopédie*. Berkov states that the article 'On the Chinese government' was part of a tradition of the study of Chinese philosophers which 'had less of the impassive nature of a science and more of the character of allusions – invulnerable to the censor – to the mores of the Court, the favourites, and the conduct of Catherine.'[63] It is difficult to prove either that the translators and publishers of the texts discussed above intended them as implied criticism of their own government, or that Russian readers in fact interpreted them in that way. But it is certain that Catherine II feared the public's tendency to read translations allegorically. Her reactions to certain translations by Nikolai Novikov, not of European works about China, but of works of Chinese literature, are a case in point.

In 1770 Novikov reworked and published, in the satirical journals that he edited, two translations by the Russian sinologist Aleksei Leontiev. The first of these was entitled 'Чензыя, китайского философа, совет данной его государю' (The Advice given by Chen-tsu, a Chinese philosopher, to his ruler). It appeared in February of 1770 in *Трутень* (The Drone), the journal through which Novikov had been presenting satirical criticism of Russian life and politics.[64] The Chinese text by Chen-tsu, a Neo-Confucian master of the twelfth century, discussed the qualities which an ideal ruler must have. Not only must he value truth, respect what is traditional in government and avoid novelty, but he must be particularly careful in his choice of advisors. Certain of the statements in the Chinese work could be read in such a way as to apply quite directly to the political events of the day in Russia, particularly to the Legislative Commission, an assembly which Catherine had called in 1767 to draft new modernised legislation for the nation, but which she had disbanded before any action had been taken. Perceptive readers of Novikov's journal could not have helped but see the veiled reference to the Commission in the following translation from Chen-tsu's 'Advice': 'If your institutions are light-minded, and consequently

[63] P. N. Berkov, 'Histoire de l'*Encyclopédie* dans la Russie du dix-huitième siècle', pp.47-58, at p.58.
[64] 'Чензыя китайского философа, совет, данной его государю', *Трутень* (Feb. 23, 1770), sheet viii, 20. The following discussion is based mainly on G. P. Makogonenko, *Николай Новиков и русское просвещение XVIII века* (Nikolai Novikov and the Russian Enlightenment of the eighteenth century) (Moscow, Leningrad 1952), pp.167-70.

unstable, then know, that not only are you not reforming your government, but it will be difficult to reform even yourself.'[65]

More daring than this was Novikov's note which followed the translation. It stated (in Berkov, *Satirical journals*, p.212):

Seeing the judicious government of our great ruler, her care for her subjects, and her unremitting labours, her institutions for the rooting of good mores, for the introducing of sciences and arts, her sagacious selection of the governing powers, her justice, her generosity, like rivers flowing abundantly over all, and in fact seeing all her enduring works, one can boldly say, that if the Chinese philosopher had lived now, he would not have written this advice to his ruler, but would have advised him to follow into the temple of eternity in the footsteps of the great Catherine.

Novikov's phrases were almost identical to those used by Catherine's flatterers, for instance, Maria Sushkova, who wrote the *Letter of a Chinese* discussed earlier. But only the most naive reader could fail to see that in this case the compliments were ironically intended. Catherine took no direct action against Novikov's periodical, but she gradually caused all of the other satirical journals, except the one in which she herself participated, to cease publication. Novikov consequently changed the nature of *The Drone*, confining his criticism to more superficial faults in Russian society. In its new form, however, the journal failed, ceasing publication in April of 1770.

Novikov persisted in his attacks. In July of 1770 in the second number of a new satirical journal which he had founded, *Пустомеля* (The Twaddler), he presented among other articles a second translation by Leontiev entitled 'Завещание Юнджена, китайского хана, к его сыну' (The Testament of Yung-cheng, the emperor of China, to his son).[66] The work consisted of advice from the emperor Yung-cheng (who ruled from 1723 to 1735) to his son who was about to inherit the throne, concerning the principles of good and just government. It emphasised the need to work hard, to be considered a worthy ruler by the nation, to maintain just courts and wise laws, and to think of the people and not only of oneself.

With this issue, the journal ceased publication. It is felt by some literary historians that Novikov's use of the 'Testament' caused the empress to close down the periodical. In 1770 Catherine's son Pavel, the heir to the throne, had become sixteen years of age, and Catherine had previously agreed that she would relinquish the throne to him at this time. The publication of the 'Testament' could have appeared to be a strong hint that the empress should now give up her power. Moreover, the following statement in the 'Testament' might easily have been interpreted to apply to the current political situation and to Catherine's position in regard to her advisers and favourites: 'Do not be deceived by flatterers and schemers and pay no attention to perverted suggestions. [...] know, that from the ruler's virtuous life comes peace and concord in the state' (in Berkov, *Satirical journals*, p.270).

[65] 'Advice by Chen-tsu', *Сатирические журналы Н. И. Новикова* (The Satirical journals of N. I. Novikov), ed. P. N. Berkov (Moscow, Leningrad 1951), pp.209-12, at p.209; see commentaries by Berkov at p.550, note 32 and in the introduction, pp.25-26.

[66] 'Завещание Юнджена, китайского хана, к его сыну', *Пустомеля* (July 1770), in P. N. Berkov, *Satirical journals*, pp.267-71.

Catherine may, on the other hand, have found the 'Testament' offensive, as G. Makogonenko points out, in that it implied that there was indeed an enlightened monarch, not in Russia but in China. In addition, the juxtaposition in the same issue of *The Twaddler* of the 'Testament' and a poem by Denis Fonvizin, 'Послание к слугам моим' (A message to my servants), pointing out some of the pitiful aspects of life in Russia, provided a bold contrast between an ideal state and Russian reality.

Makogonenko suggests therefore that it was not really the text of the 'Testament' to which the empress objected, but the way in which Novikov presented it; he notes that there was no opposition to this work when it appeared two years later as part of the book entitled *Китайския мысли* (Chinese thought), a collection of material translated from the Manchu by Aleksei Leontiev.[67] Other research has shown, however, that there are significant differences between Leontiev's version, Novikov's publication of the Chinese text, and an even earlier translation published in 1740. Novikov appears to have sharpened the tone of the work and made the content appear to apply more directly to the empress,[68] alterations which may well have made the text itself objectionable to the empress.

A third publication of a translation of a Chinese work also appears to have been interpreted by the empress as a form of criticism of her regime. This was the Russian version of the *Ta Hsüeh*, part of the *Ssu Shu* (The Four books). It was first introduced by the well-known writer Denis Fonvizin, mentioned above. Fonvizin, a leader of the Russian Enlightenment and a recognised foe of Catherine, was especially concerned with institutional reform in Russia and with the problem of improving the mores of Russian society. Attracted by the *Ta Hsüeh*, an interpretation of the teachings of Confucius, he apparently obtained the French translation during his stay in France in 1777-1778. Fonvizin's Russian version of Cibot's French translation of the classic appeared (without Fonvizin's name) in the journal *Academic news* in 1779.[69] It presented Russian readers with still another portrait of the ideal ruler, emphasising in particular the duties of the sovereign toward his people, and pointing out several of Fonvizin's favourite ideas, such as the concept that there is no difference of quality between a monarch and the lowliest of his subjects, and that the foundation of the throne is virtue.[70] The work appeared in two other Russian

---

[67] Skachkov, 'History of the study of China', pp.170-71; Skachkov, *Outline*, pp.72-73. G. P. Makogonenko, *Nikolai Novikov and the Russian enlightenment of the eighteenth century*, pp.167-70.

[68] *Chinese thought*, trans. A. Leontiev; Makogonenko does not mention the translation which had appeared thirty years earlier and which was reprinted in 1785: 'Духовная, или завещательное письмо китайскаго богдыхана Юншинг' (Last will or testamentary letter of the Chinese emperor Yung-cheng), *Calendar* (1740), pp.80-88; *Collection of compositions selected from calendars* 1 (1785), pp.114-28, 190-202; see O. L. Fishman, *The Chinese satirical novel: the Enlightenment era*, pp.163-66.

[69] Marc Raeff, *Russian intellectual history: an anthology* (New York 1966), p.87 (Raeff presents Ronald Hingley's English translation of Fonvizin's Russian version of the French translation from the Chinese!); 'Та-гио, или Великая наука' (Ta Hsüeh, or the great learning), trans. D. I. Fonvizin, *Academic news* (1779), Part 2, pp.59-101. Cited in *Union catalogue*, iii, entry 7084 (note), p.200.

[70] G. P. Makogonenko, *Денис Фонвизин, Творческий путь* (Denis Fonvizin, his way

translations within the following seven years. The first of these was done directly from the Manchu by Aleksei Leontiev, and was published in 1780 as part of his translation of the *Ssu Shu* (The Four books). It appeared again in 1786 when the first volume of *Mémoires concernant les Chinois*, which contained Cibot's French version of the classic, was translated into Russian by Mikhail Verevkin.[71]

The contents of the *Ta Hsüeh* were evidently not as offensive to Catherine as were the various texts published earlier by Novikov. Leontiev's translation had no difficulties with the censor. But Fonvizin's and Verevkin's versions of the classic appear to have been less fortunate. Fonvizin's rendering of the text itself appeared in full in *Academic news*, but there was a significant omission from one of the thirty-four notes which were part of Cibot's French translation. The part of the note which did appear in print stated: 'Kie and Tshu are the Chinese Nero and Caligula. The first is depicted in the Shu Ching and in the chronicles as a most voluptuous and luxury-loving ruler, lacking both honesty and faith, insanely fond of the magnificence of diversions and entertainments, haughty in his demands, infamous in his conduct, treacherous and cruel.'[72] But omitted was this phrase which followed the preceding material in Cibot's French translation: 'aussi cruel qu'une femme perdue de débauche, abusant avec insolence de son autorité pour opprimer les peuples, et la prostituant jusqu'à la dérision et au ridicule, pour vaquer à ses plaisirs'.[73] As one commentator has pointed out, it seems unlikely that Fonvizin himself would have removed these lines. The fact that the same phrases were also omitted from Verevkin's translation several years later also seems to indicate that the change was the work of the censor. In 1801 Fonvizin's version of the *Ta Hsüeh* appeared again in a collection of works entitled *Правдолюбец, или карманная книжка мудрого* (The Lover of truth, or the pocket book of a wise man). The original version of this book, it would appear, passed the censor, but in later editions Fonvizin's name was dropped from the translation, and eventually the *Ta Hsüeh* along with certain other selections, was omitted entirely. The potential threat contained in the text, especially when coupled with Fonvizin's name, was evidently still felt in the early years of the nineteenth century.[74]

The history of Novikov's and Fonvizin's publication of Chinese texts depicting the ideal enlightened monarch shows how such translations, when presented in a way which seemed to cast aspersions on the empress, were considered highly objectionable. But not all translations of Chinese works dealing with the mon-

in art) (Moscow, Leningrad 1961), p.195; P. N. Berkov, 'Та-Гио, или Великая наука, заключающая в себе высокую китайскую философию: комментарии' (Ta Hsüeh, or the great science, containing the high Chinese philosophy: commentaries), in D. I. Fonvizin, *Собрание сочинений* (Collected works), ed. G. P. Makogonenko, ii (Moscow, Leningrad 1959), pp.674-79.

[71] *Сы шу гей, то есть четыре книги с толкованиями* (Ssu Shu, i.e., the four books with explanations) (St Petersburg 1780-[1784]); *Mémoires*, ii.167-206.

[72] Fonvizin's translation, quoted in L. V. Krestova, 'Из истории публицистической деятельности Д. И. Фонвизина' (From the history of the publicistic activity of D. I. Fonvizin', *XVIII век* (Eighteenth century), iii (Moscow, Leningrad 1958), pp.481-89, at pp.486-87.

[73] *Mémoires concernant les Chinois*, i (Paris 1776), pp.448.

[74] Krestova, pp.480-84 and pp.486-87.

archical form of government fell into the category of dangerous material. As has been noted, Leontiev's translations of the 'Testament of Yung-cheng' and the *Ta Hsüeh*, when they appeared as part of the sinologist's collection of Chinese works, passed the censor without difficulty. Leontiev and a second Russian sinologist, A. S. Agafonov, whose objectives it would appear were purely scholarly, translated several other Chinese texts which seemed to present the general point of view that absolutism was both desirable and unalterable. These works were approved by the court, and became highly popular.[75] They included, among others, Leontiev's *Ге Янь, то есть умныя речи* (1776) (Ge Ian', or wise sayings), *Китайские поучения, изданныя от хана Юнджена* (1778) (Chinese precepts published by the emperor Yung-cheng), Agafonov's *Манжурскаго и китайскаго хана Кан-Сия книга придворных политических поучений и нравоучительных разсуждений* (1788) (The Book of political precepts and moral teachings of the Court of the Manchu and Chinese emperor K'ang-hsi), and two translations of works by the emperor Shun Chih.[76] Even if one could have read into parts of these translations hidden commentaries on the Russian political scene, the fact that they were presented to the public by recognised sinologists, rather than avowed critics of the government, evidently placed them above suspicion.

This was probably the case with certain other translated Chinese texts which dealt with other political matters. Among Leontiev's translations, for instance, are two collections of Chinese laws. But it seems unlikely that any criticism of Russian law would have been inferred from this material. It is, incidentally, noteworthy that while the *philosophes*, especially in France, continually praised the Chinese for utilising natural law as the basis of their legal system, these intellectuals were not, in fact, well acquainted with the particulars of the Chinese legal system. According to Henri Cordier's bibliography of works pertaining to China, the only substantial materials specifically concerning Chinese law that were produced in Western Europe in the eighteenth century were an essay on the Chinese legal system that appeared in 1783 in the part of the *Encyclopédie méthodique* devoted to 'Jurisprudence', and a discussion of a work on medical jurisprudence and a note on the collection of laws of the Chinese Empire in the

[75] Skachkov, 'History of the study of China', pp.171-74.

[76] *Ге Янь, то есть умныя речи*, trans. A. Leontiev (St Petersburg 1776); Yung-cheng, *Китайския поучения, изданныя от хана Юнджена*, trans. A. Leontiev (St Petersburg 1778); K'ang-hsi, *Манжурскаго и китайскаго хана Кан-Сия книга придворных политических поучений и нравоучительных разсуждений*, trans. Aleksei Agafonov (St Petersburg 1788); a second edition of this work appeared with the title: *Государь друг своих подданных, или Придворныя, политическия поучения и нравоучительныя разсуждения манжурскаго и китайскаго хана Кан-сия* (The Ruler, a friend to his subjects, or political precepts and moral teachings of the Court by the Manchu and Chinese emperor K'ang-hsi), trans. Aleksei Agafonov (St Petersburg 1795); Shun-chih, *Манжурскаго и китайскаго хана Шунь-Джия. Книга нужнейших разсуждений ко благополучию поощряющих* (The Book of the most important teachings encouraging well-being by the Manchu and Chinese emperor Shun-chih), trans. Aleksei Agafonov (St Petersburg 1788); Shun-chih, *Манжурскаго и китайскаго Шунь-Джи-хана книга Полезный и нужный образ к правлению* (The Book, 'The Useful and necessary form of government' by the Manchu and Chinese emperor Shun-chih), trans. Aleksei Agafonov (St Petersburg 1788).

Mémoires concernant les Chinois (1776-1814).[77] In Russia, on the other hand, through Leontiev's translations *Китайское уложение* (Chinese code) (1778-1779) and the three-volume *Тайцин гурунь и Ухери коли, то есть все законы и установления китайскаго (а ныне манжурскаго) правительства* (Taitsin Gurun' and Ukheri Koli, or all of the laws and regulations of the Chinese (now Manchu) government) (1781-1783), the translation of which was commissioned by the Russian government, numerous legal regulations of the Chinese empire were available to the Russian public.[78] These translations provide another illustration of the Russian government's practical interest in China. Russian intellectuals, however, were evidently not concerned with the philosophic aspects of Chinese law. The reviewer of Leontiev's book *The Chinese code*, whom one might expect to make some comment on the philosophy of the system, gives many long excerpts from the laws themselves, but is mainly concerned, it would appear, with the human interest aspects of the material.[79]

In addition to the translations which were published with no ulterior political motive, and to those which in fact attempted to discredit the Russian government, there was a third, very small category which was put forward with the propogandistic intention of praising Catherine's rule. An excerpt entitled 'From Chinese tales', published in 1775 in the journal *Собрание новостей* (Collection of news), is a case in point. Here the editor of the journal, I. F. Bogdanovich, who was a supporter of the enlightened aims of Catherine II, used a purported Chinese anecdote to ridicule the opponents of recent government measures designed to curb luxury.[80]

The most illustrious eighteenth-century Russian intellectual who took an interest in the philosophic arguments about China was the empress Catherine herself. Her manipulation of the oriental tale to glorify the concept of enlightened monarchy has already been seen. Catherine also frequently expressed her varying views concerning China in her correspondence and other writings. Chinese rationalism and the relationship between government and religion in China evidently impressed her favourably. A biographer of Catherine cites (without giving the location in Catherine's work) the following note by the empress: 'To do nothing without principle or without reason, not to allow oneself to be led by prejudice, to respect religion, but not give it any power in State matters, to banish everything that reeks of fanaticism and to draw the best out of every situation for the public good, is the basis of the Chinese empire, the

---

[77] Henri Cordier, *Bibliotheca Sinica: Dictionnaire bibliographique des ouvrages relatifs à l'Empire chinois*, i (2nd ed., Paris 1904), cols. 548 and 552.

[78] Skachkov, 'History of the study of China', p.172; *Тайцин гурунь и Ухери коли, то есть все законы и установления китайскаго (а ныне манжурскаго) правительства*, trans. A. Leontiev; *Китайское уложение*, trans. A. Leontiev (St Petersburg 1778-1779).

[79] *Санктпетербургский вестник* (St Petersburg herald), (Sept. 1779), pp.202-22.

[80] 'Из китайских повестей', *Собрание новостей* (Dec. 1775), pp.3-46. See I. Z. Serman, 'И. Ф. Богданович - журналист и критик' (I. F. Bogdanovich - journalist and critic), *XVIII век* (Eighteenth century), iv (Moscow, Leningrad 1959), pp.85-103 at p.96.

most durable of all those known on this earth. (*Political instruction* by Bielefeld: Vol. ii)'[81]

But, as has been seen already, Catherine was not a wholehearted admirer of her Eastern neighbours. She was frequently very critical of their political conduct, and she found them obstinate and often difficult to deal with. Her remarks to Voltaire concerning the French missionary accounts of China, mentioned earlier, indicate her irritation with the government, but at the same time also show her awareness that China's reputation was based at least in part on its ancient civilisation, while her own dealings were with the Manchu rulers. Catherine disagreed firmly with the idea, illustrated by Voltaire in his *Orphelin de la Chine*, that the Manchu conquerors of China had in turn succumbed to the superior civilisation of the ancient Chinese; in a letter to Voltaire in 1771, for instance, she stated, 'les Conquérans n'ont point adopté la politesse des Conquis, et ceux çi courent risque d'être entraînés par les mœurs dominantes'.[82]

The empress's commentary on Voltaire's theory represents one of the few instances of Russian debate on the Western European *philosophes*' attitude toward China; Russian intellectuals, writers, and critics, as has been noted earlier, were as generally silent in regard to the views of their colleagues in France and elsewhere as they were about the whole question of the double image of China that had taken shape in Russian literature by the end of the eighteenth century. In addition to Catherine, however, a second Russian writer did attempt to evaluate a French approach to China; again it was Voltaire's views which inspired the discussion. The Russian document, entitled 'Осведомление, или некоторое поверение Волтеровых о Китае примечаний, собранное в краткую Братищева бытность в Пекине' (Information about or verification of Voltaire's remarks about China, collected during Bratishchev's short stay in Peking),[83] is, as far as I can determine, one of the earliest detailed examinations of the sinological studies of Voltaire to be written in any country.

The work, which until recently has been largely ignored, was composed by the Russian diplomat Vasilii Bratishchev, who arrived in Peking in 1757. The envoy's on-the-spot observations were published twenty-six years later in the form of an article containing queries and answers relating to Chinese history and society.[84]

Bratishchev's report gives no indication of the source of the questions, but

---

[81] Note by Catherine II quoted in *The Memoirs of Catherine the Great*, ed. Dominique Maroger, trans. by Moura Budberg from French (London 1955), p.384. Catherine's reference may be to J. F. Bielefeld (also spelled Bielfeld), *Наставления политическия* (Political precepts), trans. from French (Moscow 1768-1775). This would appear to be a Russian translation of Bielefeld's *Institutions politiques* (The Hague 1740).

[82] See above, Introduction, note 21; Best.D17127.

[83] Vasilii Bratishchev, 'Осведомление, или некоторое поверение Волтеровых о Китае примечаний, собранное в краткую Братищва бытность в Пекине', *Опыт трудов Вольнаго Российскаго собрания при Императорском Московском университете* (Essays of the Free Russian Assembly of Moscow University), pt. 6 (1783), pp.39-62.

[84] Commentaries by the Russian sinologist Ilarion Rossokhin on Bratishchev's work, which is based, according to Rossokhin, almost entirely on the words and writings of the Jesuits in Peking, are to be found in Soviet archives. Citations to this material are given in Skachkov, *Outline*, p.394.

they are in fact based upon what was to become the first two chapters of Voltaire's *Essai sur les mœurs*.[85] It is not known who compiled the questions sent for verification to Peking, or even if it was a Russian. One of Bratishchev's answers, which indicates that the diplomat did not fully understand the question, shows, however, that the author of the queries was not Bratishchev himself.

The purpose of the compiler of the questionnaire is difficult to determine. He may have been motivated simply by the general curiosity then developing about China, or by more practical interest occasioned by Russia's political and economic ties with her neighbour. Or it may have been an interest in Voltaire, rather than in China, which prompted the verification of the French *philosophe*'s work. Perhaps it was an attempt merely to test Voltaire's accuracy as a historian. More arresting is the possibility that the compiler wanted to check Voltaire's factual acuity in order to bolster – or conversely to destroy – the philosophical implications inherent in Voltaire's work on China. Regardless of the compiler's intentions, it seems quite possible that the sophisticated segment of the Russian reading public, accustomed, as we have found, to seeing China used as a vehicle for veiled discussions of matters deemed dangerous by the government, may have attempted to read between the lines of the document.

Voltaire was a genuine admirer of the Chinese, but he also turned to China for support for several of his most basic philosophic convictions. He pointed, for instance, to the antiquity of China as proof of the inaccuracy of Old Testament chronology. Chinese written history, he pointed out, dated back to the time assigned by interpreters of the Bible to the Great Flood, yet it made no mention of the inundation. He used China's large population, which he reasoned could only have developed over a period of many thousands of years, as additional evidence of the antiquity of the nation and as a further oblique attack on Biblical accuracy. The Chinese monarchical system, which Voltaire characterised as benign and efficient, provided an example of the advantages of a patriarchal form of government, and, finally, the teachings and the morality of Confucius served as a criticism of the revealed religions of the West.[86]

A large proportion of the questions and answers in Bratishchev's report relate to three of these areas with which Voltaire was especially concerned, the antiquity of China, her large population, and Confucianism. The fourth subject, government, receives the least attention, making the religious implications all the more noticeable. Bratishchev, on the basis of Chinese reference material and conversations with Chinese officials and interpreters, Jesuit missionaries, and Russians living in Peking, makes minor corrections on some of Voltaire's statistics. On all the major points, however, he corroborates Voltaire, providing, whether he intended to or not, subtle but convincing support for the anti-Biblical, anti-clerical stands in the Chinese section of the *Essai sur les mœurs*.

The use of China as an ideological weapon by Fonvizin, Novikov, and quite

[85] This part of the *Essai sur les mœurs* appeared in Russian translation only in 1775. See note 52, above. Bratishchev's questionnaire was based upon an early French edition. See Barbara W. Maggs, 'Answers from eighteenth-century China to certain questions on Voltaire's sinology', *Studies on Voltaire* 120 (1974), pp.179-98.

[86] See A. O. Aldridge, 'Voltaire and the cult of China', and Arnold H. Rowbotham, 'Voltaire sinophile'.

possibly, the anonymous compiler of Bratishchev's questionnaire, as well as by Bogdanovich and Catherine herself shows clearly that Russian writers were following the example of the French and other Western European *philosophes*, such as Voltaire and Rousseau, who were able to use China to support widely differing points of view. Russian ideological involvement with Chinese themes and materials differed from that of Western Europe, however, in several respects, particularly in terms of quantity of publications and breadth of application, and perhaps also in regard to genuine concern about China and her culture. That the Russian *philosophes* used Chinese materials more sparingly than did their Western European counterparts is shown not only by the relatively small number of Russian philosophical works dealing with China but also by the fact that while writers in France and elsewhere made China a part of religious, linguistic, economic, judicial and literary disputes, Russian intellectuals utilised China most frequently in connection with one ideological, and at the same time practical, question – the nature of monarchy.

The limited use of China by Russian intellectuals can partly be explained by the restricted freedom of the press in Russia which made discussion of ideological matters extremely difficult. For this reason, too, it should be noted, the methodology of the Russian intellectuals was different from that of the Western European *philosophes*; adverse commentary on the part of the Russian intellectuals had to be offered quite indirectly. The Russian applications of China to ideological questions may also have been limited for another reason. As the survey of travel literature has shown, in the last few decades of the eighteenth century, when the Russian Enlightenment entered its most productive period, Chinese civilisation did not possess in Russia the untarnished image which it had had somewhat earlier in Western Europe, at the time that many of the significant French and English works concerning the 'philosophic' China were being written. Sinomania reached its height in Western Europe around 1760. But from roughly the middle of the century on, in France and England especially, the highly influential reports of travellers, which had previously been full of admiration for the Chinese, began gradually to present the Middle Kingdom in a less favourable light. In Russia, however, translations of both the early complimentary reports, and the later, less enthusiastic accounts were received together in the last few decades of the century. During this period too the reports about Russia's own missionaries, and accounts by merchants and diplomats, which on the whole presented an unfavourable picture of the Middle Kingdom, were being published. Since the image which emerged from this broad array of travel literature was not an entirely positive one, it can be argued that it simply did not provide as much inspiration for ideologues in Russia as the corresponding image did in Western Europe.[87]

The small number of writings produced by the Russian intellectuals about China suggests that Russian *philosophes* were perhaps not in fact as interested in the Middle Kingdom for its own sake as were at least some of their Western European colleagues. Russian writers did not, for instance, engage in polemics

---

[87] See also O. L. Fishman, *The Chinese satirical novel*, p.168, for a brief comparison of Western European and Russian approaches.

with each other about China itself as did prominent philosophers such as Voltaire and Rousseau, and also less well-known intellectuals, such as Alberto Fortis and G. B. Roberti, in Italy.[88] While the point can be made that many French and other Western European *philosophes* used China primarily as a device to project their own favourite theories, it cannot be denied that certain of them, Voltaire, for example, were in fact serious students of the Celestial Empire. One might question, though, whether any of the Russian *philosophes* had a genuine interest in China or whether they turned to her only because the Chinese materials provided such an excellent means of criticising or praising the Russian government in an allegorical way.

But while the ideological use of China by the Russian *philosophes* was limited in quantity and type of application, and indirect in method, it seems apparent in the final analysis that the writings of the Russian intellectuals, in combination with the fairly representative selection of translations by their French and other Western European colleagues did create for the 'philosophic' China a position of considerable importance in eighteenth-century Russian literature. Together with the China of the scholars, the philosophers' China broadened the visions of the Russian reader. The spirit of cosmopolitanism and the practice of examining other nations' concepts of government, law and religion by means of both scholarly and philosophic discussions of China became, following the Western European example, an integral part of the Russian Enlightenment. The subtle but often daring criticism of Russian life and institutions that sometimes resulted testified to the presence of a new spirit of rational inquiry in Russia and a new belief in man's ability to alter his life for the better.

[88] Sergio Zoli, *La Cina e l'età dell'illuminismo in Italia*, pp.95-111.

Conclusion

THE image of China that had developed in Russian literature by the end of the eighteenth century was a highly diverse one; the documents incorporating it were rich in factual information and ideas, and were not devoid of literary merit. While examples of stylistic excellence are perhaps few, Russia's literature about China provides on the whole rewarding reading. The travel narratives are particularly engaging, partly because of the novelty of their contents, and also because the writers of many of these works exhibit a real sense of artistic control over their material. The appealingly naive exoticism in Baikov's description of the strangeness of China, and the emotion conveyed by Lange in his various relations of his exasperating experiences with Chinese officialdom are among the outstanding instances of this type of artistic mastery. Also noteworthy stylistically is the progression in the travel narratives from the primitivism of the seventeenth century to the polished sophistication of the late eighteenth and early nineteenth centuries. The nonutilitarian literature provides even more evidence of linguistic artistry than do the travel narratives, particularly the stylistic precision of Sumarokov's poetic translation from *The Orphan of the House of Chao*, and the lyricism of Derzhavin's portrayal of the poet-musician Confucius. Among the most stylistically pleasing works is Leontiev's translation of the *Chinese ABC book* with its many formal rhetorical devices.

The documentary value of Russia's literature on China is considerable. The factual information contained in the travel accounts, while frequently presented in a disorganised manner, interspersed with subjective interpretations by the travellers, furnished readers with many details of Chinese life. More important, the translations of scholarly Jesuit works, while limited in number, made available to Russian readers some of the best Western European studies of the Middle Kingdom. The contributions of Russian historians such as Mikhail Chulkov, and of Western Europeans working in Russia, such as G. F. Müller and J. E. Fischer, were similarly important, particularly as they reflected the political relationship between Russia and China; these works added to the scholarship on China the dimensions of international politics generally lacking in Western European studies. The translations of the Russian sinologists who introduced the public to authentic works of Chinese literature, and especially to materials on history and law which were not available in Western Europe, are among the most significant Russian contributions to documentation on the Middle Kingdom.

What is perhaps most engaging about Russia's image of China in the eighteenth century is not, however, its documentary or literary values but the wealth of ideas and evaluations, often intriguingly contradictory ones, that emerges from it. The wideness of the range of opinion is brought about partly by the fact that the contributors to this literature represented many different professions and interests, and they approached China with greatly differing cultural heritages – that of Russia, of France and, to a lesser extent, of other countries of Western Europe, and of China itself. In addition, the major components of the image that took shape in the latter part of the eighteenth century had, in fact, been written over a period of about two hundred years.

Ultimately though, the differences in the attitudes expressed in this literature were a result, not so much of the nationality of a writer or the period in which he wrote, but of such factors as the occupation (and, it would seem, the success of a visitor in his endeavours in China), or of the particular goal of a writer who used the travel accounts of others for his own purposes. Those whose interests, goals and successes in China were similar more often than not agreed with each other in their attitudes toward the Chinese. For example, one segment of Russia's Chinese mirage was contributed by Western European and Russian observers who had actually visited China and either conducted political negotiations or transacted business there. In their narratives they were preoccupied with discussing the mechanics of working out agreements with Chinese officialdom, and they stressed such practical matters as the intricacies of Chinese protocol, the kowtow and gift-giving. In connection with their political and economic observations many of them presented their evaluations of the strength and stability of the Chinese government. While these writers were not completely in agreement with each other, a surprising sense of continuity emerges from their accounts. Except for the few who were unusually successful in their undertakings, Russian government officials and navigators and Western European diplomatic and naval representatives concurred in depicting the Chinese people as haughty, mercenary and often dishonest, and the Chinese bureaucrats in charge of political and commercial affairs as inscrutable and usually unco-operative. Russians joined with observers from Western Europe in the view that China was a unique land, exotic in many respects, but with serious problems, such as a weak and badly-organised government and a deficient judicial system. Similarly, Russian clergy, lacking success in their practical dealings and efforts to provide religious support to Orthodox Russians in China, were also generally unenthusiastic about their Chinese hosts.

But other groups of writers tended to register far more positive appraisals. The Jesuit missionaries, whose objectives included demonstrating to Europe the virtues of the Chinese people, and with them the French writers of travel compendiums such as Prévost, La Harpe, and La Porte, who publicised the missionaries' work, stressed entirely different aspects of China. They lauded the ideals of the Chinese people, their cultural heritage, traditional wisdom, emphasis on justice, and their concern for the welfare of the individual as shown by their patterns of family life and their social institutions. Such favourable interpretations corresponded to those of the Chinese writers Tulishen and others who, for reasons of national pride, understandably emphasised the positive attributes of their own country.

On the basis of this complimentary material most of the Western European *philosophes*, whose goal was to criticise current Western shortcomings, depicted China as an ideal social and political entity. Russian intellectuals followed the lead of their Western counterparts and adopted this interpretation with the aim of criticising the Russian Establishment. At the same time fiction writers in the West found the theme of an Eastern paradise highly attractive for literary purposes, and Russian poets and storytellers, in large part, though not with one voice, soon produced their own versions of the new utopia, Cathay.

Because of their varying points of emphasis and divergent views, the contributors to Russia's Chinese mirage produced in effect two very different Chinas. Confusing as this must have been to those Russian readers who were seriously attempting to form an impression of the Middle Kingdom, the situation was made even more perplexing by the fact that the creators of the various parts of the image seemed to ignore the existence of the other segments. There were a few exceptions: admiral Anson, the Russian navigators Lisianskii and Krusenstern, and the Orthodox missionary Gribovskii did in fact take direct issue with the idealised picture of China. The large body of Russian diplomatic reports, however, did not. Nor did most of the creators of the fictional China – or those of the *philosophes* who saw in China the blueprint for a new world – acknowledge the views of China's critics such as Anson or the Russian diplomats.

The failure of China's apologists and her detractors to discuss and attempt to refute each others' attitudes can in most cases be explained. Since the Jesuit image, for instance, was not seriously questioned for a long period of time, the missionaries themselves originally had little reason to defend their views or to quarrel with other Chinese observers. Later the Western European and Russian *philosophes* who were among China's admirers ignored the critics of the Middle Kingdom because their objective was to propagandise those aspects of Chinese civilisation which they felt were worthy of emulation in their own respective societies, not to prove China's superiority through arguments with her detractors. The writers of fiction, with few exceptions, found the untarnished utopian version of Cathay the more unique and appealing literary subject, and for artistic reasons few included any jarring elements in their descriptions of it. At the same time, among China's critics, the Russian diplomats, while showing a far from idealistic China, refrained from polemics with the creators of the other China, not because of any ideological or artistic necessities, but simply, it would seem, because their main concern was to provide accounts of their own particular successes or failures in dealing with the Chinese.

While such explanations for the creation of two independent and mutually exclusive literary Chinas in Russia can be seen in retrospect, they were in all probability not obvious to most eighteenth-century Russian readers. Lack of editorial comment on the dual nature of this image was no doubt in large part the result of Russia's intense admiration for Western Europe, especially France, from whom many of the glowing aspects of the image had come; Russia would not or could not criticise her idols, even if she disagreed with them. One can therefore only speculate on what the reaction of the ordinary Russian reader to this double image of China must have been. Was one of the two Chinas more credible than the other? Although it is impossible to answer this question definitively, there are several reasons for believing that the politically oriented works with their concomitant criticial view of the Celestial Empire may have carried more weight with Russian readers than did those which projected the idealised vision of the country.

First of all, apart from the purely scholarly works (with which the general public was probably not familiar), the travel and diplomatic narratives constituted the most numerous and the most substantial elements in the image. The majority of these works – the accounts of the governmental, commercial, and naval emissaries, both Russian and Western European – depicted a China with many faults. That a large percentage of these works was written by Russian diplomats probably made them especially credible to Russian readers. As non-fiction, actual eyewitness reports, these narratives were in all likelihood taken more seriously than were the many entertaining but generally unrealistic fictional portrayals of the Middle Kingdom. As for the works of the *philosophes*, both Russian and Western European, they did, it is true, provide impressive testimony concerning the ideal China. But quantitatively these contributions to Russia's Chinese mirage were limited. Moreover, the writings of some of the few Western Europeans who were sceptical of Chinese superiority happened to be represented among them: the translations of Rousseau and Montesquieu, for instance, may have diminished in Russia the total force of the Western European intellectuals' arguments in favour of the utopian China. While the Russian contributions to this aspect of the image were both daring and significant, their small number may have lessened the influence of the *'philosophes' China'* in Russia.

The quantitative superiority of the highly influential Russian diplomatic accounts came about, of course, as a result of the fact that Russia, unlike Western Europe, had entered into direct diplomatic relations with Peking early in the seventeenth century and had maintained these contacts on a fairly regular basis throughout the following century. The unsettled nature of these political relations between Russia and China was ultimately reflected in these narratives. Politics was also evident in other segments of Russia's Chinese mirage. For example, among the works of Russian intellectuals, scholarly accounts of the political and economic relations between Russia and China outnumber works on abstract philosophical questions. In addition, the scope of the translating activities of the Russian sinologists, extending beyond literature and philosophy to law, history, geography and economics, evidences a very practical concern with Chinese political affairs. A limited amount of political realism has even been seen to have entered Russia's belletristic literature about China.

In the consideration of this political orientation of Russia's Chinese image, the question arises as to whether there was any attempt on the part of the Russian government, or of Russian editors and translators, to deliberately mould the Russian reader's view of China through a biased selection of Russian and foreign works for publication. A rather obvious instance of negative image building can be seen in the work of the German historian Müller, who was responsible for publishing various reports unfavourable to China in the works that he edited. Müller also provided the caustic commentary on the account of the Chinese consul Tulishen. But in fact, of the total number of works by Russian specialists and travellers to China that are known to have been written prior to and during this period, a very large percentage appeared in various periodicals of the day. This would seem to suggest that there was little attempt to single out particular Russian works for publication. This, combined with the fact that a fairly representative selection of Western European commentaries (both favourable and hostile) appeared in Russian translation, would seem to indicate that there was relatively little deliberate manipulation of the image.

Looking at the various components in Russia's Chinese mirage and their relative weights in this way, one sees that the uncomplimentary view may well have predominated over the more favourable one. A consideration of the chronological development of the image lends further support to this theory. Publishing activities began late in Russia, and few works about China appeared before the middle of the eighteenth century. In the rest of Europe the Jesuit-inspired image had become established as early as the seventeenth century, and had enjoyed a long period of success before it was seriously challenged by admiral Anson's account in the middle of the following century, and was eventually widely discredited. But Russia's Chinese mirage, unlike that of Western Europe, was not cyclical. In Russia the Jesuit-inspired image appeared simultaneously, mainly in the last three decades of the century, with that projected by the older, previously unpublished Russian manuscripts and also by more contemporary works. The highly favourable picture of Cathay, rivalled from the time of its first appearance in Russia by the uncomplimentary, non-Jesuit image, was never able to flourish fully and independently on Russian soil. Russian admiration for China that may have been inspired by the Jesuit literature was kept constantly in check by the writings of China's detractors. For this reason full-fledged sinophilia such as that which evolved in France and England never developed in Russia.

Still, the idealised view of Cathay, if less credible than its counterpart, was very clearly articulated in Russian literature, and was not without influence. *Chinoiserie* or *китайщина*, a genuine appreciation of things Chinese, did indeed play a role in Russian cultural life in the last part of the eighteenth century. And the general reader, in all likelihood, became aware of the great antiquity and some of the accomplishments of Chinese civilisation. In the end, Russian readers, through their acquaintance with both visions of the Middle Kingdom, may well have arrived at a more realistic point of view and a better understanding of China than that achieved by their Western European contemporaries, who had been acquiring knowledge about the Orient over a much greater period of time.

The broad array of literature about China that was available to Russian readers of the eighteenth century not only provides insights into Russian attitudes toward the Celestial Empire, but it also reveals a great deal about Russia herself, particularly in regard to literary, intellectual and political life and to the development of Russia's own national consciousness. Drawn to Western Europe, attracted by her sinophilia, Russia at the same time stood apart, maintaining a pragmatic, political interest in the East and forming her own outlook which corresponded to these interests. Symbolic, perhaps, of Russia's position is the attitude of Catherine the Great. Like the intellectuals of the West she could praise the Chinese for their adherence to reason and their banishment of fanaticism, and for establishing the most durable empire in history. At the same time, as a political head of state, she could declare her aggressive ambition to have one day 'broken the insolence of China'.

In the area of literary life Russia's Chinese mirage, as a cross-section of the literature of the period, provides a good indication of the broad acquaintance which Russia had, through translations, of Western European, especially French, *belles-lettres*. A case in point is the work of Voltaire, nine of whose writings which touch upon China (and one satire with a Chinese theme directed against Voltaire) became known to Russian readers. Russia's desire to emulate European trends is shown clearly in her use of the patterns formulated by Western European writers who dealt with Chinese themes. Distinct examples emerge in the empress Catherine's oriental tale about a wise prince and in Sushkova's 'oriental spectator'. But the handling of the European themes is often seen to be uniquely Russian. Sushkova's use of the spectator not as an instrument of satire, but as a means of praising Russia and especially Catherine, serves as an unforgettable example of Russian independence in regard to Western patterns of literary *chinoiserie*.

Particularly noteworthy are the insights which the Russian image of China presents concerning the manifestations in Russia of the Enlightenment. The spirit of this movement, the interest in and evaluation of unfamiliar social institutions and philosophic systems, and the preoccupation with concepts such as rationalism, natural law and the nature of man, which is reflected in Western European writings not only by *philosophes* but also by travellers to China such as admiral Anson and sir George Staunton, is much less evident in the original Russian travel accounts and the work of the Russian intellectuals. The Russian diplomats and other Russian travellers were indeed concerned with such concepts as reason and justice, but they tended generally to discuss them in relation to their own experiences, rather than to analyse the philosophic premises of the Chinese system. The writings of the Russian travellers, most of whom were educated men, seem to indicate that concern with abstract principles and ideas was less widespread in Russian during this period than it was in Western Europe. The Russian *philosophes* Novikov and Fonvizin also avoided theoretical discussions of Chinese philosophy, religion or law. They were very much absorbed, however, with one abstract principle – that of the nature of monarchical government. Their subtle but daring attacks on the Russian Establishment through the use of Chinese material serve as a good illustration of the overriding concern of the Russian Enlightenment, the question of political organisation.

Russia's Chinese mirage, which reflected in this way her own intellectual, political and literary life, was, in the final analysis, considerably different from the image of China which developed in other European literatures. From the blend of Russian, Western European, and Chinese material there emerged a highly colourful, well-documented picture, an image more pragmatic in orientation and more critical in tone than its Western European counterparts. It was ultimately a uniquely Russian creation.

Appendix

Excerpt from Leontiev's *Букварь китайской* (The Chinese ABC book)

From the section entitled 'Сань дзы гин. То есть Книга троесловная' (San' dzy gin. Or the Three word book)[1]

> Знай числа, и помни
> Склады чисел и умножении.
>
> От одного десять,
> От десяти сто.
>
> От ста тысяча,
> От тысячи *вань* (десять тысяч).[2]
>
> Суть три могущества,
> Небо, земля, человек.
>
> Суть три светила,
> Солнце, луна, звезды.
>
> Суть три основания,
> Справедливость Государя и раба.
>
> Любовь отца и сына.
> Склонность мужа и жены.
>
> Весна, лето,
> Осень, зима.
>
>> Сих четырех времян,
>> Обращение неистощеваемое.
>
> Юг, север,
> Запад, восток.
>
>> Сии четыре страны,
>> Соответствуют средине.
>
> Вода, огнь,
> Древо, злато, земля (материя).[3]
>
>> Сии пять стихий,
>> Располагаются на числах.
>
> Любовь, справедливость,
> Благочиние, благоразумие, твердость.
>
>> Сих пяти вечностей,
>> Затмевать не должно.
>
> Конь, бык, баран,

---

[1] *Букварь китайской состоящей из двух китайских книжек, служит у китайцев для начальнаго обучения малолетных детей основанием* (A Chinese ABC book consisting of two Chinese booklets, which serves among the Chinese as a basis for the primary education of young children), trans. Aleksei Leontiev (St Petersburg 1779), pp.7-10.

[2] The explanation in parentheses, 'ten thousand', is Leontiev's.

[3] The explanation in parentheses, 'material', is Leontiev's.

Курица, пес, свинья.

Сии шесть скотин,
В домах содержатся нужными.

Радость, гнев,
Сетование, опасение.

Жалеть, ненавидеть, любить,
В сих семи заключаются чувства человеческия.

Кора,[4] глина, кожа,
Дерево, камень, золото.

Нить, камыш,
Составляют 8 тонов.

Прапрадед, прадед, дед,
От отца сам.

От самого сын,
От сына внук.

От внука сын,
От внукова сына сын.

Се есть девять колен,
Род человека составляющих.

Благодеяние отца, сына,
Склонность мужа, жены.

Горячность у брата большаго,
Почитание у брата меньшаго.

Различие старшаго, младшаго,
Прязнь друга, приятеля.

Осторожность до Государя,
Верность до раба.

Сии десять справедливостей,
Суть людям общественныя.

———————

Know the numbers, and remember
The sums and multiplication tables.

From one comes ten,
From ten one hundred.

From one hundred one thousand,
From one thousand *van* [ten thousand].

There are three powers,
Heaven, earth, man.

There are three luminaries,
The sun, the moon, the stars.

There are three foundations.
The justice of Ruler and slave.

The love of father and son.

[4] A note by Leontiev further defines the word *kora* as squash or gourd, without the seeds and inner part.

The attachment of husband and wife.

Spring, summer,
Fall, winter.

> The turning of these four seasons
> Is unending.

South, north,
West, east.

> These four cardinal points,
> Are relative to the middle.

Water, fire,
Wood, gold, earth [material]

> These five elements
> Are arranged by number.

Love, justice,
Decency, wisdom, steadfastness.

> These five eternities,
> Must not be replaced.

Horse, bull, ram,
Chicken, dog, pig,

> These six animals,
> Are kept as necessities in the households.

Happiness, anger,
Lamentation, fear.

To pity, to hate, to love,
> The human emotions consist of these seven things.

The gourd, clay, leather,
Wood, stone, gold.

The thread, the reed
> Constitute the eight tones.

Great great-grandfather, great-grandfather, grandfather,
Oneself from the father.

From oneself the son,
From the son the grandson.

From the grandson a son,
From the grandson's son a son.

> These are the nine generations,
> Composing the family of man.

The good deed of father, of son,
The attachment of husband, of wife.

The fervour of the elder brother,
The respect of the younger brother.

The distinction between senior, junior,
The good will of a friend, an acquaintance.

Prudence toward the Ruler,
Rectitude toward the slave.

These ten justices
Are common to man.

Excerpts from Leontiev's *Уведомление о чае и о шелке* (Information about tea and silk)

Number 37 Бабочки вышли (The Butterflies have emerged)[5]

> Из гнездышков из сеток прекрасны метлячки,
> На свет вышли беленки, а были червячки.
> По парочкам сошедшись, далеко не летят
> Яйчками своими, как золотом кропят,
> Вот плод от них остался нам черви возрастут,
> Червь каждой будет с шелком, камку после соткут.
> Как бабочки посохли, куда бы их девать?
> Всех на воду пускают, других уж будут ждать.

———————

> From the little nests, from the nets, beautiful butterflies
> Have come out into the light white,
>   but they were once worms.
> Having joined in pairs, they do not fly far.
> They sprinkle their eggs like gold.
> Their offspring have remained for us; the worms will grow.
> Each worm will have silk; later a silken fabric
>   will be woven.
> When the butterflies have withered, what will become
>   of them?
> They let them all out on the water; they will
>   already be awaiting others.

[5] *Уведомление о чае и о шелке. Из китайской книги ‹Вань-Боу Кюань› называемой* (Information about tea and silk. From the Chinese book entitled 'Van'-Bou Kiuan'), trans. Aleksei Leontiev (St Petersburg 1775), p.33.

Bibliography

Abbreviations used in the bibliography

THE following abbreviations have been used for the titles of Russian journals and publishers:

AI   *Академическия известия* (Academic news)
DRV   *Древняя российская вивлиофика* (Ancient Russian library)
ES   *Ежемесячныя сочинения к пользе и увеселению служащия* (Monthly compositions for use and enjoyment). Title varies: also, *Ежемесячныя сочинения и известия о ученых делах* (Monthly compositions and news of scholarly matters)
NES   *Новыя ежемесячныя сочинения* (New monthly compositions)
PDRN   *Продолжение Древней российской вивлиофики* (Continuation of the Ancient Russian library)
RV   *Русский вестник* (Russian herald)
SLRS   *Собеседник любителей российскаго слова* (Colloquy of the amateurs of the Russian word)
SSVM   *Собрание сочинений, выбранных из месяцословов на разные годы* (Collection of compositions selected from monthlies of various years)
SV   *Сибирский вестник* (Siberian herald)

General references and bibliographies

Cordier, Henri, *Bibliotheca sinica: dictionnaire bibliographique des ouvrages relatifs à l'Empire chinois*. 2nd ed. rev., corr. & aug. Paris 1904-1908

Cox, Edward G., *A reference guide to the literature of travel*. Seattle 1935-1949

Neustroev, Aleksandr Nikolaevich, *Историческое розыскание о русских повременных изданиях и сборниках за 1703-1802 гг.* (Historical research results on Russian periodical publications and collections for 1703-1802). St Petersburg 1875

– *Указатель к русским повременным изданиям и сборникам за 1703-1802 гг.* (Index to Russian periodicals and collections for 1703 to 1802). St Petersburg 1898. Reprint: Cleveland 1963

Описание изданий, напечатанных при Петре I (Сводный каталог Государственной публичной библиотеки имени М. Е. Салтыкова-Щедрина и Библиотеки Академии наук СССР со сведениями об изданиях 1689-1725 гг.) (Description of publications printed during the reign of Peter I [Union catalogue of the State Public Library named after M. E. Saltykov-Schedrin and of the Library of the Academy of Sciences of the USSR with information about publications of 1689-1725). Comp. T. A. Bykova and M. M. Gurevich, and *Дополнения и приложения* (Additions and supplements). Moscow, Leningrad 1955-1972

Русский биографический словарь (Russian biographical dictionary). St Petersburg 1896-1918

Skachkov, P. E., *Библиография Китая* (Bibliography of China). Moscow, Leningrad 1932. 2nd ed., rev. & enl. Moscow 1960

Сводный каталог русской книги гражданской печати XVIII века 1725-1800 (Union catalogue of the Russian book of the eighteenth century 1725-1800). Editorial Board: I. P. Kondakov and others. Compilers: E. I. Katsprzhak and others. Institutional sponsors: Министерство Культуры РСФСР (Ministry of Culture of the USSR), Государственная библиотека СССР имени В. И. Ленина (State Library of the USSR named after V. I. Lenin), and other libraries. Moscow 1963-1967, and *Дополнения, Разыскиваемые издания, Уточнения* (Supplements, Additional editions, Clarifications). Vol. 6. Editorial Board: N. M. Sikorskii and others. Moscow 1975.

Всесоюзная государственная библиотека иностранной литературы (All Union State Library of foreign literature). *Китайская художественная литература: Библиография русских переводов и критической литературы на русском языке* (Chinese artistic literature: Bibliography of Russian translations and of critical literature in Russian). Comp. P. E. Skachkov and I. K. Glagoleva. Moscow 1957.

Primary sources

Akademiia nauk SSSR. Institut Kitaevedeniia. (Academy of Sciences of the USSR. Intitute of sinology). *Русско-китайские отношения, 1689-1916; официальные документы* (Russo-Chinese relations, 1689-1916; Official documents). Comp. P. E. Skachkov and V. S. Miasnikov. Moscow 1958

(Amiot, Joseph Marie), 'О начале похода' (The Principle of attack). Trans. Sofronii Gribovskii. Excerpted from Amiot, *L'Art militaire des Chinois* (Paris 1772). *Военный журнал* (Military journal), Bk. 11 (1818), pp.1-5

Amiot, Joseph Marie, *Vie de Koung-tsée, appellé vulgairement Confucius. Mémoires concernant l'histoire, les sciences, les arts, les mœurs, les usages, etc. des Chinois. Par les missionaires de Pékin.* Paris 1776-1814. xii (1786)

(Amiot, Joseph Marie) Amio, Zh. M. *Житие Кунг-Тцеэа или Конфуциуса.* Trans. of above work by M. I. Verevkin. St Petersburg 1790

Anson, George, *Путешествие около света, которое в 1740, 41, 42, 43, 44, годах совершил адмирал лорд Ансон.* Comp. Richard Walter. Trans. of *A voyage round the World, in the years 1740, 1741, 1742, 1743, 1744.* St Petersburg 1751

Anson, George, *A voyage round the World, in the years 1740, 1741, 1742, 1743, 1744.* Comp. Richard Walter. 2nd ed. London 1748

Baier, T. Z., *Museum sinicum, in quo sinicae linguae et litteraturae ratio explicatur.* St Petersburg 1730

Baikov, F. I., 'Путешествие российского посланника Федора Исаковича Байкова в Китай, 7162 (1654) года июня 25 дня' (Journey of the Russian envoy Fedor Isakovich Baikov to China, 25 June 1654). DRV, no. 4 (1788), pp.120-42. Also appeared in SV (1820)

– 'Статейный список' (Journal). Trans. J. F. Baddeley. In Baddeley, John Frederick, *Russia, Monogolia, China.* London 1919 ii.135-53

– 'Статейный список' (Journal). In N. F. Demidova and V. S. Miasnikov, *Первые русские дипломаты в Китае (‹Роспись› И. Петлина и статейный список Ф. И. Байкова)* (The First Russian diplomats in China [I. Petlin's 'Description' and F. I. Baikov's Journal]). Moscow 1966, at pp.113-45

Bailly, J. S., 'Письма о начале наук и народов азийских'. Evidently a translation of *Lettres sur l'origine des sciences, et sur celle des peuples de l'Asie, adressées à m. de Voltaire* (London 1777). *Растущий виноград* (The Growing grapevine) (June 1785), p.40; (Sept. 1785), p.13; (Oct. 1785), p.5; (Nov. 1785), p.37; (Oct. 1786), p.9; (Nov. 1786), p.1; (Dec. 1786), p.5. Cited in Neustroev, p.110

Bakmeister, I., *Опыт о Библиотеке и Кабинете редкостей и истории натуральной Санктпетербургской императорской Академии наук* (Essay on the Library and the Rare Objects and Natural History Room of the St Petersburg Imperial Academy of Sciences). St Petersburg 1779

Bantysh-Kamenskii, N., *Дипломатическое собрание дел между российским и китайским государствами с 1619 по 1792-й год* (Diplomatic collection of affairs between the Russian and Chinese States from 1619 to 1792). Kazan 1882

Barrow, John, *Travels in China*. London 1804

(Bell, John) Bell, Dzhon, *Белевы путешествия чрез Россию в разныя асиятския земли; а именно: в Испаган, в Пекин, в Дербент и Константинополь.* Translation of Bell, *Voyages*, below. Trans. M. Popov. St Petersburg 1776
– *Travels from St Petersburg in Russia to diverse parts of Asia*. Glasgow 1763
– *A journey from St Petersburg to Pekin, 1719-22.* Ed. J. L. Stevenson. Edinburgh 1965
– *Voyages depuis St Petersbourg en Russie, dans diverses contrées de l'Asie*. Paris 1766

Bichurin, N. Ia., *Описание Пекина* (Description of Peking). St Petersburg 1829

(Bilfinger, Georg Bernhard) Bil'finger, G. B., *Опыт древней китайцов философии о их нравоучении и правлении, с приложением Проповеди* (Essay on the ancient philosophy of the Chinese regarding their moral teachings and government supplemented with a sermon). St Petersburg 1794

'Благодетель и мудрец' (The Benefactor and the sage). In *Полезное и увеселительное чтение для юношества и для всякаго возраста* (Useful and amusing reading for youth and all ages). Ed. Ia. Blagodarev. Moscow 1788. pp. 82-107. Also in *Чтение для вкуса, разума и чувствований* (Reading for taste, intelligence, and sensibility). No. 1. (1792), pp.107-31

Bogdanovich, I. F., 'Из Китайских повестей' (From Chinese tales). *Собрание новостей* (Collection of novelties) (Dec. 1775), pp.43-46

Bouvet, Joachim, 'Histoire de l'empereur de la Chine'. Trans. by J. Crull in *The Present condition of the Muscovite empire, till the year 1699* (London 1699). Russian trans. in F. O. Tumanskii, *Собрание разных записок и сочинений [...] о жизни [...] Петра Великаго* (Collection of various notes and works on the life of Peter the Great). St Petersburg 1787-1788. i (1787)

Brand, Adam, *Beschreibung der Chinesischen Reise*. Hamburg 1698
– *A journal of the embassy from their majesties John and Peter Alexievitz, emperors of Muscovy, etc., over land into China*. London 1698

Bratishchev, Vasilii, 'Осведомление, или некоторое поверение Волтеровых о Китае примечаний, собранное в краткую Братищева бытность в Пекине' (Information about or verification of Voltaire's remarks about China, collected during Bratischev's short stay in Peking). In *Опыт трудов Вольнаго Российскаго собрания при Императорском Московском университете* (Essays of the Free Russian Assembly of Moscow University), Pt. 6 (1783), pp.39-62
Букварь китайской состоящей из двух китайских книжек, служит у китайцев для начальнаго обучения малолетных детей основанием (A Chinese ABC book consisting of two Chinese booklets, which serves among the Chinese as a basis for the primary education of young children). Trans. Aleksei Leontiev. St Petersburg 1779.

Carpini, Giovanni de Plano, 'The journey of friar John of Pian de Carpini 1245-1247'. In *Contemporaries of Marco Polo*. Ed. Manuel Komroff. London 1929. pp.27-71

(Carpini, Giovanni de Plano) Karpini, Dzh., *Любопытнейшее путешествие монаха францисканскаго ордена Жана дю План Карпина, посыланнаго в 1246 году в достойнстве легата и посла от папы Иннокентия IV к татарам* (The Very interesting journey of the Franciscan monk Giovanni de Plano Carpini sent in 1246 as legate and consul to the Tatars by pope Innocent iv). Moscow 1795

(Castillon, Jean) Kastiion, Zhan, *Китайские, японские, сиамские, тонквинские и прочие анекдоты, в которых наипаче описываются нравы, поведения, обычаи и религии сих различных асийских народов*. Trans. of Castillon, *Anecdotes chinoises, japonoises, siamoises, tonquinoises, etc.* Moscow 1791

Catherine ii, 'Le Czarowitsch Feveh, second Conte russe'. In F. M. Grimm, *Correspondance littéraire, philosophique et cri-*

tique par Grimm, Diderot, Raynal, Meister, etc. Paris 1882. xvi.85-95

– Letter of 6 November 1790 to the prince de Ligne. In *Les Lettres de Catherine II au prince de Ligne.* Ed. the princess Charles de Ligne. Bruxelles, Paris 1924. p.134

– *Märchen von Zarewitsch Fewei.* Berlin, Stettin 1784

– *The Memoirs of Catherine the Great.* Ed. Dominique Maroger. Trans. from French by Moura Budberg. London 1955

– *Опера комическая Февей, составлена из слов скаски, песней руских и иных сочинений* (The Comic opera Fevei, composed from the words of the tale, of Russian songs and from other works). St Petersburg 1786

– *Письма и бумаги императрицы Екатерины II хранящияся в Императорской Публичной Библиотеке.* (Letters and papers of empress Catherine II preserved in the Imperial Public Library). Ed. A. F. Bychkov. St Petersburg 1873

– *Сказка о царевиче Февее* (The Tale of Prince Fevei). St Petersburg 1783

– 'Сказка о царевиче Февее' (The Tale of Prince Fevei), and 'Опера комическая Февей' (The Comic opera Fevei). In *Сочинения императрицы Екатерины II* (The Works of the empress Catherine II). Ed. A. Smirdin. St Petersburg 1849-1850. i (1849), pp.261-78 and pp.461-93

Catiforo, Antonio (Katiforo, Antonio), *Житие Петра Великаго, императора и цамодержца бцероцціихого* (The Life of Peter the Great, All-Russian emperor and ruler). St Petersburg 1772

Chambers, William, *A dissertation on oriental gardening [...] to which is annexed an explanatory discourse, by Tan Chetqua, of Quang-chew-fu, gent.* 2nd ed. with additions. London 1773

(Chambers, William) Uil'iam Cheimbers, *О китайских садах. Перевод из книги сочиненной г. Чамберсом содержащей в себе описание китайских строений, домашних их уборов, одеяний, махин и инструментов.* Trans. of Chambers, *Designs of Chinese buildings, furniture, dresses, machines and utensils [...] to which is annexed a description of their temples, houses, gardens, etc.* (London 1757). St Petersburg 1771

'Чензыя, китайского философа, совет, данной его государю' (The Advice of

Chen-tsu, a Chinese philosopher, to his ruler). *Трутень* (The Drone) (23 Feb. 1770), sheet VIII, 20. Also in P. N. Berkov (ed.), *Сатирические журналы Н. И. Новикова* (The Satirical journals of N. I. Novikov). Moscow, Leningrad 1951. pp.209-12

Chinesische Gedanken, nach der von Alexei Leontieff aus der manschurischen Sprache verfertigten russischen Übersetzung. Ins Deutsche übersetzt. Weimar 1776; 1778; 1796

Chuang Tzu, *Chuang Tzu: basic writings.* Trans. Burton Watson. New York, London 1964

Chulkov, Mikhail, *Историческое описание российской коммерции при всех портах и границах от древних времян до ныне настоящаго и всех преимущественных узаконений* (Historical description of Russian commerce at all ports and borders from early times to the present and of all preferential legislation). St Petersburg 1781-1788

Clerc, Nicolas Gabriel, *Yu le Grand et Confucius, histoire chinoise.* Soissons 1769

Confucius Sinarum philosophus, sive scientia sinensis latine exposita. Studio et opera Prosperi Intorcetta. Ed. Philippe Couplet. Paris 1687

Defoe, Daniel, *The Compleat English gentleman.* London 1890

– *The Farther adventures of Robinson Crusoe.* London 1719. Reprint, London 1925

(Defoe, Daniel) Defo, Daniel', *Жизнь и приключения Робинзона Круза природнаго агличанина* (The Life and adventures of Robinson Crusoe, an Englishman by nationality). Trans. Iakov Trusov. St Petersburg 1st ed. 1762-1764; 3rd ed. 1787; 4th ed. 1797

(Dentrecolles, François Xavier) Dantrekol', F. K. *Подробное описание, 1) как китайцы делают свой фарфор; 2) как китайцы разводят и кормят шелковых червей для получения от них лучшаго и многожайшаго шелку [...] В пользу имеющих, или желающих завести в Российской империи подобные заводы* (Detailed description of 1. how the Chinese make their porcelain; 2. how the Chinese cultivate and feed silk worms in order to obtain the best and the most silk from them [...] for the use of those having or wishing to introduce into the Russian empire similar industries). Trans. G. Smirnov. Moscow 1790

Депей китаец (Depei, the Chinese). Trans. A. Leontiev. St Petersburg 1771

Derzhavin, Gavriil, 'К первому соседу' (To the first neighbour) *Сочинения Державина* (Works of Derzhavin). Ed. I. Ia. Grot. St Petersburg 1864. i.102-106.

– 'На взятие Измаила' (On the taking of Izmail). *Works of Derzhavin*, i.341-61

– 'Памятник герою' (Monument to a hero). *Works of Derzhavin*, i.428-35

– 'Развалины' (The Ruins). *Works of Derzhavin*, ii.92-101

– *Записки* (Notes). *Works of Derzhavin*, vi.405-842

'Дневные записки караванного пути через Наунскую дорогу от Цурукайту до Пекина в 1736 году' (Journal of the caravan route by way of the Naun Road from Tsurukhaitu to Peking in 1736). AI, (April 1781), pp.466-505; (May 1781), pp.602-31

(Dodsley, Robert [supposed author]) Dodsli, R. *Экономия жизни человеческой, или сокращение индейскаго нравоучения*. Trans. E. & P. Tsitsianov from Dodsley, *The Economy*, below. Moscow 1765 & 1769; 1781; 1791

Dodsley, Robert (supposed author). *The Economy of human life*. Translated from an Indian manuscript, written by an ancient Bramin. London 1807. The Library of Congress catalog lists editions in '1749?' and 1750

(Dodsley, Robert [supposed author]) Dodsli, R. *Китайский мудрец, или Наука жить благополучно в обществе*. Trans. by S. P. Kolosov of *The Economy of human life*. St Petersburg 1773; 1777; 1785

– *Книга премудрости и добродетели, или Состояние человеческой жизни*. Trans. of *The Economy of human life*. Moscow 1786; 1794

– 'Устроение человеческой жизни'. Trans. of *The Economy of human life*. *Полезное увеселение* (Useful amusement) (Feb. 1762), pp.57-68; (April 1762), pp.147-73

'Другой Кандид или Друг истины' (The Other Candide or the friend of truth). In *Зимния вечеринки, другой Кандид, или Друг истины* (Winter evenings, The Other Candide, or the Friend of Truth).

Trans. I. N. Vodop'ianov. Moscow 1789

Du Halde, Jean Baptiste, *Ausführliche Beschreibung des chinesischen Reichs und der großen Tartarey*. Trans. from the French. Rostok 1747-1749

– *Description géographique, historique, chronologique, politique, et physique de l'Empire de la Chine*. Paris 1735.

(Du Halde, Jean Baptiste) Diu Gal'd, Zh. B., *Географическое, историческое, хронологическое, политическое и физическое описание Китайския империи и Татарии Китайския*. Trans. of Du Halde, *Description*, above. St Petersburg 1774-1777

– 'Известие о шелковых заводах, каким образом они учреждены в Китае и о прочем туда принадлежащем, переведеное из дю Гальдова описания Китайского государства. С приобщением некоторых, от прапорщика и китайского языка переводчика Лариона Россохина, учиненных примечаний' (News about silk factories, how they are established in China, and other relevant information, translated from Du Halde's Description of the Chinese government. With a supplement containing notes by ensign and translator of Chinese Ilarion Rossokhin). ES (May 1757), pp.387-461

'Духовная или завещательное письмо китайскаго богдыхана Юншинг' (Last will or testamentary letter of the Chinese emperor Yung-cheng). *Календарь* (Calendar), (1740), pp.80-88; SSVM, 1 (1785), pp.114-28, 190-202

(Fischer, Johann Eberhard) Fisher, I. E., 'Рассуждение о разных именах китайского государства и о ханских титулах' (Discussion of the various names of the Chinese State and imperial titles), ES (Oct. 1756), pp.311-27

– *Сибирская история с самаго открытия Сибири до завоевания сей земли российским оружием* (Siberian history from the actual discovery of Siberia to the conquest of this land by Russian arms). St Petersburg 1774

(Foucquet, Jean-François, trans.), 'Китайский катехизис, или разговор китайца Ку-зю, ученика Конфуциева, с принцем Ку, счном короля Лу, платившего дань китайскому императору Гюнвану за 417 лет до христ. эры' (Chinese catechism or a conversation of the Chinese Ku-ziu, a student of Confucius, with prince Ku, son of king Lu, who had paid the tax to the Chinese emperor Giunvan, in 471 B.C.). *Минерва* (Minerva), Pt. 1 (1806), pp.17-25. *Новый Пантеон отечественной словесности* (New Pantheon of literature of the fatherland), Pt. 3 (1819), pp.58-66

Ге Янь, то есть умныя речи (Ge Ian', or wise sayings). Trans. A. Leontiev. St Petersburg 1776; 1779

(Gerbillon, Jean François), Gerbillon, Io. F., 'Описание и известие о Великой Татарии' (Description and news of Great Tartary). Commentary by G. F. Müller. *Календарь* (Calendar) (1744-1747). SSVM, 1 (1785), pp.227-50

[Godunov, Petr Ivanovich], 'Ведомость о Китайском государстве' (Information about the Chinese government). PDRN, 7 (1791), pp.198-224

Godunov, Petr Ivanovich, *Ведомость о китайской земле* (Information about the land of China). In P. E. Skachkov, 'Ведомость о китайской земле', *Страны и народы Востока* (Lands and peoples of the East). Issue 2. Moscow 1961. pp.206-19

(Goldsmith, O.), '‹Китайская повесть› (из english книги *The Citizen of the World, or letters from a Chinese philosopher*)' ('Chinese tale' [from the English book *The Citizen, etc.*]). ES (Oct. 1763), pp.348-53

Gonzáles de Mendoça, Juan, *Historia de las cosas mas notables, ritos y costumbres, del gran reyno dela China*. Rome 1585

(Gribovskii), Sofronii, 'Известие о Китайском, ныне Манджуро-Китайском государстве' (News about the Chinese, now Manchu-Chinese, government). *Чтения в Императорском Обществе истории и древностей российских при Московском университете* (Papers of the Imperial Society of History and Antiquities of Russia at Moscow University), No. 1 (1861), pp.23-119

– 'Путешествие архимандрита Софрония Грибовскаго от Пекина до Кяхты в 1808 г.' (The Journey of archimandrite Sofronii Gribovskii from Peking to Kiakhta in 1808). SV 1 (1823), pp.1-14, 15-30, 31-44, 45-62

– 'Уведомление о начале бытия россиян в Пэйдзине и о существовании в оном грекороссийской веры' (Information about the beginning of the presence of the Russians in Peking and on the existence there of the Greco-Russian faith). In *Материалы для истории Российской духовной миссии в Пекине* (Materials for the history of the Russian religious mission in Peking). Ed. N. I. Veselovskii. St Petersburg 1905. pp.1-47

– 'Записка, без подписи, о трудностях, с которыми приходится считаться архимандриту в Пекине при обращении китайцев в христианство' (Note, unsigned, concerning the difficulties facing an archimandrite in Peking in converting the Chinese to Christianity). In Veselovskii, *Materials for the history of the Russian religious mission*, pp.59-64.

(Grosier, Jean Baptiste). Groz'er, 'Описание китайских войск и военного их порядка' (Description of the armed forces of the Chinese and their military organisation). NES, 28 (Oct. 1788), pp.47-55

Gueullette, Thomas Simon, 'L'Histoire d'Outzim-Ouchantey, Prince de la Chine'. *Les Mille et un quarts d'heure, contes tartares*. In *Le Cabinet des fées, ou collection choisie des contes des fées, et autres contes merveilleux*. Ed. C. J. Mayer. Genève, Paris 1785-1789. xxi (1786), pp.198-339

(Gueullette, Thomas Simon) Gëllet, Toma Simon, *Тысяча и одна четверть часа, повести татарския*. Trans. of Gueullette, *Les Mille, etc.*, above. Moscow 1765-1766; 2nd printing, 1777-1778

(Ides) Evert Ysbrandszoon. *Driejaarige Reise naar China*. Amsterdam 1704

Ides, Evert Ysbrandszoon, 'Проезжая посланному до китайского государства Елизарию Избранту 7200 г.' (Official papers of the envoy to the Chinese government Ysbrants Ides 7200). In F. O. Tumanskii, *Собрание разных записок и сочинений [...] о жизни Петра Великаго* (Collection of various notes and works on the life of Peter the Great). St Petersburg 1787-1788. i, pt. 2 (1787), pp.71ff

– 'Путешествие и журнал [...] Ебергарда Избраннедеса' (The Journey and the journal [...] of Everard Ysbrants Ides). DRV, No. 4, pt. 8 (1789), pp.360-475; Pt. 9 (1789), pp.387-461.

– *Three years travels from Moscow over-land to*

China. London 1706

Историческое и географическое описание Китайской империи, с изъяснением различных названий Китая (Historical and geographical description of the Chinese empire with explanations of the various names of China). Moscow 1789

'История Хины или китайская' (Chinese history). *История, генеология и география – Примечания к ‹Ведомостям›* (History, genealogy, and geography – Commentary on 'The News'), No.13-18 (1731)

'Известие о новых книгах' (News about new books). Review of *Букварь китайской. Санктпетербургский вестник* (St Petersburg herald), Pt. 6 (1780), pp.369-72

'Известие о новых книгах. Китайское уложение' (News about new books. The Chinese code). Review of *Китайское уложение* (Chinese code). *Санктпетербургский вестник* (St Petersburg herald) (Sept. 1779), pp.202-22

Johnstone, C. (Johnston), *The Pilgrim: or, a picture of life. In a series of letters, written mostly from London, by a Chinese philosopher, to his friend at Quang-Tong. Containing remarks upon the laws, customs, and manners of the English and other nations*. London [1775]

(Johnstone, Charles) Dzhonston, Charlz, *Пильгрим, то есть по обещанию странствующий, или Картина жизни*. Trans. of Johnstone, *The Pilgrim: or, a picture of life*. Trans. by N. N. Moscow 1793.

(Jouve, Joseph) Zhuv, Zhozef, *История о завоевании Китая манжурскими татарами*. Trans. by A. P. from Jouve, *Histoire de la conquête de la Chine par les Tartares mancheoux*. Moscow 1788

(K'ang-hsi) Kansi, *Государь друг своих подданных, или Придворныя, политическия поучения и нравоучительныя разсуждения манжурскаго и китайскаго хана Кан-сия, собранныя сыном его ханом Юн-джином* (The Ruler – a friend to his subjects, or political precepts and moral teachings of the Court by the Manchu and Chinese emperor K'ang-hsi, collected by his son, the emperor Yung-cheng). Trans. Aleksei Agafonov. St Petersburg 1795

– *Манжурскаго и китайскаго хана Кан-*

Сия книга придворных политических поучений и нравоучительных разсуждений собранная сыном его ханом Юн-джином (The Book of the political precepts and moral teachings of the Court of the Manchu and Chinese emperor K'ang-hsi collected by his son the emperor Yung-cheng). Trans. Aleksei Agafonov. St Petersburg 1788

Kantemir, Antiokh, 'Сатира II. На зависть и гордость дворян злонравных. Филарет и Евгений' (Satire II. On the envy and pride of wicked nobles. Filaret and Evgenii). *Поэты XVIII века, Библиотека поэта, Малая серия* (Poets of the 18th century, Library of the poet, Small series). 3rd ed. Leningrad 1958. i.137-50

Kircher, Athanasius, *China monumentis*. Amsterdam 1667

'Китай. Многолюдство. Армия. Полиция. Земледелие. Из путешествия аглинскаго Посла Лорда Макартнея' (China. Populousness. Army. Police. Agriculture. From the journey of the English ambassador lord Macartney). *Политический журнал* (Political journal), Pt. 2 (1796), pp.21-33

'Китайские анекдоты' (Chinese anecdotes). *Друг юношества* (The Friend of youth), No. 1 (1810), pp.75-87; No. 10 (1810), pp.100-109; No. 11 (1810), pp.54-73

'Китайские стихотворения: Спокойствие Пастуша (песня). Песня' (Chinese poems: The Little Shepherd's Calm [song]. Song). Trans. V. Olin from *Choix des lettres édifiantes, écrites des missions étrangères. Журнал древней и новой словесности* (Journal of ancient and modern literature), 4, pt. 4 (1819), pp.159-65

Китайския мысли (Chinese thought). Trans. A. Leontiev. St Petersburg 1772

Китайское уложение (Chinese code). Trans. A. Leontiev. 2 pts. St Petersburg 1778-1779

Klaproth, Iu., 'Заметки о китайско-русской границе, собранные Юлием Клапротом во время путешествия по оной в 1806 году' (Notes on the Chinese-Russian border, compiled by Julius Klaproth during a trip along it in 1806). *Северный архив* (Northern archives), No. 9 (1823), pp.184-204; No. 10 (1823), pp.253-77; No. 11 (1823), pp.328-46; No.

12 (1823), pp.413-32

(Kozel'skii, Iakov Pavlovich), *Китайский философ или Ученые разговоры двух индийцов Калана и Ибрагима* (The Chinese philosopher or scholarly conversations of two Indians, Kalan and Ibrahim). St Petersburg 1788.

– 'Рассуждения двух индийцев Калана и Ибрагима о человеческом познании' (The Discussions of two Indians, Kalan and Ibrahim, about human knowledge). Excerpts. In *Избранные произведения русских мыслителей второй половины XVIII века* (Selected works of Russian intellectuals of the second half of the 18th century). Moscow 1952. i.552-620

– *Разсуждения двух индийцов Калана и Ибрагима о человеческом познании* (The Discussion of two Indians, Kalan and Ibragim, about human knowledge). Second edition of *Китайский философ*, etc. St Petersburg 1788

Краткое хронологическое росписание китайских ханов; из книги Всеобщаго зерцала, с показанием леточисления китайскаго и римскаго, от начала Китайской империи по 1786 год (A short chronological list of the Chinese emperors from the book, the Universal mirror, with an indication of the Chinese and Roman dates, from the beginning of the Chinese empire to 1786). Trans. A. Agafonov. Moscow 1788

Krizhanich, Iurii, *Повествование о Сибири* (Report on Siberia). SV 17 (1822), pp.1-24, 25-46, 47-68; 18 (1822), pp.69-92

(Krusenstern, Adam Johann von) Kruzenshtern, Ivan Fedorovich, *Путешествие вокруг света в 1803, 4, 5 и 1806 годах* (Voyage around the World in the years 1803-1806). St Petersburg 1809-1813

Krusenstern, Adam Johann von, *Reise um die Welt in den Jahren 1803, 1804, 1805, und 1806*. St Petersburg 1810-1812; 2nd printing, Berlin 1811-1812

– *Voyage round the World in the years 1803, 1804, 1805, and 1806*. Trans. Richard Hoppner. London 1813

(Lacroix, Louis Antoine Nicolle de) Lakrua, L. A. N., *Географическое описание Азии, с присовокуплением к главным местам оныя политической и естест-* *венной истории* (A geographic description of Asia with a supplement of political and natural history for its main places). Translation of a chapter from *Géographie moderne*. Moscow 1789

La Harpe, Jean François de, *Abrégé de l'Histoire générale des voyages*. Paris 1780-1801

(La Harpe) Lagarp, Zh. F., *История о странствиях вообще по всем краям земнаго круга, сочинения господина Прево, сокращенная новейшим расположением чрез господина Ла-Гарпа* (A general history of voyages to all parts of the Earth, by Prévost, abridged with a new arrangement by mr. La Harpe). Trans. M. Verevkin. Moscow 1782-1787

Lange, Lorents, (Abridgement of narrative concerning the caravan of 1715-1716). In F. C. Weber, *Das veränderte Rußland*. Franckfurth 1721. pp.72-116. Also in A. F. Prévost, *Histoire générale des voyages*. Paris 1749. xx.288-314. See also Shafranovskaia, T. K., *Путешествие Лоренца Ланга в 1715-1716 гг.*

– 'Дневные записки караванного пути через Наунскую дорогу от Цурухайту до Пекина в 1736 году' (Journal of the caravan route by way of the Naun Road from Tsurukhaitu to Peking in 1736). AI (April 1781), pp.466-505; (May 1781), pp.602-31

– 'Ежедневная записка пребывания г. Ланга, агента [...] при дворе Пекинском, в 1721 и 1722 годе' (Daily notes on the stay of mr Lange, agent, at the Court of Peking in 1721-22). In John Bell, *Белевы путешествия*, above under 'Bell'. iii.i-viii, 1-150

– 'Journal of Lange's residence at Peking in 1727-28 (Third journey)'. In John Dudgeon, *Historical sketch of the ecclesiastical, political and commercial relations of Russia with China*. Peking 1872. Appendix. Also in reprint, 1940.

– *Journal of the residence of mr de Lange, agent of his Imperial Majesty of All the Russias, Peter the First, at the Court of Peking, during the years 1721 and 1722*. In John Bell, *Travels* (1763) and (1788), above under 'Bell'. ii.223-423

– 'Tagebuch einer in den Jahren 1727 und 1728 über Kjachta nach Peking unter Anführung des Agenten Lorenz Lange gethanen Karawanenreise'. In Pallas, *Neue nordische Beyträge zur physikalischen und geographischen Erd- und Völkerbeschreibung Naturgeschichte und Ökonomie.* St Petersburg, Leipzig 1781-1796. ii, ch. 7, pp.83-159

La Porte, Joseph de, *Le Voyageur français ou la connoissance de l'ancien et du nouveau monde.* Paris 1768-1795

(La Porte, Joseph de) La Port, Zhozef de, *Всемирный путешествователь, или Познание Стараго и Новаго света.* Trans. of La Porte, *Le Voyageur*, above. St Petersburg 1778-1794. 2nd ed., 1780-1786; 3rd ed., 1799-1816

Le Clerc, Nicolas Gabriel. *See* Clerc, Nicolas Gabriel

Lecomte, Louis Daniel, *Nouveaux mémoires sur l'état présent de la Chine.* Paris 1696-1698

Leibniz, Gottfried Wilhelm von, *Selections.* Ed. Philip P. Weiner. New York 1951
– 'Preface' to *Novissima Sinica* in *Opera omnia*. Ed. L. Dutens. Genève 1768. iv.78-86

Leontiev, A., *Описание китайской шахматной игры* (Description of the Chinese chess game). St Petersburg 1775

Lisianskii, Iurii, *Путешествие вокруг света в 1803, 4, 5, и 1806 годах.* (A voyage around the World in 1803-1806). St Petersburg 1812

(Lisianskii, Iurii) Urey Lisiansky, *A voyage round the World in the years 1803, 4, 5, and 6.* Trans. U. Lisianskii. London 1814

Lomonosov, M. V., 'Ода [...] Императору Петру Феодоровичу' (Ode to the emperor Peter Feodorovich). *Полное собрание сочинений* (Complete works). Moscow, Leningrad 1950-1959. viii (1959), pp.751-60
—Lomonosov, M. V., 'Письмо о пользе стекла' (Letter on the usefulness of glass). *Полное собрание сочинений* (Complete works). Moscow, Leningrad 1950-1959. viii (1959), pp.508-22

(Lorenzi, Giovanni Battista) Lorentsi, Dzhovanni Battista, *Идол китайский, шутливая музыкальная драмма представленная на новом Сарскосельском театре августа дня 1779 – L'Idolo chinese, dramma giocoso per musica da rappresentarse nel nuovo teatro di sarsco selo il giorno d'augosto 1779.* Trans. V. A. Levshin. St Petersburg

1779
– *Идол китайский, шутливая музыкальная драмма, представленная на новом Сарскосельском театре июля дня 1779 года.* Trans. by V. A. Levshin of *L'Idolo chinese*. St Petersburg 1779

Macartney, George, *An embassy to China.* Ed. J. L. Cranmer-Byng. Hamden, Conn. 1963

Mailla, Joseph Anne Marie Moyriac de, *Histoire générale de la Chine, ou annales de cet empire traduites du Tong-Kien-Kang-Mou.* Paris 1777-1785

Материалы для истории Российской духовной миссии в Пекине (Materials for the history of the Russian religious mission in Peking). Ed. N. I. Veselovskii. St Petersburg 1905

Mémoires concernant l'histoire, les sciences, les arts, les mœurs, les usages, etc. des Chinois. Par les missionaires de Pékin. Paris 1776-1814

Mendoça. *See* Gonzáles de Mendoça

Meng, Ssu-ming, 'The E-lo-ssu kuan (Russian hostel) in Peking'. *Harvard journal of Asiatic studies* 23 (1960-61), pp.19-46

Millot, Claude François Xavier, *Histoire moderne.* Pt. 4 of *Histoire générale. Œuvres.* Paris 1816-1820. vii (1820)

(Millot, Claude François Xavier) Millo, Klod Fransua Ksav'e, *О состоянии Асии и новейших переменах Китая, Японии, Персии, и Мунгалии в последния времена.* Trans. by Ivan Ikonnikov of 'De l'état et des principales révolutions de l'Asie dans les derniers siècles' from *Histoire générale*

'Монолог из китайскои трагедии, называемой Сирота' (Monologue from the Chinese tragedy entitled 'The Orphan'). Retranslated from the German by A. P. Sumarokov. *Трудолюбивая пчела* (The Busy bee) (Sept. 1759), p.570

Montesquieu, Charles de Secondat de, *De l'esprit des lois. Œuvres.* Ed. R. Caillois. Paris 1949-1951. ii (1951), pp.227-1037

(Montesquieu, Charles de Secondat de) Montesk'ë, Sharl' Lui de, *О разуме законов.* Trans. of *De l'esprit des lois* by Vasilii Kramarenkov. St Petersburg 1775

Müller, G. F., *Eröffnung eines Vorschlages zu Verbesserung der Russischen Historie.* St Petersburg 1732-1764. Vol. x, Supplement. *Sammlung Russischer Geschichte.*

Dorpat 1816

- 'История о странах при реке Амуре лежащих, когда оныя состояли под Российским владением' (History of the lands located on the Amur River, when they belonged to Russia). ES (July-October 1757), p.3 *passim*
- 'Изъяснение сумнительств находящихся при постановлении границ между Российским и Китайским Государствами 7197 года' (An explanation of the ambiguities involved in the establishment of the boundaries between the Russian and Chinese states in the year 7197 [1689]). ES (April 1757), pp.305-21
- 'О первых Российских путешествиях и посольствах в Китай' (The First Russian travellers and embassies to China). ES (July 1757), pp.15-55
- *Описание Сибирскаго царства и всех произшедших в нем дел, от начала а особливо от покорения его Российской державе по сии времена* (Description of the Siberian realm and all that has taken place there from the beginning but especially from its conquest by Russian arms to the present time). Bk. 1. Trans. V. Lebedev and I. Golubtsov. St Petersburg 1750. Bk. 2, *Сибирская история* (Siberian history). Trans. I. Golubtsov. ES, 20 (Jan.-June 1764), pp.3-43, 99-135, 195-237, 291-324, 387-418, 483-528

'О Китайском посольстве в Россию' (On the Chinese embassy to Russia). *Примечания на ‹Ведомости›* (Remarks on 'The News'), (1730), p.195

О китайском правлении. Взято из Энциклопедии, сочиненной собранием ученых мужей (On the Chinese government. Taken from the *Encyclopédie* composed by a society of learned men [Diderot and d'Alembert]). Trans. Ivan Zhdanovskii. Moscow 1789

'О книгах: Китайский мудрец или наука жить благополучно в обществе' (About books: the Chinese sage or the science of living successfully in society). *Санктпетербургския ученыя ведомости* (St Petersburg scholarly news), No. 21 (1777), pp.167-68; No. 22 (1777), pp.169-71

'*О некоторых обыкновениях Китайских. Отрывок из путешествия в Китай Английского Посла Граф Макартнея*' (Various customs of the Chinese. Excerpt from the journey to China of the English ambassador lord Macartney). *Вестник Европы* (Herald of Europe) 15 (1805), pp.195-206

'О садах в Китае' (On Gardens in China). *Экономический магазин* (Economic magazine), Pt. 25 (1786), pp. 321, 337, 353

Обстоятельное описание происхождения и состояния маньджурскаго народа и войска, в осми знаменах состоящаго. (Detailed description of the origin and state of the Manchu people and their army, consisting of eight banners). Trans. I. K. Rossokhin & A. L. Leontiev. St Petersburg 1784

Описание жизни Конфуция, китайских философов начальника (Description of the life of Confucius, the leading Chinese philosopher). Ed. Philippe Couplet, corrector Shcheglov. Moscow 1780

(Ornatskii), Amvrosii. 'Краткое описание Китайскаго Пекинскаго монастыря' (A short description of the Chinese Peking monastery). In *История Российской иерархии* (History of the Russian Church hierarchy). Moscow 1807-1815. ii (1810), pp.439-500

(Ornatskii), Amvrosii, 'Schicksale der russischen Kirche in China'. In Müller, *Eröffnung*, above. x, *Sammlung* (1816), pp.277-96

Pallas, Peter Simon, *Sammlungen historischer Nachrichten über die Mongolischen Völkerschaften*. St Petersburg 1776-1801

(Pastoret, Claude Emmanuel Joseph Pierre) Pastore, Klod Emmaniuel' Zhosef P'er, *Зороастр, Конфуций и Магомет, сравненные как основатели вер, законодатели и нравоучители, с приобщением табелей их догматов, законов и нравственности*. Trans. of *Zoroastre, Confucius et Mahomet, comparés comme sectaires, législateurs et moralistes*. Moscow 1793

Pauw, Cornelius de, *Recherches philosophiques sur les Egyptiens et les Chinois*. Berlin 1773

Pensées morales de divers auteurs chinois, recueillies et traduites du latin et du russe [de Léontieff] par Levesque. Paris 1782

Переводы из Энциклопедии (Translations from the *Encyclopédie*). Moscow 1767

'Переводы с китайского языка. I Перевод

с китайской печатной копии снятой с найденного в земле камня. II Перевод с китайской газеты публикованной в 5 день 2 луны 31 года царствования Хана Кансия (1692) коя содержит в себе Езуитскую челобитную, и по челобитной решительную резолюцию' (Translations from the Chinese. I Translation from a Chinese printed copy taken from a stone found in the earth. II Translation from a Chinese newspaper published on the fifth day of the second month of the thirty-first year of the reign of the emperor K'ang Hsi [1692] which contains a Jesuit petition and an affirmative reply to the petition). Trans. Aleksei Leontiev. ES, (Dec. 1764). i at pp.516-27 and ii at pp.528-36

Petlin, Ivan, 'Роспись' (Description). In N. F. Demidova and V. S. Miasnikov, *Первые русские дипломаты в Китае (‹Роспись› И. Петлина и статейный список Ф. И. Байкова)* (The First Russian diplomats in China [Petlin's 'Description' and F. I. Baikov's Journal]. Moscow 1966 at pp.41-58

– 'Роспись Китайскому государству и по обинскому и иным государствам, жилым и кочевым улусам и великой Обе реки и дорогам' (Description of the Chinese nation and other governments, towns and nomadic settlements along the Ob and the Great Ob River and routes). SV 2 (1818), pp.211-46

– 'Статейный список' (Journal). Trans. J. F. Baddeley. In John Frederick Baddeley, *Russia, Mongolia, China*. London 1919. ii.73-84

(Pope, Alexander) Pop, Aleksandr, *Храм славы* (The Temple of Fame). Trans. M. M. Kheraskov. Moscow 1761

– *Храм славы из творений славнаго Попе* (The Temple of Fame from the work of the famous Pope). Trans. Pavel L'vov. St Petersburg 1790

Pope, Alexander, *The Poems of Alexander Pope*. Ed. John Butt. New Haven 1966

Prévost. *See* La Harpe

Prévost, Antoine François, *Histoire générale des voyages*. Paris 1746-1779

Проповедь о Христе спасителе в Китайском царстве, изображенная китайским писмом в 781 году по рождестве Христове на камне (A sermon about Christ the Saviour in the Chinese empire inscribed on stone in Chinese characters in the year 781 A.D.). Trans. A. Leontiev. St Petersburg 1784

Pushkin, A. S., *Полное собрание сочинений* (Complete works). Moscow, Leningrad 1937-1949

'Путешествие добродетели' (The Journey of virtue). *Утренний свет* (The Morning light), 2 (1778), pp.239-66; 3 (1778), pp.97-184, 191-263. *Путешествие добродетели, или Странствование по свету юнаго китайскаго царевича с философом предводительствовавшим и научившим онаго; в новейшия времена случившееся* (The Journey of virtue, or travels around the World of a young Chinese prince with a philosopher who guides and teaches him; which happened in modern times). Trans. A. K. Moscow 1782

Radishchev, A. N., *Избранные сочинения* (Selected works). Moscow, Leningrad 1949

– 'Письмо о китайском торге (1792)' (Letter on the Chinese trade [1792]). *Полное собрание сочинений А. Н. Радищева* (Complete collection of the works of A. N. Radishchev). Ed. A. K. Borozdin and others. St Petersburg 1907. ii.201-42

(Ramsay, Andrew Michael) Ramzai, E. M., *Новое Киронаставление, или Путешествия Кировы с приложенными разговорами о богословии и баснотворстве древних*. Trans. by A. Volkov of *Les Voyages de Cyrus, avec un discours sur la mythologie*. Moscow 1765

– *Новая Киропедия, или Путешествия Кировы*. Trans. of Volkov corrected by S. S. Bobrov. Moscow 1785

Ramsay, Andrew Michael, *The Travels of Cyrus. To which is annexed, a discourse upon the theology and mythology of the pagans*. London 1757

(Raynal, G. T. F.) Reinal, G. T. F., 'Политическия разсуждения о китайцах' (Political considerations about the Chinese). Trans. Vasilii Zuev. *Растущий виноград* (Growing grapevine), (Dec. 1785), pp.46-64; (Feb. 1786), pp.54-74; (March 1786), pp.60-74; (April 1786), pp.86-95; (May 1786), pp.90-98; (June 1786), pp.78-84; (July 1786), pp.60-76; (Aug. 1786), pp.84-92; (Sept. 1786), pp.69-86

'Разговор Китайского посла с русским чиновником' (Conversation of the Chinese consul with a Russian official). RV, 12 (Dec. 1810), 1-14

Ripa, Matteo, *Memoirs of father Ripa, during thirteen years residence at the Court of Peking in the service of the emperor of China*. Selected and trans. from the Italian by Fortunato Prandi. New ed. London 1855

Rossiiskaia imperatorskaia dukhovnaia missiia, Pekin (Imperial Russian ecclesiastical mission, Peking). *Труды членов Российской духовной миссии в Пекине* (Works by the members of the Russian ecclesiastical mission in Peking). St Petersburg 1852-1866

Rousseau, Jean-Jacques, *Discours sur les sciences et les arts*. Ed. G. R. Havens. New York, London 1946

– 'Economie (morale et politique)'. *Encyclopédie, ou dictionnaire raisonné des sciences, des arts et des métiers*. Ed. Denis Diderot. Lausanne, Berne 1779-1786. xi (1779), pp.776-96

(Rousseau, Jean-Jacques) Russo, Zhan Zhak, *Гражданин, или Разсуждение о политической экономии*. Trans. of the article 'Economie (morale et politique)' from Diderot's *Encyclopédie*. Trans. V. Medvedev. St Petersburg 1787

Rousseau, Jean-Jacques, *Julie, ou la nouvelle Héloïse*. *Œuvres complètes*. Ed. Bernard Gagnebin and Marcel Raymond. Paris 1964. ii

(Rousseau, Jean-Jacques) Russo, Zhan Zhak, *Новая Елоиза*. Trans. by Pavel Potemkin of pt. 1 of *La Nouvelle Héloïse*. Moscow 1769

– *Новая Елоиза*. Trans. by Petr Andreev of pt. 2 of *La Nouvelle Héloïse*. St Petersburg 1792

– *Новая Елоиза*. Trans. of pts. 1-2 of *La Nouvelle Héloïse*. St Petersburg 1792-1793

– *Разсуждение, удостоенное награждения от Академии Дижонской в 1750 году*. Trans. by Pavel Potemkin of *Discours sur les sciences et les arts*. Moscow 1768; 1787

– *Речь Ж. Ж. Руссо, удостоенная в 1750 году от Дижонской академии награждения*. Trans. by M. Iudin of *Discours sur les sciences et les arts*. St Petersburg 1792

– *Статья о политической экономии, или государственном благоучреждении*. Trans. by A. I. Luzhkov of 'Economie (morale et politique)' from Diderot's *Encyclopédie*. St Petersburg 1777

Русско-китайские отношения в XVII веке. Материалы и документы (Russo-Chinese relations in the 17th century. Materials and documents). Eds. N. F. Demidova, V. S. Miasnikov and others. Moscow 1969-1972

S., M., 'О благоговении сыновнем у китайцев, почерпнуто из последних известии христианских проповедников, находящихся в Пекине и издано в Париже прошлого 1779 года' (Filial piety in China, taken from the latest news of the Christian missionaries in Peking and published last year, 1779, in Paris). AI, Pt. 4 (April 1780), pp.516-28

S., M. (Sushkova, Maria), 'Письмо Китайца к Татарскому Мурзе, живущему по делам своим в Петербурге' (Letter of a Chinese to a Tatar nobleman living in St Petersburg on business). SLRS, Pt. 5 (1783), pp.3-8

'Сад Сеэ-Ма-Куанга. Поэма' (The Garden of Ssŭ-ma Kuang. A poem). Trans. of 'Le Jardin de Sée-ma-kouang' from *Mémoires concernant les Chinois* (above). ii (1777), pp.643-50. *Записки, надлежащия до истории* (below). iv (1787), pp.339-45

Сборник постановлений и распоряжений по цензуре с 1720 по 1862 год (Collection of decrees and decisions on censorship from 1720 to 1862). St Petersburg 1862. Cited in I. Aisenshtok, p.785

Schnitscher, J. C., *Berättelse om Ajuckiniska Calmuckiet, eller om detta Folkets Ursprung, huru de kommit under Ryssamas Lydno, deras Gndar, Gndsdyrkan och Prester [...] deras Politique och Philosophie, etc*. Stockholm 1744

– 'Nachricht von den Ajuckischen Calmücken.' Trans. from the Swedish. In G. F. Müller, *Eröffnung eines Vorschlages* St Petersburg 1760. iv.275-364

(Schnitscher, J. C.), 'Записка Шведского Капитана И. Х. Шничера, который был у Китайских посланников бывших в 1714 году у Аюки-Хана в провожатых, с копией ландкарты в Пекине напечатанной' (Note by the Swedish captain J. Ch. Schnitscher who escorted the Chinese consuls who visited Aiuki Khan in 1714, with a copy of a map printed in Peking). ES (Nov. 1764), pp.428-40

(Shun-chih) Shun'-Dzhi, *Манжурскаго и китайскаго хана Шунь-Джия. Книга нужнейших разсуждений ко благополучию поощряющих*. (The Book of the most important teachings encouraging well-being by the Manchu and Chinese emperor Shun-chih). Trans. A. Agafonov. St Petersburg 1788

– *Манжурскаго и китайскаго Шунь-Джи-хана книга Полезный и нужный образ к правлению*. (The Book, 'The useful and necessary form of government' by the Manchu and Chinese emperor Shun-Chih). Trans. Aleksei Agafonov. St Petersburg 1788)

(Smorzhevskii, Feodosii), 'Об иезуитах в Китае. (Отрывок из китайских записок иеромонаха Феодосия Сморжевскаго)' (The Jesuits in China. [Excerpt from the Chinese notes of the priest Feodosii Smorzhevskii]). Contributed by E. F. Timkovskii. SV, Pt. 19 (1822), pp.107-32, 181-210; Pt. 20 (1822), pp.227-54, 295-310, 329-56

Smorzhevskii, Feodosii, 'Выписка из замечаниев о Пекинских духовных миссиях' (Extract from remarks on the Peking ecclesiastical missions). In Veselovskii's *Materials* at pp.65-71

Spafarii, N. G., *Описание первые части вселенныя, именуемой Азии, в ней же состоит Китайское государство с прочими его городы и провинции* (Description of the first part of the universe, called Asia, in which is located the Chinese State with its various cities and provinces). Kazan 1910

– 'Spathary: his embassy to China, 1675-77'. Trans. J. F. Baddeley. In John Frederick Baddeley, *Russia, Mongolia, China*. London 1919. ii.242-422

– 'Статейный список' (Journal). In Iu. V. Arsenev, 'Статейный список посольства Н. Спафария в Китае 1675-1678 гг.' (Journal of the embassy of N. Spafarii in China 1675-1678). *Вестник археологии и истории* (Herald of archaeology and history), 17 (1906). Also published separately in the same year

Старинныя письма китайскаго императора к российскому государю (Old letters from the emperor of China to the Russian sovereign). Ed. Matvei Komarov. Moscow 1787

Staunton, George Leonard, *An authentic account of an embassy from the king of Great Britain to the emperor of China*. 2nd ed. London 1798

(Staunton, George Leonard) Stonton, Dzhordzh; (George Macartney) Dzhordzh Makartnei, *Путешествие во внутренность Китая и в Татарию, учиненное в 1792, 1793, 1794 гг. лордом Макартнеем* (The Journey into the interior of China and Tartary made by lord Macartney in the years 1792-1794). Trans. from the French. Moscow 1804-1805

(Stritter, Johann Gotthelf) Shtritter, I. G., 'Историческое и географическое описание г. Пекина' (Historical and geographical description of the city of Peking). *Исторический и географический месяцослов* (Historical and geographic monthly), 20 (1781), pp.151-87. SSVM, 5 (1790), pp.1-33

Sushkova. *See* S., M. 'Письмо'

Sviateishii Pravitel'stvuiushchii Vserossiiskii Sinod (Most Holy Governing All-Russian Synod). 'Инструкция от Святейшаго Правительствующаго Всероссийскаго Синода' (Instructions from the Most Holy Governing All-Russian Synod). In Veselovskii, *Materials*, pp.53-58

Сы шу гей, то есть четыре книги с толкованиями (Ssu Shu, i.e., the four books with explanations). Trans. A. Leontiev. St Petersburg 1780-[84]

Swift, Jonathan, *Gulliver's travels*. Ed. Harold Williams. London 1926

'Tagebuch einer im Jahre 1736 unter Anführung des Kanzleyraths Lange und des Commissars Firsof von Zuruchaitu durch die Mongoley nach Peking verrichteten Karawanenreise'. In Peter Simon Pallas, *Neue nordische Beyträge zur physikalischen und geographischen Erd- und Völkerbeschreibung, Naturgeschichte und Ökonomie*. Leipzig, St Petersburg 1781-1796. ii, ch. 8, pp.160-207

'Та-Гио, или Великая наука' (Ta Hsüeh, or the great learning). Trans. D. I. Fonvizin. AI (1779), Part 2, pp.59-101

Тайцин гурунь и Ухери коли, то есть все законы и установления китайскаго (а ныне манжурскаго правительства (Taitsin Gurun' and Ukheri Koli, or all of the laws and regulations of the Chinese [now Manchu] government). Trans. A. Leontiev. St Petersburg 1781-1783

'Tchao Chi cou ell oder der junge Waise aus dem Hause Tchao. Eine Chinesische Tragödie'. In Du Halde, *Ausführliche Beschreibung*, above, iii.420-44

(Temple, W.) Templ, U. 'О народных недовольствах' (Of popular discontents). In *Опыт о народных недовольствах* (Essay on popular discontents). Trans. P. P. Kurbatov. St Petersburg 1778

– 'О здравии и о жизни долголетней' (On health and long life). In *Опыт*, previous entry

Tindal, Matthew, *Christianity as old as the Creation*. London 1730

Тшуанг-Тзе и Тиена, или Открытая неверность повесть китайская, с приобщением трех повестей из книги, называемой Превраты щастия (Chuang Tzu and Tiena (?) or open infidelity, a Chinese story, with three stories from the book, Reversals of fortune). Trans. from the French by A.V.K.P.A.: P.Tr.P.P.V. St Petersburg 1785

(Tulishen), 'Auszug einer Chinesischen Reise-Beschreibung von Peking durch Sibirien nach der Astrachanischen Calmückey'. German trans. based on French trans. by A. Gaubil in Müller, *Eröffnung*, above, at i.327-48

– *Narrative of the Chinese embassy to the Khan of the Tourgouth Tartars*. Trans. George Thomas Staunton. London 1821

– 'Описание путешествия, коим ездили китайские посланники в Россию, бывшие в 1714 г. у калмытского хана Аюки на Волге' (Description of a journey to Russia by the Chinese consuls who visited the Kalmuk Khan Aiuki on the Volga in 1714). Trans. A. Rossokhin. ES, 2 (1764), pp.3-48, 99-150, 195-234, 291-353, 387-413

– 'Прибавление к китайскому путешественному описанию, которое находится в оной же китайской книге' (Supplement to the Chinese travel description, which is in the same Chinese book). ES, (Nov. 1764), pp.414-27

– *Путешествие китайскаго посланника к калмытскому Аюке хану, с описанием земель и обычаев российских* (The journey of the Chinese consul to the Kalmuk Khan Aiuki with a description of the Russian lands and customs). Trans. A. Leontiev. St Petersburg 1782; 1788

– 'Relation chinoise'. Abridged trans. by A. Gaubil in E. Souciet, *Observations mathématiques, astronomiques, géographiques, chronologiques, et physiques, tirées des anciens livres chinois; ou faites nouvellement aux Indes et à la Chine; par les pères de la Compagnie de Jésus*. Paris 1729. i.148-75

Turgot, A. R. J., 'Questions sur la Chine adressées a deux Chinois, suivies de Réflexions sur la formation et la distribution des richesses'. In *Œuvres et documents*. Ed. G. Schelle. Paris 1913-1923. ii; [1st ed., Paris 1776]

Уведомление о чае и о шелке. Из китайской книги Вань Боу Кюань называемой (Information about tea and silk from the Chinese book entitled *Van'-Bou Kiuan'*). Trans. A. Leontiev. St Petersburg 1775

Vigel, F. F. *Записки (Издание ‹Русского архива›. Дополненное с подлинной рукописи)* (Memoirs, 'Russian archives' edition. Supplemented from the original manuscript). Moscow 1891-1892

Voltaire, F. M. A., *Correspondence and related documents. The Complete works of Voltaire*. Ed. Theodore Besterman. Genève, Banbury, Oxford 1968-1977

– *An essay upon the civil wars of France*. 2nd ed. London 1728

(Voltaire, F. M. A.), 'Естественный закон поэма'. Trans. by I. I. Vinogradov of 'Poème sur la loi naturelle'. In *Жизнь славнейшаго г. Вольтера* (The Life of the most famous Voltaire). St Petersburg 1787. pp.77-126

(Voltaire, F. M. A.) Vol'ter, F. M. A., *Философическия речи о человеке*. Trans. by I. G. Rakhmaninov of 'Discours en vers sur l'homme, vi'. St Petersburg 1788

– *Генриада, героическая поэма г. Волтера, переведенная с французскаго языка стихами*. Trans. in verse by A. I. Golitsyn of *La Henriade*. Moscow 1790

Генрияда, героическая поэма в десяти песнях. Trans. by Iakov Kniazhin of *La Henriade*. St Petersburg 1777

– 'Генриады'. Trans. from *Le Temple de l'Amitié* and *La Henriade*. AI, Pt. 5 (1780), pp.85-96

– *Китайский сирота – трагедия*. Trans.

into Russian verse by Vasilii Nechaev of *L'Orphelin de la Chine*. St Petersburg 1788

Voltaire, F. M. A., *Notebooks I. The Complete works of Voltaire* 81. Ed. Theodore Besterman. Genève 1968

(Voltaire, F. M. A.), *Новое расположение истории человеческаго разума*. Trans. of *Nouveau plan d'une histoire de l'esprit humain*. St Petersburg 1775

– 'О славе. Разговор с китайцем'. Trans. by A. L. Dubrovskii of 'Gloire. III Entretien avec un Chinois'. ES, 4 (Sept. 1756), pp.303-07. *Прохладные часы* (Cool hours) Pt. 2, (1793), pp.71-77

Voltaire, F. M. A., *L'Orphelin de la Chine. Œuvres complètes*. Ed. Moland. Paris 1877-1885. v (1877), pp.291-358

(Voltaire, F. M. A.) Vol'ter, F. M. A., 'Отрывки из Разговор о человеке'. Excerpts from 'Discours en vers sur l'homme'. *Иртышь* (Oct. 1789), p.34

Voltaire, F. M. A., *Poème sur la loi naturelle. Œuvres complètes*. Ed. Moland. Paris 1877-1885. ix (1877), pp.439-64

– *Précis du siècle de Louis XV. Œuvres complètes*. Ed. Moland. Paris 1877-1885. xv (1878), pp.145-435

(Voltaire, F. M. A.) Vol'ter, F. M. A., *Принцесса Вавилонская*. Trans. by F. Polunin of *La Princesse de Babylone*. [Moscow] 1770

– 'Разговор Иокт-шина, китайского императора, с иезуитом Риголетом'. Manuscript translation of 'Relation du bannissement des jésuites de la Chine (L'Empereur de la Chine et le frère Rigolet)'. Cited in P. R. Zaborov, 'Вольтер в русских переводах XVIII века' (Voltaire in Russian translations of the eighteenth century). Academy of Sciences of the U.S.S.R., Institute of Russian Literature (Pushkin House), *Эпоха просвещения: из истории международных связей русской литературы* (The Age of Enlightenment: from the history of the international ties of Russian literature). Leningrad 1967. pp.110-207, at p.206

Voltaire, F. M. A., 'Relation du bannissement des jésuites de la Chine' ('L'Empereur de la Chine et le frère Rigolet'). *Œuvres complètes*. Ed. Moland. Paris 1877-1885. xxvii (1879), pp.1-16

(Voltaire, F. M. A.) Vol'ter, F. M. A.,

Задиг или Судба, восточная повесть; и Свет каков есть, видение Бабука, писанное им самим. Trans. by I. L. Golenishchev-Kutozov of *Zadig* and *Le Monde comme il va*. St Petersburg 1765, 1788, 1795. ES, 9 (Jan. 1759), pp.58ff.

Вторый Кандид, уроженец китайской, или Друг истинны, южная повесть (Candide the second, a native of China, or the friend of truth, a southern story). Trans. Petr Vel'iaminov. St Petersburg 1774

Walter. *See* Anson

(Wieland, Christoph Martin) Viland, Kristof Martin, *Золотое зеркало, или Цари Шешианские, истинная повесть*. Trans. of *Der goldene Spiegel, oder die Könige von Scheschian*. Moscow 1781

(Yung-cheng), Iunchzhen, *Китайския поучения, изданныя от хана Юнджена для воинов и простаго народа, в 2 году царствования его* (Chinese precepts published by the emperor Yung-cheng for soldiers and common people in the second year of his reign). Trans. A. Leontiev. St Petersburg 1788

Записки, надлежащия до истории, наук, художеств, нравов, обычаев, и проч. китайцев, сочиненныя проповедниками веры христианской в Пекине. Trans. of *Mémoires concernant [...] les Chinois*, above. Moscow 1786-1788

Записки о русском посольстве в Китай (1692-1695) (Notes on the Russian embassy to China (1692-1695)). Comp. M. I. Kazanin. Moscow 1967

'Завещание Юнджена, китайского хана, к его сыну' (The Testament of Yungcheng, the emperor of China, to his son). *Пустомеля* (The Twaddler) (July 1770). In *Сатирические журналы Н. И. Новикова*. Ed. P. N. Berkov (Satirical journals of N. I. Novikov). Moscow, Leningrad 1951. pp.267-71

Житие Кунг-Тсеэа или Конфуциуса, как именуют его европейцы (The Life of Kung-Tsee or Confucius as he is called by Europeans). Trans. by M. I. Verevkin of Amiot, *Vie de Koung-tsee*, above

Зимния вечеринки, другой Кандид, или Друг истины (Winter evenings, the other Candide or the friend of truth). Trans. I. N. Vodop'ianov. Moscow 1789

'Зсе-ма-коанг, или испытанная верность'

(Ssŭ-ma Kuang or fidelity put to the test). Trans. P. L'vov, *Приятное и полезное препровождение времени* (Pleasant and useful pastime). Pt. 16 (1797), pp.257-70, 273-80

Secondary sources

Adams, Percy G., *Travelers and travel liars, 1660-1800*. Berkeley, Los Angeles 1962

(Adoratskii), Nikolai. 'Православная миссия в Китае за 200 лет ее существования' (The Orthodox mission in China during the 200 years of its existence). Kazan 1887. *Православный собеседник* (The Orthodox companion). (Feb.-Oct. 1887)

Aisenshtok, I., 'Французские писатели в оценках царской цензуры' (French writers in the evaluations of the tsarist censorship). *Литературное наследство* (Literary heritage). Vols. xxxiii-xxxiv. Moscow 1939, pp.769-858

Aldridge, A. O., *Voltaire and the century of light*. Princeton 1975

– 'Voltaire and the cult of China'. *Tamkang review* 2, no. 2, and 3, no. 1 (Oct. 1971-April 1972), pp.25-49

Alekseev, M. P., 'Пушкин и Китай' (Pushkin and China). In *А. С. Пушкин и Сибирь* (A. S. Pushkin and Siberia). Moscow, Irkutsk 1937. pp.108-45

– *Сибирь в известиях западно-европейских путешественников и писателей* (Siberia in the narratives of Western European travellers and writers). 2nd ed. Irkutsk 1941

Allen, Beverly Sprague, *Tides in English taste (1619-1800): a background for the study of literature*. Cambridge, Mass. 1937

Appleton, William W., *A cycle of Cathay: the Chinese vogue in England during the seventeenth and eighteenth centuries*. New York 1951

Arsen'ev, Iu. V., 'О происхождении ‹Сказания о великой реке Амуре›' (On the origin of the 'Tale of the Great River Amur'). *Известия Русского географического общества* (News of the Imperial Russian Geographic Society) 18, Issue 4 (1882), pp.245-54

Atkinson, Geoffroy, *Les Relations de voyages du dix-septième siècle et l'évolution des idées*. Paris [1924]

Aurich, Ursula, *China im Spiegel der deutschen Literatur des 18. Jahrhunderts*. Germanische Studien, Heft 169. Berlin 1935

Baddeley, John Frederick, *Russia, Mongolia, China*. London 1919

Bartol'd, Vasilii Vladimirovich, *История изучения Востока в Европе и в России*. (The History of the study of the orient in Europe and in Russia). 2nd ed. Leningrad 1925

Belevitch-Stankevitch, Henriette, *Le Goût chinois en France au temps de Louis XIV*. Paris 1910

Berkov, P. N., 'Histoire de l'Encyclopédie dans la Russie du dix-huitième siècle'. *Revue des études slaves* 44 (1965), pp.47-58

– *История русской журналистики XVIII века* (History of Russian journalism in the eighteenth century). Moscow 1952

– 'Сатирические журналы Н. И. Новикова' (The Satirical journals of N. I. Novikov). Intro. to *Сатирические журналы Н. И. Новикова*. Ed. P. N. Berkov. Moscow 1951. pp.7-42

– 'Та-Гио, или великая наука, заключающая в себе высокую китайскую философию: Комментарии' (Ta Hsüeh, or the great science, containing the high Chinese philosophy: commentaries). In D. I. Fonvizin. *Собрание сочинений* (Collected works). Ed. G. P. Makogonenko. Moscow, Leningrad ii (1959), pp.674-79

Bredon, Juliet, *Peking*. Shanghai 1931

Bridges, Richard M., 'A possible source for Daniel Defoe's *The Farther adventures of Robinson Crusoe*'. *British journal for eighteenth-century studies* 2 (1979), pp.231-36

Burgess, Malcolm, 'Fairs and entertainers in 18th-century Russia'. *The Slavonic and East European review* 38 (Dec. 1959), pp.95-113

Cahen, Gaston, *Histoire des relations de la Russie avec la Chine sous Pierre le Grand (1689-1730)*. Paris 1912

Carré, Jean Marie, 'Avant-propos'. M. F. Guyard. *La Littérature comparée*. Paris 1951

Cary-Elwes, Columba, *China and the Cross*.

London 1957

Ch'en Shou-yi, 'Daniel Defoe, China's severe critic'. *Nankai social and economic quarterly* 8 (Oct. 1935), pp.511-50

Chenakal, V. L., 'М. В. Ломоносов о странах Востока' (M. V. Lomonosov on the countries of the East). In *Из истории науки и техники в странах Востока: сборник статей* (From the history of science and technology in the countries of the East: collection of articles). Issue 2. Moscow 1961. pp.190-94

Chinard, Gilbert, *L'Amérique et le rêve exotique dans la littérature française au dix-septième et au dix-huitième siècle*. Paris 1913

Čiševskij, Dmitrij, *History of Russian literature from the eleventh century to the end of the Baroque*. The Hague 1960

Conant, Martha Pike, *The Oriental tale in England in the eighteenth century*. New York 1908

Connaissance de l'étranger: mélanges offerts à la mémoire de Jean-Marie Carré. Paris 1964

Cordier, Henri, *Histoire générale de la Chine et de ses relations avec les pays étrangers*. Paris 1920

Cross, Anthony G., 'Don't shoot your Russianists; or, Defoe and Adam Brand'. *British journal for eighteenth-century studies* 3 (1980), pp.230-33

Dai, David Wei-Yang, 'Confucius and Confucianism in the European Enlightenment'. Diss. University of Illinois, 1979

Dawson, Raymond, *The Chinese chameleon: an analysis of European conceptions of Chinese civilization*. London 1967

Demidova, N. F. and V. S. Miasnikov, *Первые русские дипломаты в Китае («Роспись» И. Петлина и статейный список Ф. И. Байкова)* (The First Russian diplomats in China [I. Petlin's 'Description' and F. I. Baikov's Journal]). Moscow 1966

Dottin, Paul, *Daniel Defoe et ses romans*. London 1924

Dudgeon, John, *Historical sketch of the ecclesiastical, political and commercial relations of Russia with China*. Peking 1872; 1940

Etiemble, René, 'De la pensée chinoise aux philosophes français'. *Revue de littérature comparée* 30 (1956), pp.465-78

– *Les Jésuites en Chine (1552-1773): la querelle des rites*. Paris 1966

– *L'Orient philosophique au dix-huitième siècle*.

Paris 1961

Fishman, Ol'ga Lazarevna, *Китайский сатирический роман: эпоха Просвещения* (The Chinese satirical novel: the Enlightenment era). Moscow 1966

Florinsky, Michael T., *Russia, a history and an interpretation*. New York 1957

Florinskii, V. M., 'Прибавления' (Appendices) to Nikolai Bantysh-Kamenskii, *Дипломатическое собрание дел между Российским и Китайским государствами с 1619 по 1792-й год* (Diplomatic collection of affairs between the Russian and Chinese States from 1619 to 1792). Kazan 1882. pp.513-44

Foust, Clifford M., *Muscovite and mandarin*. Chapel Hill 1969

Franke, Wolfgang, *China and the West*. Trans. R. A. Wilson. Columbia 1967

Fu, Lo-shu (ed.), *A documentary chronicle of Sino-Western relations (1644-1820)*. Association for Asian Studies: Monographs and papers, no. 22. Tucson 1966

Gal'perin, A. L., 'Русская историческая наука о зарубежном Дальнем Востоке в XVII в. – середине XIX в. (Краткий обзор)' (Russian historical scholarship about the foreign Far East from the 17th century to the mid-19th century: a short survey). *Очерки по истории русского востоковедения* (Essays on the history of Russian orientology) 2 (1956), pp.3-35

Glazik, J., *Die Russisch-Orthodoxe Heidenmission seit Peter dem Grossen. Missionswissenschaftliche Abhandlungen und Texte* 19. Munster 1954

Gukovskii, Grigorii A., 'The empress as writer'. In *Catherine the Great: a profile*. Ed. Marc Raeff. New York 1974. pp.64-89

Guy, Basil, *The French image of China before and after Voltaire*. Studies on Voltaire 21 Genève 1963

– 'Rousseau and China'. *Revue de littérature comparée* 30 (1956), pp.531-36

Honour, Hugh, *Chinoiserie: the vision of Cathay*. London 1961

Ikonnikov, A., *Китайский театр и «китайщина» в Детском селе* (The Chinese theatre and *chinoiserie* at Detskoe Selo). Moscow 1931

Избранные произведения руцких мыслителей второй половины XVIII века (Selected works of Russian thinkers of the eighteenth century). Ed. I. Ia.

Shchipanov. Moscow 1952

Jost, François, 'Literary exoticism'. In François Jost, *Introduction to comparative literature*. Indianapolis 1974. pp.109-26

Kirby, E. Stuart, *Russian studies of China: progress and problems of Soviet sinology*. Totowa, New Jersey 1976

Kogan, Iu. Ia., 'Из истории распространения антихристианских памфлетов Вольтера в России в XVIII веке' (From the history of the distribution of anti-Christian pamphlets of Voltaire in 18th-century Russia). In *Вопросы истории религии и атеизма: сборник статей* (Questions in the history of religion and atheism: collection of articles). Moscow 1955. iii.237-77

– *Просветитель XVIII века Я. П. Козельский* (An Enlightenment figure of the eighteenth century, Ia. P. Kozel'skii). Moscow 1958

Korostovets, I., '*Русская духовная миссия в Пекине*' (The Russian ecclesiastical mission in Peking.) *Русский архив* (Russian archives) 9 (1893), pp.57-86

Krestova, L. V., '*Из истории публицистической деятельности Д. И. Фонвизина*' (From the history of the publicistic activity of D. I. Fonvizin). *XVIII век* (The Eighteenth century). Moscow, Leningrad 1958. iii.481-89

Kubacheva, V. N., '*Восточная повесть*› в русской литературе XVIII – начала XIX века' (The Oriental tale in Russian literature of the 18th and early 19th centuries). *XVIII век* (The Eighteenth century). Moscow, Leningrad 1962. v.295-315

Labriolle, François de, 'Le Prosveščenie russe et les *lumières* en France (1760-1798)'. *Revue des études slaves* 45 (1966), pp.75-92

Lach, Donald F., *Asia in the making of Europe*. Chicago 1965-1977

– 'China and the era of the Enlightenment'. *Journal of modern history* (June 1942), pp.209-23

– 'Leibniz and China'. *Journal of the history of ideas* 6 (1945), pp.436-55

Latourette, Kenneth Scott, *The Chinese: their history and culture*. 4th ed. New York, London 1964

– *A history of Christian missions in China*. New York 1929

Lensen, George Alexander (ed.), *Russia's*

eastward expansion. Englewood Cliffs 1964

Liu, James J. Y., *The Art of Chinese poetry*. Chicago 1962

McConnell, Allen, *A Russian 'philosophe': Alexander Radishchev, 1749-1802*. The Hague 1964

Maggs, Barbara W., 'Answers from eighteenth-century China to certain questions on Voltaire's sinology'. *Studies on Voltaire* 120 (1974), pp.179-98

– '"The Jesuits in China": views of an eighteenth-century Russian observer'. *Eighteenth-century studies* 8 (Winter 1974/75), pp.137-52

Makogonenko, G. P., *Денис Фонвизин: творческий путь* (Denis Fonvizin: his way in art). Moscow, Leningrad 1961

– *Николай Новиков и русское просвещение XVIII века* (Nikolai Novikov and the Russian Enlightenment of the 18th century). Moscow, Leningrad 1952

Mancall, Mark, *Russia and China: their diplomatic relations to 1728*. Harvard East Asian Series 61. Cambridge, Mass. 1971

Martino, Pierre, *L'Orient dans la littérature française au dix-septième et au dix-huitième siècle*. Paris 1906

Mason, Mary G., *Western concepts of China and the Chinese. 1840-1876*. New York 1939

Материалы для истории Российской духовной миссии в Пекине (Materials for the history of the Russian religious mission in Peking). Ed. N. I. Veselovskii. St Petersburg 1905

Maverick, Lewis A., *China a model for Europe*. San Antonio, Tex. 1946

Monnier, André, *Un publiciste frondeur sous Catherine II: Nicolas Novikov*. Paris 1981

Mornet, Daniel, 'Les imitations du *Candide* de Voltaire au dix-huitième siècle'. *Mélanges offerts par ses amis et ses élèves à m. Gustave Lanson*. Paris 1922. pp.298-303

Mungello, David E., *Leibniz and Confucianism: the search for accord*. Honolulu 1977

Ovchinnikov, R. V., '‹Рапорт› М. В. Ломоносова и других академиков в Сенат о переводе ‹Истории Китайского государства›' (The 'Report' of M. V. Lomonosov and other academicians to the Senate on the translation of the 'History of the Chinese State'). *Исторический архив* (Historical archives), no. 6 (1961), pp.234-35

Parry, Albert, 'Russian (Greek Orthodox)

Missionaries in China, 1689-1917: their cultural, political and economic role'. *Pacific historical review* 9 (Dec. 1940), pp.401-24

Pavlovsky, Michel N., *Chinese-Russian relations*. New York 1949

Petrov, V. P., *Российская Духовная миссия в Китае* (The Russian ecclesiastical mission in China). Washington, D.C. 1958

Pinot, Virgile, *La Chine et la formation de l'esprit philosophique en France (1640-1740)*. Paris 1932

Primakovskii, A. P., 'О русских переводах произведений Монтескье' (On Russian translations of works by Montesquieu). *Вопросы философии* (Problems of philosophy), no. 3 (1955), pp.138-39

Radovskii, M. I., 'Первая веха в истории русско-китайских научных связей' (The First milestone in the history of Russian-Chinese scholarly relations). *Вестник Академии наук СССР* (Herald of the Academy of Sciences of the USSR), no. 9 (1959), pp.95-97

Raeff, Marc, *Origins of the Russian intelligentsia: the eighteenth-century nobility*. New York 1966

– (ed.), *Russian intellectual history: an anthology*. New York 1966

Reichwein, Adolf, *China and Europe: intellectual and artistic contacts in the eighteenth century*. Trans. J. C. Powell. New York 1925

– *China und Europa: geistige und künstlerische Beziehungen im 18. Jahrhundert*. Berlin 1923

Riasanovsky, Nicholas V., 'Asia through Russian eyes'. In *Russia and Asia: essays on the influence of Russia on Asian peoples*. Ed. Wayne S. Vucinich. Stanford 1972. pp.3-29

Rice, Tamara Talbot, 'The conflux of influences in eighteenth-century Russian art and architecture: a journey from the spiritual to the realistic'. In *The Eighteenth century in Russia*. Ed. J. G. Garrard. Oxford 1973. pp.267-99

Rogger, Hans, *National consciousness in eighteenth-century Russia*. Cambridge, Mass. 1960

Rose, Ernst, Review of Ursula Aurich, *China im Spiegel der deutschen Literatur des 18. Jahrhunderts. Germanic review* 12 (1937), pp.70-72

Rowbotham, Arnold H., 'A brief account of the early development of sinology'.

Chinese social and political science review 7, no. 2 (1921-1923), pp.113-38

– 'China and the age of Enlightenment in Europe'. *Chinese social and political science review* 19 (1935-1936), pp.176-201

– *Missionary and mandarin: the Jesuits at the Court of China*. Berkeley 1942

– 'Voltaire sinophile'. *PMLA* 47 (1932), pp.1050-65

Русско-китайские отношения в XVII веке: материалы и документы (Russo-Chinese relations in the 17th century: materials and documents). Comp. N. F. Demidova and V. S. Miasnikov. Moscow 1972. ii.69-641

Русско-китайские отношения в XVIII веке: Материалы и документы (Russo-Chinese relations in the 18th century: materials and documents). Comp. N. F. Demidova and V. S. Miasnikov. Moscow 1978. i

Sebes, Joseph, *The Jesuits and the Sino-Russian treaty of Nerchinsk (1689): the diary of Thomas Pereira, S. J.* Rome 1961

Serman, I. Z., 'И. Ф. Богданович – журналист и критик' (I. F. Bogdanovich – journalist and critic). *XVIII век* (The Eighteenth century). Moscow, Leningrad 1959. iv.85-103

Shafranovskii, K. I. and T. K. Shafranovskaia, 'Сведения о китайских книгах в библиотеке Академии наук в XVIII в.'. (Report on Chinese books in the Library of the Academy of Sciences in the eighteenth century). In Akademiia nauk SSSR, Biblioteka (Academy of Sciences of the USSR, Library), *Научные и культурные связи библиотеки АН СССР со странами зарубежного Востока* (Scholarly and cultural ties of the Library of the Academy of Sciences of the USSR with foreign countries of the East). Leningrad, Moscow 1957. pp.83-93

Shafranovskaia, T. K., 'О поездках Лоренца Ланга в Пекин' (Lorents Lange's journeys to Peking). *Советское китаеведение* (Soviet sinology) 4 (1958), pp.155-59

– 'Поездка лекаря Франца Елачича в 1753-1756 гг. в Пекин для пополнения китайских коллекций кунсткамеры' (The Journey of the physician Franz Elachich in 1753-1756 to Peking for rebuilding the

Chinese collection of the Kunstkamera). In *Из истории науки и техники в странах Востока: сборник статей* (The history of science and technology in the East: collection of articles). Ed. A. T. Grigor'ian. Issue 2. Moscow 1961. pp.126-31

Shafranovskaia, T. K. and K. I. Shafranovskii, 'Приобретение в начале XVIII в. китайских книг российским резидентом в Китае Лоренцом Лангом' (The Acquisition, at the start of the 18th century, of Chinese books by the Russian Agent in China, Lorents Lange). In *Страны и народы Востока* (Lands and peoples of the East) Issue 1. Moscow 1959. pp.295-301

Shafranovskaia, T. K., 'Путешествие Лоренца Ланга в 1715-1716 гг.в Пекин и его дневник' (The Journey of Lorents Lange in 1715-1716 to Peking and his journal). In *Страны и народы Востока* (Lands and peoples of the East) Issue 2. Moscow 1961. pp.188-205

Shklovskii, Viktor, *Матвей Комаров, житель города Москбы* (Matvei Komarov, Resident of Moscow). Leningrad 1929

Shtrange, M. M., 'Энциклопедия Дидро и ее русские переводчики' (Diderot's *Encyclopédie* and its Russian translators). In Академия наук СССР, Институт истории (Academy of Sciences of the USSR, Institute of History), *Французский ежегодник: статьи и материалы по истории Франции. 1959* (French yearbook: articles and materials on the history of France. 1959). Moscow 1961. pp.76-88

Shvarts, V. S., *Пригороды Ленинграда* (The Suburbs of Leningrad). Leningrad, Moscow 1961

Sipovskii, V. V., *Из истории русского романа и повести (Материалы по библиографии, истории и теории русского романа* (The History of the Russian novel and short story [Materials on the bibliography, history and theory of the Russian novel]). St Petersburg 1903. i, part 2

Skachkov, P. E., 'История изучения Китая в России в XVII и XVIII вв. (краткии очерк)' (History of the study of China in Russia in the 17th and 18th centuries – a brief outline). In Akademiia nauk SSSR, Institut istorii (Academy of Sciences of the USSR, Institute of History), *Международные связи России в XVII-XVIII вв. (Экономика, политика и культура)* (International ties of Russia in the 17th and 18th centuries – economics, politics and culture). Moscow 1966. pp.152-80

– *Очерки истории русского китаеведения* (Outline of the history of Russian sinology). Moscow 1977

– 'Первый преподаватель китайского и маньчжурского языков в России' (The First teacher of the Chinese and Manchu languages in Russia). *Проблемы востоковедения* (Problems of oriental studies), no. 3 (1960), pp.198-201

– 'Ведомость о китайской земле' (Information about the land of China). In *Страны и народы Востока* (Lands and peoples of the East). Issue 2. Moscow 1961. pp.206-19

Strenina, A. V., 'У истоков русского и мирового китаеведения (Россохин и Леонтьев и их труд ‹Обстоятельное описание происхождения и состояния маньчжурского народа и войска, в осьми знаменах состоящего›)' (At the sources of Russian and world sinology [Rossokhin and Leontiev and their work 'Detailed description of the origin and state of the Manchu people and their army, consisting of eight banners']). *Советская этнография* (Soviet ethnography), no. 1 (1950), pp.170-77

Taranovich, V. P., 'Иларион Россохин и его труды по китаеведению' (Ilarion Rossokhin and his sinological works). *Советское востоковедение* (Soviet studies of the East), no. 3 (1945), pp.225-41

Treadgold, Donald W., *The West in Russia and China: religious and secular thought in modern times.* Cambridge 1973

Tscharner, Eduard Horst von, *China in der deutschen Dichtung bis zur Klassik.* München 1939

– 'China in der deutschen Dichtung des Mittelalters und der Renaissance'. *Sinica* 9, Heft 1 (1934), pp.8-31

– 'China in der deutschen Dichtung, i Barock'. *Sinica* 12, Heft 3/4 (1937), pp.91-129

– 'China in der deutschen Dichtung, ii Aufklärung und Rokoko'. *Sinica* 12, Heft 5/6 (1937), pp.181-207

– 'China in der deutschen Literatur des

klassischen Zeitalters'. *Sinica* 9, Heft 5 (1934), pp.185-98 and 269-80

– 'Die Erschließung Chinas im 16. und 17. Jahrhundert'. *Sinica* 9, Heft 2 (1934), pp.50-77

Val'denberg, V. E. [Waldenberg], *Госу-дарственные идеи Крижанича* (Krizhanich's ideas about the State). St Petersburg 1912

Veselovskii, N. I. *See Materials*

Vucinich, Wayne S. (ed.), *Russia and Asia: essays on the influence of Russia on the Asian peoples*. Stanford, California 1972

Waley, Arthur, *Yuan Mei, eighteenth-century Chinese poet*. London 1956

Widmer, Eric, '"Kitai" and the Ch'ing empire in seventeenth-century Russian documents on China'. *Ch'ing-shih wen-t'i*, 2, no. 4 (Nov. 1970), pp.21-39

– *The Russian ecclesiastical mission in Peking during the eighteenth century*. Cambridge, Mass. 1976

Zaborov, P. R., *Русская литература и Вольтер: XVIII – первая треть XIX века* (Russian literature and Voltaire: the eighteenth to the first third of the nineteenth century). Leningrad 1978

– 'Вольтер в русских переводах XVIII века' (Voltaire in Russian translations of the eighteenth century). In *Эпоха просвещения: из истории международных связей русской литературы* (The Age of Enlightenment: from the history of the international ties of Russian literature). Leningrad 1967. pp.110-207

Записки о русском посольстве в Китай (1692-1695) (Notes on the Russian embassy to China 1692-1695). Comp. M. I. Kazanin. Moscow 1967

Zoli, Sergio, *La Cina e l'età dell'illuminismo in Italia*. Bologna 1974

Index